SAGE was founded in 1965 by Sara Miller McCune to support the dissemination of usable knowledge by publishing innovative and high-quality research and teaching content. Today, we publish over 900 journals, including those of more than 400 learned societies, more than 800 new books per year, and a growing range of library products including archives, data, case studies, reports, and video. SAGE remains majority-owned by our founder, and after Sara's lifetime will become owned by a charitable trust that secures our continued independence.

Los Angeles | London | New Delhi | Singapore | Washington DC | Melbourne

Social Work EDUCATION

Social Work EDUCATION

Indigenous Perspectives

Edited by
SANJOY ROY

Los Angeles | London | New Delhi
Singapore | Washington DC | Melbourne

First published in 2021 by

SAGE Publications India Pvt Ltd
B1/I-1 Mohan Cooperative Industrial Area
Mathura Road, New Delhi 110 044, India
www.sagepub.in

SAGE Publications Inc
2455 Teller Road
Thousand Oaks, California 91320, USA

SAGE Publications Ltd
1 Oliver's Yard, 55 City Road
London EC1Y 1SP, United Kingdom

SAGE Publications Asia-Pacific Pte Ltd
18 Cross Street #10-10/11/12
China Square Central
Singapore 048423

Published by Vivek Mehra for SAGE Publications India Pvt Ltd. Typeset in 10.5/13 pt Bembo by Zaza Eunice, Hosur, Tamil Nadu, India.

Library of Congress Control Number: 2020948144

ISBN: 978-93-5388-637-0 (HB)

SAGE Team: Rajesh Dey, Shipra Pant and Rajinder Kaur

To
all the graduate, postgraduate students, research scholars
and practitioners
of social work and allied disciplines
who are actually working as the change agents.

Thank you for choosing a SAGE product!
If you have any comment, observation or feedback,
I would like to personally hear from you.

Please write to me at **contactceo@sagepub.in**

Vivek Mehra, Managing Director and CEO, SAGE India.

Bulk Sales

SAGE India offers special discounts
for purchase of books in bulk.
We also make available special imprints
and excerpts from our books on demand.

For orders and enquiries, write to us at

Marketing Department
SAGE Publications India Pvt Ltd
B1/I-1, Mohan Cooperative Industrial Area
Mathura Road, Post Bag 7
New Delhi 110044, India

E-mail us at **marketing@sagepub.in**

Subscribe to our mailing list
Write to **marketing@sagepub.in**

This book is also available as an e-book.

Contents

List of Figures   ix
List of Tables   xi
List of Abbreviations   xiii
Foreword by Stephen M. Marson   xvii
Acknowledgements   xxi

Introduction
Sanjoy Roy   1

Part 1: Major Themes in Social Work Practice

Chapter 1   Medical and Psychiatric Social Work Practice:
             Glimpses and Reflections
             K. Sathyamurthi   15
Chapter 2   Social Work Practice with Families
             and Children
             Archana Kaushik   28
Chapter 3   Emergence and Development of Professional
             Social Work in Correctional Settings
             Sanjoy Roy   52

Part 2: Major Practice Areas in Social Work

Chapter 4   Palliative Care: Emerging Field of
             Social Work Practice
             Tushti Bhardwaj   69
Chapter 5   Social Work and Counselling: Contemporary
             and Emerging Practice Areas
             Shashi Rani   84

Chapter 6   Social Intervention through Social Enterprises:
             A Sustainable Approach to Social Work
             Preeti Jha   101
Chapter 7   Environment, Climate Change and
             Social Work: Imperatives for Practice
             Neera Agnimitra   119
Chapter 8   Social Work and Terrorism
             Basem Youssief Mohamed ELmoazen   143
Chapter 9   Disaster Management in India:
             Perspectives from Social Work Practice
             Subhasis Bhadra   161
Chapter 10   Integrated Social Work Intervention with
             Drug Dependents: Cure to Care
             Kirti Arya and Ravi Ranjan Kumar   189
Chapter 11   Social Casework with Juvenile Delinquents:
             A Psychosocial Model
             Mohd. Shakil and Asif Khan   204

Conclusion
Sanjoy Roy   216

About the Editor and Contributors   225
Index   230

List of Figures

2.1 Violation of Child Rights   41
2.2 Broad Categorization of Services for Children   42

3.1 Major Correctional Institution Types in India   60

4.1 Approaches to Palliative Care   72
4.2 Palliative Care Models   73
4.3 Pictorial Assessment of Pain   74
4.4 Foundational Measures for a Successful
     National Programme   80

6.1 Structure of the Organization   112
6.2 Models Followed in the Organization   113

9.1 Extended Cycle of Disaster Management   169
9.2 Role of Social Workers in Disaster Management   185

10.1 Key Reasons for Drug Dependence   191
10.2 A Hypothetical Time Scale of Drug
     Use Career of a Typical IDU   195

List of Figures

List of Tables

3.1 Different Roles of Social Workers in
    Correctional Settings   61

10.1 Classification of Drugs   192
10.2 Adverse Effects of Drugs on Vulnerable Populations   198

List of Abbreviations

ACA	American Counselling Association
AIDS	Acquired Immune Deficiency Syndrome
ALIMCO	Artificial Limbs Manufacturing Corporation of India
BAC	British Association for Counselling
BBB	Build Back Better
BPRD	Bureau of Police Research and Development
CASW	The Canadian Association of Social Workers
CB	Civil Defense
CBRN	Chemical, Biological, Radiological and Nuclear
CHC	Community Health Centers
CISM	Crisis Incident Stress Management
CMS	Centers for Medicare and Medicaid Services
CNS	Central nervous system
DISE	District Information System for Education
DM	Disaster management
DRC	Drug De-addiction and Rehabilitation Centres
DRR	Disaster risk reduction
GER	Gross enrolment ratio
GOI	Government of India
HIV	Human Immunodeficiency Virus
HVCR	Hazard, Vulnerability, Category and Risk
IASC	Inter-agency Standing Committee
IASSW	International Association of Schools of Social Work
ICDS	Integrated Child Development Services
IDNDR	International Decade for Natural Disaster Reduction
IFSW	International Federation of Social Workers
IGNOAPS	Indira Gandhi National Old Age Pension Scheme
IIPA	Indian Institute for Public Administration
IPOP	Integrated Programme for Older Persons
LIC	Life Insurance Corporation

MBA	Master of Business Administration
MDG	Millennium Development Goals
MHFA	Mental Health First Aid
MoSPI	Ministry of Statistics and Programme Implementation
NAPCC	National Action Plan on Climate Change
NASW	National Association of Social Workers
NCRB	National Crime Records Bureau
NDMA	National Disaster Management Authority
NDPS	Narcotic Drugs and Psychotropic Substances
NDRF	National Disaster Response Force
NFHS	National Family Health Survey
NGO	Non-governmental organization
NHS	National Health Service
NNPC	Neighborhood Network in Palliative Care
NOVA	National Organization for Victim Assistance
NPDM	National Policy on Disaster Management
NPDRR	National Platform for Disaster Risk Reduction
NPHCE	National Programme for Health Care of the Elderly
NPOP	National Policy on Older Persons
OD	Organization development
PAR	Participatory action research
PDR	People's Democratic Republic
PFA	Psychological First Aid
PHC	Primary health centers
PIP	Programme Implementation Plans
PMVVY	Pradhan Mantri Vaya Vandana Yojana
SC	Sub-centers
SDG	Sustainable development goals
SDMA	Sate Disaster Management Authority
SDTT	Sir Dorabji Tata Trust
SFA	Stress First Aid
SRS	Sample Registration System
TISS	Tata Institute of Social Sciences
U5MR	Under-5 Mortality Rate
UN	United Nation
UNCRC	United Nations Convention on the Rights of the Child
UNDP	United Nations Development Programme

UNICEF	United Nation Children's Fund
UNIFEM	The United Nations Development Fund for Women
UTs	Union territories
WHO	World Health Organization

Foreword

India has an impressive cultural history of care for the troubled that extends long before the existence of formal social work education (Chatterjee, 2010). Raja Ram Mohan Roy, well known within India, but unfortunately unrecognized within the Western world, made profound strives towards advocacy for humanity and educational resources. He instigated a reform movement to engage Indians to embrace values that stressed kindness and generosity to those who are less fortunate. Internationally revered, Mahatma Gandhi was the fountainhead who demonstrated and guided Hindu culture to what, today, embodies social work values. In fact, Gandhi has had the single most profound impact on the articulation of contemporary social work values and ethics of any single person in world history. Clearly, India has a solid history of advocacy for humanity followed by efforts to systematize such humanitarian concerns within the academic arena. For example, the internationally respected *Indian Journal of Social Work* is the second oldest scholarly social work journal within our world.

Within India, we see an impressive array of publications for advancing academic social work on a microscopic level that has international implications (e.g., Desai, 2000). This brings us to the book entitled *Social Work Education: Indigenous Perspectives* edited by Dr Sanjoy Roy, Associate Professor of Social Work at the University of Delhi. Once again, we witness India's advancement of the social work profession—not just for India but for the worldwide community of social workers. Dr Roy is following the tradition of the many Indian social work luminaries of the past as noted above.

Dr Roy has collected the writings of top national and international scholars and has edited a book that provides cutting-edge information and analysis on topical areas of interest to social work education in India and throughout the English-speaking world. The topics included do not merely cover current interests but also offer a peek into the future of educational enterprises.

Dr Roy has recruited authors to address subject matters within the chapters that capture unique perspectives of social work practice and research. Some of these chapters have the potential of providing a paradigm shift in the manner in which social workers see successful intervention in our rapidly changing world. This world, as noted by Dr Roy, includes the impact of global warming and other natural events that have an impact on the human condition and the way in which social services can be delivered in a troubled world. With great and extraordinary profound insight, some authors link social service delivery to economic issues and climatic changes. Such writings will have a great impact on the international community of social workers.

Unlike most of the edited books in academic social work, Dr Roy's presentation does not include an emphasis in clinical social work. Rather, he is even-handed and comprehensive in the chapters he selected. He recruited authors with highly diverse specialty areas. These specialties afford the reader an insight into the vast array of present and future social work practice in the areas of business models, services to family and children, gerontology, juvenile delinquency, end-of-life care, the natural environment impact on humanity, social service delivery within terrorism, disaster management, substance abuse, correctional social work and clinical social work. Dr Roy is thorough and comprehensive in his approach to providing an edited book for both academic and practicing social workers. This editedbook is an extremely valuable addition to the growing indigenous literature on social work education, and it will surely provide a wealth of information as well as valuable insights for students, academicians, research scholars and practitioners.

In the end, I can say that Dr Roy's work has made a significant contribution to advancing the social work profession in India and the entire world.

Stephen M. Marson, MSW, PhD, ACSW
Professor Emeritus, Sociology and Criminal Justice Department
University of North Carolina, North Carolina, USA
Editor of *The Journal of Social Work Values and Ethics,* USA

REFERENCES

Chatterjee, A. (2010). Objective helping, Hegel and three Indian reformers in colonial civil society prefacing the personalytical history of social work. *Indian Journal of Social Work*, 71(2), 145–166.

Desai, M. (2000). Curriculum planning for history of philosophies of social work. *Indian Journal of Social Work*, 61(2), 221–239.

Acknowledgements

The chapters compiled in this edited book, titled *Social Work Education: Indigenous Perspectives*, are written mostly by senior academicians from India and overseas. All the chapters are written with sincerity by experts from the essential and emerging domains of field practice and the relevant issues—starting from the historical background, their importance in social work, where and how social work skills, techniques, methods and models could be used in these domains and the role of social workers in dealing with these issues in each of these broad domains.

I am truly thankful to Professor Stephen M. Marson (MSW, PhD, ACSW), Professor Emeritus, Sociology and Criminal Justice Department, University of North Carolina, USA, and Editor of *The Journal of Social Work Values and Ethics*, USA, for providing me a very thoughtful Foreword for this book.

I am really grateful to SAGE Publications for publishing this book. I am deeply appreciative of the wholehearted cooperation and professionalism of the entire team at SAGE Publications for helping to improve the quality of the book to international standards. I am also thankful to the contributors for writing high-quality chapters for the book, which I am sure will be immensely and enormously valuable for academicians, practitioners and advanced students of social work and related disciplines.

Introduction

Sanjoy Roy

AIMS AND SCOPE OF THE BOOK

This book is especially designed to provide a critical view on the existing practices of social work education and discusses the contemporary issues and practices that are yet to be given special attention in the social work discipline, particularly in India. It discusses and highlights the role of social workers in dealing with or tackling them.

This book is made up of some of the works that leading social work educators have written, based on their research and experiences to meet the emerging/contemporary concerns in social work education. All the chapters of this book provide a historical perspective on the concerned issue taken up in the chapter and identify the relevant social work skills, techniques and methods that may be useful in tackling that issue. They also provide a sound academic foundation of the concerned issue with critical analysis of the existing literature, with a view to stimulate readers to think, debate and reflect on the issue. It also marks a distinction from other books, especially in its coverage of diverse and emerging issues that were hitherto neglected in the social work discipline. To quote a few examples, it includes palliative care and social work, climate change and social work and terrorism and social work. The insights of the educators that have been presented in different chapters of this book will not only arouse interest in readers on various emerging issues in social work discipline but also advance their learning levels on the same.

While claiming to be the voice of all social workers in indigenous perspectives, this book provides experiences, observations and case examples of some of the best educators of India which other educators, in addition to social work students, may also find useful. The book will also help to develop an interest in the general public to pursue a career in social work discipline and get professional recognition of their work. It will thus create a pool of qualified social workers who would be well educated and trained with the ability to translate social work knowledge, skills and values into practice. Further, this book attempts to provide a vision for contemporary social workers working in different situations dealing with complex human relations. In providing this vision, it keeps in view the broad vision of the social work discipline that is reflected in the definition of social work promulgated jointly by the International Federation of Social Workers (IFSW) and International Association of Schools of Social Work (IASSW). This definition states:

> Social work is a practice-based profession and an academic discipline that promotes social change and development, social cohesion, and the empowerment and liberation of people. Principles of social justice, human rights, collective responsibility and respect for diversities are central to social work. Underpinned by theories of social work, social sciences, humanities and indigenous knowledge, social work engages people and structures to address life challenges and enhance wellbeing. (IFSW and IASSW, 2014)

SOCIAL WORK PROFESSION AND ITS VARIOUS METHODS

Social work is a practice-based discipline which imbibes in students' scientific knowledge, skills, values, principles, philosophies, methods and models during classroom teaching, which they are supposed to apply in their occupational career while rendering professional services and aid to individuals, groups or communities (Mishra, 1994; Roy, 2015). Social work teaching largely consists of six methods—social casework, social group work, community organization, social work research, social welfare administration and social action. The first three are called primary methods and the remaining three secondary methods. Each of these methods is designed to serve specific purpose(s). Social casework as a primary method is regarded as a problem-solving process in which the social caseworker helps an individual overcome his personal limitations, solve his problems, and adjust properly with the society at large (Perlman, 1957; Richmond, 1922). Social group work, another primary method, is a process in which social group worker helps various types of groups to solve their specific problems and enhance their social functioning in the society (Konopka, 1963; Trecker, 1948). Community organization, another primary method of social work, is a process in which community social worker helps community identify its problems and solve them primarily by mobilizing resources available within its locality.

Social work research is one of the three secondary methods of social work which a social worker uses to scientifically explore or understand an individual's, group's or community's problem(s) and help the concerned accordingly. It thus enriches the primary methods of social work (Das, 2010; Fortune & Reid, 2017). Social welfare administration is another secondary method of social work which a social worker uses to understand the welfare machinery of the state and help the target group avail the benefits of its various schemes, programmes and policies (Chowdhry, 1992; Sachdeva, 1992). Social action is the third and last secondary method of social work, which a social worker applies usually as a last resort when other methods of social work seem inadequate to help the target group. By using this method, social worker arouses consciousness in the people about their pertinent social problem(s) and helps them take organized collective action to resolve it within the democratic or constitutional framework (Kumar, 1997; Siddiqui, 1984).

GAPS BETWEEN THEORY AND PRACTICE IN SOCIAL WORK

Social work has consistently proved to be a successful discipline, both in developed countries and in developing countries. Among others, it has contributed to the preparation of a large number of professional social work personnel (Gore, 1959), enhancement of people's participation in the community development programmes (Estes, 1997), expansion and promotion of social justice among newly emerged vulnerable groups (Pathare et al., 2015), resolution of a number of environmental problems and various types of disasters (Bhatt & Agnimitra, 2014), treatment of various health problems (Gehlert & Browne, 2012) and empowerment of disadvantaged groups and advancement of society (Parker & Crabtree, 2018). However, social work, like any other discipline, is fraught with several limitations. First, the social work discipline is largely an 'imported' discipline from Western countries. Over the years, the fact that it, in its present form, is less suited to the (different) problems and needs of the developing countries has come to surface. Second, it has so far failed to establish itself as a well-recognized discipline and is still not taught in many universities. Third, it still remains excluded from the subject list of various competitive examinations and thus offers fewer prospects of employment. Fourth, the social work perspective until today has evolved as a perspective of the dominant classes of the respective countries and so lacks diversity. Fifth, the primary methods of social work are fully imported from the West, while secondary methods to a great extent encompass indigenous knowledge of the respective countries. Thus, a gap exists between primary and secondary methods of social work.

This book attempts to bridge some of these gaps and many others through various novel means suggested in each chapter to address the specific problems discussed in them.

INDIGENOUS PERSPECTIVES IN SOCIAL WORK

The indigenization of social work education is not a new phenomenon; it rather began with the emergence of the social work discipline itself. But the pace of indigenization was very slow in the beginning in most of the countries. For example, in India, the curriculum of social work education incorporated, from its very beginning, the contents on the Indian history and philosophy of social work, Indian social problems, family and child welfare, welfare and development of disadvantaged groups and fieldwork in India's villages (Kulkarni, 1993). However, it was only after 1971 that the indigenization of social work education acquired a character of almost a movement, not only in India but also all over the world. In 1971, this term was first used in the context of social work education by the United Nations in one of its field surveys of social work training, referring to the inappropriateness of Western social work theories in non-Western countries (Nimmagadda & Martell, 2016). Since then, the indigenization movement of social work education has acquired a worldwide character, and today the native scholarship of almost all developing countries of Asia, Africa and South America talk of the need of indigenization of social work education to make it a culturally relevant discipline. They argue that the contents and pedagogy of social work education in developing countries are largely replicas of the Western social work syllabi, which are unsuited to the needs of most of these countries due to their peculiar characteristics. Among others, they cite that most of these developing countries are predominantly rural, with the vast majority of the population being poor, unlike Western countries which are predominantly industrialized with a significant majority of urban population (Dominelli, 2012).

Indigenous perspectives broadly refer to the perspectives that emerge from within the cultures of the country. Indigenous perspectives in social work thus mean that social work knowledge should arise from within the cultures, reflect local traditions and practices, be interpreted within the local frames of reference, and thus be locally relevant and culturally sensitive (Gray & Hetherington, 2013). This means learning to value the local worldview and developing a contextualized understanding of the social problems, so that any knowledge does not assume universal hegemony and application. It also means evaluating any knowledge from the local standpoint, bringing necessary correction or adaptation in them and making them locally relevant. It, however, must not be understood as the outright rejection of any non-local knowledge. It simply means the legitimization of locally relevant, diverse perspectives along with the global knowledge perspectives. It must also be noted here that indigenous perspectives should not be in singular but always in plural. This is because a modern country/society usually consists of heterogeneous social groups whose cultures and perspectives may differ from one another.

Indigenous perspectives are often equated with 'multicultural perspectives' (see Gonzalez & Congress, 2013; Sue, 2006). But there is a significant difference between the two. The former refers to the perspectives from within the cultures of the country, while the latter refers to the coexistence of different perspectives, whether indigenous or not. Therefore, precaution should be taken to use them interchangeably. And, as far as possible, both should not be used interchangeably unless the context otherwise permits. There is also debate over whose knowledge should count as 'indigenous' (Briskman, 2014; Gray et al., 2013). As noted above, a modern country is made of diverse social groups who have settled in the country at different points of time. In history, they were different warring groups who fought against each other to control the resources. But, after the emergence of modern nation-states and adoption of the modern Constitution, they have consented to live together peacefully. Yet, the conflicts of interest exist among them over a range of matters. Under such circumstances, determining 'indigenous communities' is a highly controversial matter and therefore 'indigenous perspectives' too. Today, each community tends to claim indigenous origin of itself and is eagerly ready to recognize its perspective as 'indigenous'. In such situations, recognizing one perspective, including what is called national perspective, as indigenous may provoke others to become aggressive to gain recognition of their perspectives also as indigenous. The solution therefore lies with the recognition of multiple indigenous perspectives within one country/nation.

The discourse of indigenization of social work education has been carried forward over the years, but so far it has not been able to make a substantive impact on the redesigning of course curriculum and field work practicum of social work education. The following reasons may be attributed for this failure:

1. The early intellectuals in these countries came predominantly from the ruling class, which approached the societal issues from functionalist perspective due to their conservative ruling-class ideology.
2. These intellectuals initially blocked the diverse representation of social groups in higher education institutions/universities and consistently denied the legitimacy of other perspectives.
3. These intellectuals primarily relied on the reinterpretation of the age-old mythological documents and tried to give them a scientific

character to re-legitimize their ruling ideologies in the modern times.

4. This created a wide gap between the social realities of ancient times and that of modern times.

5. The early theories were thus developed based on these 'manufactured scientific realities' which did not correspond to the empirical social realities of the modern times.

6. It was after a long time that people from the bottom layer of society reached the higher education institutions. Such people mostly carried out empirical research from subaltern perspectives or perspectives from below.

7. This generated a body of empirically grounded scientific knowledge that stood in direct confrontation with the earlier body of manufactured scientific knowledge.

8. This has created gaps between theory and practice of social work education in contemporary times.

9. These gaps are now being sought to be filled in through what has today come to be called the 'indigenization' of social work education.

10. However, there is also a resurgence of the ideological imperialist movement of ruling-class intellectuals to impose their conservative ideology on the rest of the population in the name of 'indigenization'.

GENERIC SOCIAL WORK VERSUS SPECIALIZED SOCIAL WORK

There is growing debate over generic versus specialized social work all over the world. Generic social work refers to imparting the whole set of knowledge of social work to all students in order to enable them to work with various types of client groups in a variety of settings and at all levels, addressing their various personal and social problems. Specialized social work, on the other hand, refers to the training of social workers in a specific domain of social work knowledge (Leighninger, 1980). When social work education began, it was mostly centred around the dissemination of generic social work knowledge. This included the teaching and practice of the six core methods of social work as discussed in the preceding section. Specialization was not introduced at that time. But from the last few decades, there is growing realization of specialization within the social work discipline. The proponents of specialized social work argue that the generalist approach to social work is sufficiently not equipped to deal with the specific problems of different social groups of society, and that these specific problems require different sets of knowledge and skills to solve them (Raeymaeckers, 2016). The supporters of generic social work, on the other hand, argue that social workers must have knowledge of as wide variety of fields as possible, for they have to work with multiple groups (such as individual, family, youth, elderly and women) and in multiple settings (such as rural, urban, industrial, capitalist, organizational and so on; Tolson et al., 2003). Over the years, a section of advocators of both generic and specialized social work has come to realize that social work education is incomplete in the absence of either of them. Hence, a proper balance of both generic and specialized social work is needed. In view of this, many universities, departments and institutes offer specialized social work education in addition to generic social work education. For example, in India, postgraduate social work education consists of two years, of which the first year is devoted to providing generic social work knowledge to all students, and in the second year, they are given opportunity to opt for one specialized subject among a set of specializations. These specialized courses include gender studies, tribal studies, disaster studies, health system studies, developmental studies, cultural studies, human ecology, public policy and governance, education, criminology, medical and psychiatric social work, clinical social work and so on.

This book also marks a shift from generic social work to specialized social work in the face of the growing realization of the importance of domain-specific knowledge.

STRUCTURE OF THE BOOK

The book is organized into two major parts: (a) Major Themes in Social Work Practice, which includes chapters on medical and psychiatric social work practice; social work practice with families and children; and emergence and development of professional social work in correctional settings; and (b) Major Practice Areas in Social Work, which includes chapters on palliative care; social work and counselling;

social intervention through social enterprises; environment, climate change and social work; social work and terrorism; disaster management in India; integrated social work intervention with drug dependents; and social case work with juvenile delinquents.

The book is divided into 11 chapters. Each of these chapters provides critical analysis of a specific theme or practice identified by its author as relevant to social work. The authors have written their respective chapters keeping in view the following points: (a) the relevance of the issue or topic in the social work discipline; (b) the historical background of the concerned issue/topic; (c) the need of solving the concerned issue; (d) the identification and application of suitable social work skills, techniques, methods, therapies and models to solve the concerned issue and (e) the identification of a set of roles of professional social workers in dealing with the concerned issue.

CENTRAL THEMES AND ARGUMENTS OF THE BOOK

The central theme of the book revolves around the identification of the contemporary issues and practices of social work education and the critical analysis of each of them from indigenous perspectives. This includes (a) re-examination of medical and psychiatric social work practice and recognition of the importance of fieldwork in them; (b) identification of the scope and challenges of the social work profession in working with families and children; (c) roles and professional obligations of social workers while working with various types of correctional settings; (d) approaches, models and agents of palliative care in India; (e) psychosocial approaches and application of various social work therapies in counselling; (f) emergence of social enterprises as self-sustainable models in social work; (g) social work response to environmental problems and environmental justice mandate of social work; (h) social work response to terrorism and its remedies; (i) role of social workers in disaster management; (j) importance of client-centric approach in drug rehabilitation and (k) importance of the psychosocial model in the treatment of juvenile delinquents.

The main argument of this book is that the social work profession must move from its focus on traditional issues and practices to contemporary issues and practices to meet the emerging needs of society. It should also develop and employ indigenous perspectives along with the adaptation of Western or non-indigenous perspectives to approach country-specific problems. In the absence of indigenous perspectives, the social work discipline would long remain a 'Western-imported discipline' with progressively lesser practical utility for developing countries. At the same time, it must be ensured that 'indigenization' does not slip into 'ethnocentrism', 'parochialism' and 'regionalism'. Instead, it must retain, promote and foster 'universalism', 'multidimensionalism' and 'modernism'. The success of indigenization of social work education would depend on its ability to integrate what is universally accepted and what is locally relevant.

UTILITY OF THE BOOK

This book is a blend of theory and practice of social work education. Readers are encouraged to read this book as an active participant in the discussions of various contemporary issues and challenges of social work and augment their ability to apply social work knowledge, skills, values, principles, techniques, theories and models in the practical settings. In this way, readers' knowledge will become deeply entrenched as part of their own development. This book also provides a number of key examples, case studies and problem-solving approaches to enhance the readers' understanding of the specific issues and challenges dealt in each chapter. It will enable the readers understand the key issues from indigenous perspectives with their historical roots, why they are important in social work, when and how social work skills, techniques, methods, and models could be effectively applied, what key roles social workers would require to play in dealing with those issues and so on. Each chapter ends with a brief summary and a list of suggestions for references and further reading on the topic.

REFERENCES

Bhatt, S., & Agnimitra, N. (Eds.). (2014). *Social work response to environment and disasters*. Shipra Publications.

Briskman, L. (2014). *Social work with indigenous communities: A human rights approach*. Federation Press.

Chowdhry, D. P. (1992). *Social welfare administration*. Atma Ram & Sons.

Das, D. K. L. (2010). *Practice of social research*. Rawat Publications.

Dominelli, L. (2012). Globalization and indigenization: Reconciling the irreconcilable in social work? In K. Lyons, T. Hokenstad, M. Pawar, N. Huegler, & N. Hall (Eds.), *The SAGE handbook of international social work* (pp. 39–55). SAGE Publications.

Estes, R. J. (1997). Social work, social development, and community welfare centres in international perspective. *International Social Work, 40*(1), 43–55.

Fortune, A. E., & Reid, W. J. (2017). *Research in social work* (3rd ed.). Rawat Publications.

Gehlert, S., & Browne, T. (Eds.). (2012). *Handbook of health social work*. John Wiley & Sons.

Gonzalez, M. J., & Congress, E. P. (Eds.). (2013). *Multicultural perspectives in social work practice with families* (3rd ed.). Springer Publishing Company.

Gore, M. S. (1959). Contribution of social work education to the preparation of village level workers. *Social Welfare in South-East Asia, 2*(2), 22–26.

Gray, M., & Hetherington, T. (2013). Indigenization, indigenous social work and decolonization: Mapping the theoretical terrain. In M. Gray, J. Coates, M. Y. Bird, & T. Hetherington (Eds.), *Decolonizing social work*. Routledge.

Gray, M., Coates, J., Bird, M. Y., & Hetherington, T. (Eds.). (2013). *Decolonizing social work*. Routledge.

IFSW [International Federation of Social Workers] and IASSW [International Association of Schools of Social Work]. (2014). *Global definition of social work*. https://www.ifsw.org/global-definition-of-social-work/

Konopka, G. (1963). *Social group work: A helping process*. Prentice-Hall.

Kulkarni, P. D. (1993). The indigenous base of social work profession in India. *Indian Journal of Social Work, 54*(4), 555–565.

Kumar, H. (1997). *Social work, social development and sustainable development*. Regency Publications.

Leighninger, L. (1980). The generalist-specialist debate in social work. *Social Service Review, 54*(1), 1–12.

Mishra, P. D. (1994). *Social work: Philosophy and methods*. Inter-India Publications.

Nimmagadda, J., & Martell, D. R. (2016). Home-made social work: The two-way transfer of social work practice knowledge between India and the USA. In M. Gray, J. Coates, & M. Y. Bird (Eds.), *Indigenous social work around the world: Towards culturally relevant education and practice* (pp. 141–152). Routledge.

Parker, J., & Crabtree, S. A. (2018). *Social work with disadvantaged and marginalized people*. SAGE Publications.

Pathare, S., Bhatt, S., & Varghese, J. (Eds.). (2015). *Social justice and social work profession in India*. Manas Publishers and Distributors.

Perlman, H. H. (1957). *Social casework: A problem-solving process*. The University of Chicago.

Raeymaeckers, P. (2016). A specialist's perspective on the value of generalist practice: A qualitative network analysis. *Journal of Social Work, 16*(5), 610–626.

Richmond, M. E. (1922). *What is social case work?* Russell Sage Foundation.

Roy, S. (2015). *Methods and development of social work.* Discovery Publishing House.

Sachdeva, D. R. (1992). *Social welfare administration in India.* Kitab Mahal Publishers.

Siddiqui, H. Y. (1984). *Social work and social action: A developmental perspective.* Harnam Publications.

Sue, D. W. (2006). *Multicultural social work practice.* John Wiley & Sons.

Tolson, E. R., Reid, W. J., & Garvin, C. D. (2003). *Generalist practice: A task-centered approach* (2nd ed.). Columbia University Press.

Trecker, H. B. (1948). *Social group work: Principles and practices.* The Woman's Press.

PART 1

Major Themes in Social Work Practice

Chapter 1

Medical and Psychiatric Social Work Practice

Glimpses and Reflections

K. Sathyamurthi

INTRODUCTION

Social work is a profession based on scientific knowledge and practice. It is also an academic discipline intended to promote change and development in society, through the creation of social cohesion, and to ensure general welfare of the people. Social work as a profession aims to improve the well-being of individuals and to help them satisfy their basic human needs. This is especially true of those who are vulnerable, oppressed and living in poverty, and is also rooted in the set of core values and ethical standards of the discipline. The six core values of social work are social justice, dignity and worth of the person, importance of human relationships, integrity, and competence.

Social work paradigms range from the clinical to the ecological and further to the progressive. The developments in the social work paradigms occur from time to time due to the painstaking care taken by academic institutions and associations, in order to meet the mission of the social work profession (NASW, 2005, 2008). In 1955, a National Association of Social Workers (NASW) was set up in the USA through the merger of seven organizations and cornerstone of the social work profession in the USA (Desai, 2004).

The Tata Institute of Social Sciences (TISS) pioneered social work education in India in 1936, which was followed by the establishment of 34 more institutions in the next four decades. Many indigenous specializations were offered in the final year of postgraduation in social work.[1]

Recently, TISS has expanded by starting new schools, such as schools of social work, management and labour welfare, human ecology, health systems studies, media and cultural studies, education, habitation studies and development studies. New specializations in social work are being offered in many schools of social work apart from the abovementioned indigenous specializations. In general, most of the social work departments in colleges and universities are still following the indigenous specializations such as community development, human resource development, medical social work (MSW) and psychiatric social work (PSW), social work with families, welfare of the weaker sections and human rights, and youth welfare and development.

According to the clinical social work (CSW) paradigm, some people cannot adjust to the larger forces due to psychosocial problems. Clients are considered persons with dysfunctional conditions (NASW, 2005, 2008).

PSW is a specialized branch of social work that is concerned with theoretical as well as practical aspects of clinical work practice with any individuals, groups and communities having difficulty in dealing with their psychological, emotional and intellectual problems by themselves. Social workers specializing in this area also need substantial working knowledge of psychiatry, which primarily deals with problems of the mind and associated disorders. The essential purpose of PSW is to help people with problems of the mind and/or with behaviour problems. In precise terms, psychiatric social workers deal with the problems of 'mind' and 'brain' and their solutions.

---

[1] http://ijsw.tiss.edu/greenstone/collect/ijsw/index/assoc/HASH0b6a/fac99 d45.dir/doc.pdf

CSW includes two broad dimensions: medical social work (MSW) and PSW. Medical and psychiatric social workers attempt to understand the behaviour of people when they are ill, see disease potentialities within individuals and their families, find resources in the community, discover the environmental effects associated with the disease, and create insight into their problems, bringing out a social diagnosis and suggesting the means of treatment, together with the physical and other psychological methods, which should help people revive their strength and become active citizens.

MSW is commonly known as the field in which social workers work with individuals and groups in clinical and community settings, which are typically hospitals, outpatient clinics, community health agencies, skilled nursing facilities, long-term care facilities or hospices. They provide care, primarily by assessing the psychosocial functioning of patients and their families, and intervening as necessary in case they need psychosocial help.

On the other hand, PSW is a challenging field of professional practice which aims at working with individuals having problems of various kinds. Such individuals are often unable to manage their situation due to factors such as emotional distress, which may be a source of further problems for themselves and the society at large.

ORIGIN AND HISTORY

The first psychiatric social worker was appointed in 1907 at The Johns Hopkins Hospital at Baltimore, Maryland, USA. Psychiatric care was initiated in 1908, and the Department of Social Services was started in 1912. By 1983, the service strength had been extended by appointing 11 social workers in the Adolf Meyer building in Cranston, Rhode Island. Medical social workers in the early stage of practice, until the profession was officially renamed in the 1960s, were originally called hospital almoners. The Institute of Almoners was initially formed in 1945 in Britain and was renamed the Institute of Medical Social Workers in 1964.[2]

---

[2] https://en.wikipedia.org/wiki/Medical_social_work

A. S. Desai (1985) notes in *The Foundations of Social Work Education in India and Some Issues* that Dr J. M. Kumarappa, who became the director of TISS in 1941, visited the USA for assessing how social work education was being pursued there. Based on his assessment, the generic curriculum followed in TISS was changed to a specialization-oriented curriculum (Desai, 1985). The social work specializations were the branches of other subjects. Thus, MSW and PSW were established in 1948. The family and child welfare specialization was initiated in 1949 by an American specialist in child development on an invitation by an American social work professional; both specializations were headed by an Indian faculty trained in the USA. Later the group and community organizations were established in 1952, headed by an alumnus who received training in the USA.

In November 1970, the WHO seminar on the 'Organisation and Future Needs of Mental Health Services in India' recommended the creation of the post of social worker in all district hospitals, with opportunities for promotion in the medical college to an assistant professor. During 1973, the first conference of the Indian Society of Psychiatric Social Work was held in the premises of the School of Social Work, Kashi Vidyapeeth, and C. P. Goyal was elected as the first president. Many problems in regard to the nomenclature of psychiatric social workers, pay scales, cadre and recruitment rules, duties and functions were thoroughly discussed, followed by a second conference at Madras in 1974 with much more grandeur and activity. The society also started a journal called *Indian Journal of Psychiatric Social Work*, which was devoted to the publication of research literature in the field (Ramana, 1981).

By 1975, more emphasis was being laid on psychological and psychiatric aspects in the treatment of illnesses. Social workers were being expected to play their part in the psychiatric multidisciplinary team with competence, and to discuss social diagnostic problems and suggest psychosocial treatment programmes together with traditional rehabilitation and follow-ups. In 1976, a committee was appointed by NIMHANS through which the syllabus was further modified to incorporate modern trends in the field of mental health, as per which the social worker was expected to equip himself not for institution work but for handling the community aspects, on which more emphasis was increasingly being laid (Ramana, 1981).

TRENDS IN CLINICAL SOCIAL WORK

CSW focuses on the mental, emotional and behavioural well-being of individuals, couples, families and groups. CSW professionals diagnose and treat people with mental disorders in collaboration with other mental health professionals. Clients who have emotional and behavioural disturbances need to be treated in various institutional and non-institutional care service settings. CSW centres work with a holistic approach with multi-dimensional focus through psychotherapeutic interventions and also strengthen the client's relationship to their environment for a viable treatment plan.

CSW is a practice area of social work which focuses on core phases such as assessment, diagnosis, treatment and prevention of mental illness as well as emotional and other behavioural problems. In an international practice, CSW (or PSW or social work practice) is a licenced profession, and it has been accredited by the respective national councils or associations for providing care services. In the Indian context, neither the government nor the professional organizations have initiated the licensing process, which hinders the practice at large.

The aforementioned practice areas of the specialization of MSW and PSW began case management in the early 20th century. This continues even in the present context, where the health settings are often different. Also, other related disciplines such as child welfare, adolescent welfare, women welfare, family related services, intellectual disabilities related to cognition from childhood to adolescence, industrial healthcare services and community-based care and support in rural, urban and tribal settings have come up in a big way.

Social work practice initially started as a not-for-profit service, and all the fields of the specialization have incrementally become professional in nature. In the present context of corporate social responsibility, medical and psychiatric social workers play a very prominent role in providing preventive and rehabilitative services. This will pave the way for social workers to understand the culture and diversity of individuals, groups and communities. This will also help them determine which approaches are better suited to the expectations and needs of different individuals, groups and communities (NASW, 2013).

SKILLS, TECHNIQUES AND METHODS

Social work has both very specific and very general skills and techniques, such as observation, recording, counselling, interview and participatory learning and action. These need to be used as part of both its primary methods at the micro or meso level, such as social casework, social group work and community organization, and its secondary methods at the macro level such as social action, social welfare administration and social action.

In the early 20th century, PSW practice was modified using the psychodynamic perspective from psychiatry, with social casework as the primary practice approach. This was done by expanding the foundations or theoretical background of social casework, as emphasized in social action, planning and policy (NASW, 2013).

The emerging concept and practices in the international perspectives, such as 'psychological first aid'(PFA) as an evidence-informed modular approach to help children, adolescent, adults and families in the immediate aftermath of disaster and terrorism, as well as mental health first-aid practices, are gaining momentum in the practice of MSW and PSW in India. Social workers use various primary and secondary methods for identifying and defining problems or needs of individuals, groups and families. The following are the techniques used in the social casework for managing the clients:

- Client or person-centred approach
- Case worker–client relationship
- Person-in-environment focus
- Strengths perspective

- Teamwork
- Client intervention at the micro, meso and macro levels.

MODELS

Social workers make use of several models as part of their interventions. The most appropriate models used in MSW and PSW are as follows.

Problem-solving Model

A problem-solving model is a systematic approach, which was identified by H. H. Perlman, to review the strengths and weaknesses, identify evidence-based instructional interventions by collecting data, monitor progress and evaluate the effectiveness of interventions. For generating potential solutions for the implementation, monitoring and evaluation of the effectiveness of the interventions, a six-step process suitable in CSW—comprising problem formulation/identification, root cause(s) analysis, initiation, development and implementation of the alternative solutions and evaluation of the outcome with regard to the purposes of the process—is used. This helps free the client to focus on the tasks related to the solution of his/her problem, by involving his ego in the work designated to deal with the problem and to mobilize internal and external psychological resources in the service of finding satisfactory solution(s) to his/her problems.

Behavioural Modification Model

Integrating behaviour modification models into the primary care settings has the potential to facilitate change in the client's behaviour. Improved health behaviour may be achieved by:

- Individualizing intervention to client characteristics and needs
- Setting goals and problem-solving methods together with clients
- Multiple follow-up contacts

Supporting the client in adapting to the social and physical environment and utilizing opportunities for closer integration with the larger direct instruction model, mastery learning and programmed instruction model are some common models in behaviour modification.[3]

Crisis Intervention Model

This model relates to psychological care during emergency to assist individuals in crisis situations to restore their psychosocial and biological functioning and minimize their psychological trauma. The seven critical stages in the process that have been identified are as follows:

- Planning and assessment
- Establishing a collaborative relationship
- Identifying problems
- Exploring feelings and emotions
- Generating alternative and coping strategies
- Restoration of functioning and development of the implementation action plan
- Follow-up action.[4]

Public Health Model

Public health model is a paradigm of the traditional medical model of individual care within the context of multiple determinants of health. This is epidemiological in nature and attempts to prevent or reduce illness or social problems in a given population by identifying the risk indicators and by targeting policies and interventions to minimize the long-term effects of the problems (World Health Organization, 2006). This model of disease prevention and intervention operates at three levels—primary, secondary and tertiary.[5]

---

[3] https://wikieducator.org/Behaviour_Modification_Model

[4] https://triggered.edina.clockss.org/ServeContent?rft_id=info:doi/10.1093/brief-treatment/mhi030

[5] https://aifs.gov.au/cfca/publications/defining-public-health-model-child-welfare-services-context

FIELD-BASED PRACTICE IN MEDICAL AND PSYCHIATRIC SOCIAL WORK

In general health settings, there were several indigenous practices carried out by various researchers and practitioners in India and across the world. In the MSW and PSW field, there are several practice models which have been developed by individuals and practitioners.

In Tamil Nadu, TT Ranganathan Clinical Research Foundation[6] started in 1980 as a day care centre for treating alcoholics. In 1989, the therapeutic services were extended to drug-dependent persons as well by Dr Shanthi Ranganathan's foresight and determination.

The Banyan[7] started as a non-governmental organization in 1993. It has since then expanded its services to three states and has a variety of holistic mental health solutions to address multifaceted components of distress. Ms Vandana, founder, and Ms Vaishnavi, co-founder, began the services with the aim to create a sustainable model of mental health care and support services to the needy through shelters, hospitals, community-based care with the inclusiveness principle of care to the acute medical, psychiatric and psychological services to the people.

Schizophrenia Research Foundation (SCARF India[8]) was founded in 1984 by a group of mental health professionals and philanthropists headed by Padma Bhushan Dr M Sarada Menon. This is now a Collaborating Centre of the World Health Organization (WHO) for Mental Health Research and Training.

Apart from the above organizations, several governmental and non-governmental organizations in India are working in the field of MSW and PSW. These organizations practice both the indigenous and other models to prevent and treat mental illness and rehabilitate the individual in his larger group and community.

---

[6] http://www.addictioncentreindia.org/
[7] https://thebanyan.org/
[8] https://www.scarfindia.org/

ROLE OF SOCIAL WORKERS

Professionally qualified social workers have an understanding about healthcare with a multidisciplinary team due to formal education, work and academic expertise. Social workers have a formal role as educators. The roles of professional social workers in hospitals include educator, motivator, patient care provider, facilitator, counsellor, therapist and palliative care coordinator. Social workers in psychiatry are involved in imparting psycho-education to the patients and family members and also assisting in creating a discharge plan by linking the available resources to the patients and families in the institution and community. Psychiatric social workers (also variously called clinical social workers, medical social workers and case managers) assist in providing care and treatment to individual patients or clients, groups and families based on their strengths and liabilities. Social workers are involved in evaluating the patient's family situation and reinforcing the social support systems that are available to the patients.[9]

The core functions, roles and responsibilities of social workers vary according to the programmes or objectives, level or degree of client engagement, as well as client's priorities and strengths. One of their major roles is to develop the implementation of a care plan to monitor the delivery of services right up to the termination of treatment and follow-up.

CLINICAL SOCIAL WORK TODAY:
GLIMPSES AND REFLECTIONS

Clinical social workers find employment opportunities in various functions such as case management, care continuum, healthcare services, health planning, managed care and providing support for health insurance. These functions are more prevalent for the medical social workers. While psychiatric social workers are also engaged in some of these functions, they are also involved in a major way in psychosocial case diagnosis and therapy.

---

[9] https://www.sochealth.co.uk/1946/07/16/work-psychiatric-social-worker/

In CSW practice, at the micro level, the individuals are addressed at the level of their bio-psychosocial and spiritual status, and the social systems in the community and society at large are addressed at the macro level of intervention. Though these seem to be simple primary functions of clinical social workers, in reality there exist lots of challenges. First, lack of awareness of the functions of medical social workers among the healthcare services proves to be a major barrier. The medical social worker's functions overlap with those of other paraprofessionals. Second, the advocacy role of the medical social worker, on behalf of the client, is often perceived by the healthcare services to be in conflict with their organizational interests.

According to Barker (2013), the care continuum includes the specialized home-based health services which a seriously or chronically ill or injured person might need. In general, it addresses the need for both the medical care and the other services that promote the patients' well-being.

Medical and psychiatric social workers are more frequently employed in the hospices, where their functions are crucial. However, social workers in these fields face secondary trauma and so PFA in such contexts is evidently most useful for both the client and the social worker or caregiver.

Medical social workers in many healthcare settings are confined to providing continuity of care since their service is limited by the organizations. Home visits and community visits to create health awareness are usually restricted by such organizations.

In healthcare settings, social workers have to work in accordance with the brief of a multidisciplinary team that includes physicians, social workers, psychologists, nurses and hospital attendants. Cohesion between the team members is vital, but always lacking. The role of clinical social workers in health planning in India is hardly evident, as its significance is not felt in the government system. Also, the social workers lack awareness about the scope of their work in health planning.

In the international scenario, healthcare and insurance are very much in place in many countries for the patients who seek effective services. Also, the practice and recognition of qualified psychiatric and medical social workers is very well organized and structured in the USA, the UK and other countries, which help those professionals work effectively. In India, healthcare coverage and insurance on similar lines is an emerging trend, as the scope of social work is not yet felt sufficiently both by the system and by the social workers. In many hospitals in India, however, medical social workers are working very effectively in the insurance and rehabilitation domain.

Qualified social workers should accept and practice the case management services based on their individual competences in relation to the patient or client perspective, as these will vary in spite of their education. He/she should look for professional development refresher courses, certification and other prerequisites to enhance their knowledge and competences. To be competent in the practice of MSW or PSW, the social worker needs to attain the requisite training and gather sufficient experience to adequately help the individual patients achieve quality of life and well-being. This can only be accomplished through care and support, in keeping with the dignity and worth of an individual.

CONCLUSION

Social work is a profession that aims at the well-being of people irrespective of the differences in their specific status. Social work education enables the students to understand the true meaning of social work and its concepts. Though we now have access to a large number of sources of literature specific to the field, these are mostly rooted in western culture. The practice of social work has evolved in India over the last eight decades, but still depends on the western models, as indigenous approaches are not given due credit in the social work curriculum. Several research studies in the field have suggested working models based on indigenous specifications, which can be incorporated in the social work education teaching material and implemented during fieldwork in relation to individuals, the community and society. Clinical social workers in India should be aware of what is happening in other countries. However, instead of just imitating the work done by others, they should try to evolve their own models in conjunction with local systems and demands.

REFERENCES

Barker, R. L. (2013). *The social work dictionary* (6th ed.). NASW Press.

Cox, David, & Pawar, Manohar. (2006). *International social work: Issues, strategies, and programs.* SAGE Vistaar.

Desai, Manu. (1985). *An anthology of short stories for social work education.* Tata Institute of Social Sciences.

Desai, Murali. (2004). *Methodology of progressive social work education.* Rawat Publication.

NASW. (2005). *NASW standards for clinical social work.* Author.

NASW. (2008). *NASW code of ethics.* Author.

NASW. (2013). *NASW standards for social work case management.* Author.

Ramana, K. V. (1981). *Social work education and social work practice in India.* Association of Psychiatric Social Workers.

World Health Organization. (2006). *Preventing child maltreatment: A guide to taking action and generating evidence.* WHO Press. whqlibdoc.who.int/publications/2006/9241594365_eng.pdf

Chapter 2

Social Work Practice with Families and Children

Archana Kaushik

INTRODUCTION

Family is considered the bastion of human civilization. The family system has universal presence, although its structures and functions vary from society to society and time to time. It is taken as the basic unit of society—the building block. The family is not merely a biological group; rather, it is a primary social institution. It provides for the basic needs, sense of security, love, care and warmth. The family unit is one of the most vital and influential aspects in an individual's life. Invariably, the institution of family lays the foundation of basic personality dispositions. Morals, values and interpersonal skills learnt during early socialization in the family system generally have bearing on an individual's behaviour patterns throughout his/her life.

The highly diverse and dynamic nature of the institution of family poses challenges for the scholars and social scientists in defining it. The family is largely defined from two viewpoints—structural and functional. Structurally, from the traditional definition of three to four generations living together under one roof and having food cooked in a common hearth (which was later termed joint family) to husband and wife living with their unmarried children (nuclear family), the normative family pattern has seen a substantial change. In the contemporary world, various alternative family patterns are observed, such as 'dual income no kid' families or 'live-in couples' without marriage, which raises questions whether children are necessary or sufficient to define family, or any civil or religious ceremony is needed to conceptualize family. Moreover, homosexual relationships are gradually gaining acceptance, defying the notion that a man and a woman are at the core of a family.

When seen from the functional perspective, it is often held that the institution of family came into existence basically to meet the needs of nurturance and socialization of children. Traditionally, a family unit used to perform several functions such as carrying out economically gainful activities (e.g., farming and weaving), providing education and skill development to children, socialization, health management, recreation and several others. Gradually, many of these functions are taken over by schools, hospitals/dispensaries, factories, workplaces, mass media, peers, cinema and so on. In the present times, with more and more women getting employed outside the household, even childcare is given over to crèches and nannies. These changes in the family system have far-reaching implications on the lives of individual members, including children.

> Family-centred care is defined as 'a philosophy of care in which the pivotal role of the family is recognized and respected ... [in which] families should be supported in their natural care-giving and decision-making roles ... [in which] parents and professionals are seen as equals' (Brewer et al., 1989, p. 1056)

Further, children are considered the biggest asset of any nation. Nelson Mandela stated, 'There can be no keener revelation of a society's soul than the way in which it treats its children.' They signify the potential resource of a society. With more than 400 million children, India is home to the largest number of children in the world. Unfortunately, not every child is blessed with loving parents and stable home life. Some children are forced to cope with upheaval and problems at home, such as neglect and abuse, due to inherent problems such as parental alcoholism and drug addiction as well as poverty. A large proportion of children in the country are malnourished, illiterate, living amidst poverty, forced into labour bondage (instead of being in school), trafficked for exploitative practices such as beggary and flesh trade, and are subjected to abuse, violence and discrimination based on gender, caste, community and class.

HISTORICAL EVOLUTION OF SOCIAL WORK WITH FAMILIES AND CHILDREN

Family-centred social work practice can be traced back to the 1950s. In 1975, Bronfenbrenner mentioned the impact of involvement of family on the educational outcomes and overall development of children. However, until the late 1980s the family social work practice did not gain much popularity. Shelton et al. (1987) observed that in the second half of the 1980s a series of papers on the core elements of family-centred practice was published by the US Association for the Care of Children's Health. These core elements entailed recognizing the vital significance of the family in the child's life; facilitating collaboration of parents and professionals in diverse activities ranging from individual care to programme development, implementation and evaluation; respecting the racial, ethnic and socio-cultural diversity of families; recognizing the strengths and different coping strategies of individual families; continuous sharing of complete and unbiased information with parents in supportive ways and so on. This drew the attention of the social work fraternity in the area of family-centred practice. In between, Hartman and Laird in 1983 provided 'family-centred social work practice' based on the ecological model or systems approach. It has proved highly beneficial and paved way for other family-centred social work practitioners to develop various models of family assessment and interventions. In the 1990s, with the development of early childhood care and education, as well as early intervention with young children with disabilities, family-centred social work practice gained momentum. Similarly, Dunst et al. (1991, p. 115) have defined family-centred practice as 'a combination of beliefs and practices that define particular ways of working with families that are consumer driven and competency enhancing'. Three key elements were included in this— one, there is an emphasis on strengths and not deficits; two, the efforts are geared towards family's control over required and desired resources and promoting choices; and three, developing a collaborative relation between professionals and parents (Dunst et al., 1994).

On examining the evolution of family-centric social work in Indian context, it can be found that professional social work started in India in 1936 with the establishment of Sir Dorabji Tata Graduate School of Social Work (now called Tata Institute of Social Sciences, [TISS]) in Mumbai. In 1947, the Indian Conference of Social Work developed the social work curriculum for India in consultation with the Council on Social Work Education, through the Technical Cooperation Mission Programme, USA. Professional social work education in India has, more often than not, received the criticism of being 'borrowed knowledge' from the West and so inadequate to address the social problems of Indian settings. However, as Kulkarni (1993) asserts, social work education has evolved as a graft on the indigenous knowledge and ancient heritage rather than an independent transplant. In fact, Dr Manshardt, one of the founders of social work education in India, emphasized that the *Indian-ness* in social work must be amalgamated into the academic curriculum, field practicum and social work research (see Manshardt, 1936, p. 2). The curriculum content of American social work was initially borrowed while the indigenization happened at a snail's pace. However, in the beginning phase, among other areas, social work with families and children was being taught as a small portion of the paper on 'fields of social work or areas of social work practice' at the college and university levels, which soon was changed to a separate paper on 'Family and Child Welfare' (Desai, 1987, pp. 208–219). Alongside, Christian missions as well as philanthropic and voluntary organizations working with the physically and mentally handicapped, orphans, the destitute and the poor created demand for courses such as family and child welfare for the employment of social work graduates.

In the fieldwork practicum, at the start, focused target groups were families and children and juvenile delinquents. Gradually, student trainees expanded work on families and children on a whole range of issues and problems using different methods of social work practice. With time, MPhil and PhD on various topics including aspects of family functioning, communication and interaction patterns also widened the scope of family-centric social work theorization and practice.

Moreover, the Indian Conference of Social Work (renamed the Indian Council of Social Welfare), since 1947, has been developing rich indigenous literature on social work through the compilation of thematic papers by social workers in annual sessions, published under the gamut of 'Social Work Forum'. Other agencies, such as the National Institution of Public Cooperation and Child Development and All India Conference of Women and Indian Council of Child Welfare, are also contributing to indigenous literature in similar ways. Much of the work relates to social work with families and children (see Desai, 2010). The publication of *Encyclopaedia of Social Work in India* and the regular publication of nearly 15 social work journals, including Indian Journal of Social Work, are among several other initiatives in developing indigenous social work literature, covering significant topics and areas of practice including families and children.

Social work educational institutions have developed field action projects to meet praxis and practice needs. TISS opened the first child guidance clinic in India, which was followed by other schools of social work. However, not much literature could be developed from field action projects despite having huge scope (Desai, 2019). After the creation of the Family Social Work Unit at TISS, Murli Desai compiled numerous research studies and bibliographies on varied aspects of Indian families. Ample work was done, through seminars, workshops, empirical research and curriculum planning, that not only enriched family social work in numerous ways—family policy, family laws, family life education and social work with families—but also resulted in the emergence of four courses for the specialization in family social work as contextualized in Indian settings.

Over the years, a range of family assessment and practice models and frameworks have been gradually developed, experimented and improvised. Though the list is exhaustive, the salient ones are Beavers Systems Model, Circumplex Model of Marital and Family Systems, McMaster Model, Family Capacity Model, Friedman Family Assessment Model, Darlington Family Assessment Model, Family Systems Theory/Model, Family Cycle of Health and Illness Model, Calgary Family Assessment Model and Calgary Family Intervention Model, Family Systems Stressor-Strength Inventory and several more.

These models have wide applicability to culturally diverse family groups. In the postmodern times, with the prevalence of heterogeneity, plurality and diversity, these models are based on universally applicable aspects such as communication, cohesiveness, flexibility, boundary, decision-making patterns, problem-solving approach and such others, rather than emphasis on structural and functional aspects of family systems. These models invariably measure parameters of the family's functioning as a continuum, divided into different levels, rather than dichotomous variables. Due to such characteristic features, these family assessment and intervention models are equally applicable for traditional, normative, as well as alternative family systems.

In the evolution of social work, the child remained an integral part of all the interventions—be it visits by teachers or development of methods of casework and groupwork. In India, traditionally, the care of children has been bestowed with the family and the community. The joint family system used to be the social safety net, and in case of death and disability of the parents, other family members would take care of the child. After independence, the government in its first five-year plan provided financial assistance to NGOs to meet certain needs of children in terms of crèche facility, education and health. Gradually, children's institutions were established by the government. From the Third Five-Year Plan, integrated services on education, health and nutrition for children were initiated on an experimental basis. Childcare committees were established by the Central Social Welfare Board to find out the needs of children. In 1995, Integrated Child Development Services (ICDS) was started, first on pilot basis in 33 blocks and later expanded in the whole country. In 1991, after India's signing of the United Nations Conventions on Rights of Children, several policies and laws related to children such as the Juvenile Justice (JJ) Act were amended on the basis of the child rights framework.

RELEVANCE OF SOCIAL WORK INTERVENTIONS WITH FAMILIES AND CHILDREN

Social work profession, since its inception, has responded to varied problems and challenges faced by families and children. The disciple has evolved strong conceptual and theoretical base of examining various facets of problems in well-being of families and children along with specialized skills and areas of practice. International Federation of Social Work (2019) has highlighted family well-being as one of the salient goals in its recent definition of social work profession. As an enabling profession, social work plays a pivotal role in the fields of family and child welfare.

Although every family experiences problems at one point or another, some problems are potent enough to make the family system dysfunctional. These problems can also put an excessive amount of stress on individual members of a family. In the contemporary world, changing family structure and functions have posed serious threats to the security and safety of families, especially children and older people. The informal support system from kith and kin, which used to act as buffer at the time of crisis in family relationships, is gradually vanishing. In urban areas, increasing impersonality and alienation is the fallout of diminishing social support systems. Since family is the basic unit of society, almost all humans are part of a family in their lifetime and so any problem experienced by individuals impacts their family. In addition, family is a dynamic notion. Almost all the problems encountered by humans influence their roles and relationships in the family. This shows that the scope of social work with families is nearly omnipresent. Social workers working in the fields of health, education, social welfare, disaster, conflict and peace, rural–urban development, indigenous communities and such others are directly or indirectly dealing with families.

Further, family is of pivotal significance for human beings. Human infants cannot survive without the protection and nurturance of the family. It provides for all their needs, from survival needs to developmental opportunities. A child is socialized and develops perspectives, attitudes, ideas, perceptions and personality in the family itself. Children thrive when parents actively promote their positive growth and development. When family relations go dysfunctional, its implications may range from mild to severe in consequence on children and other members, depending upon the causes of the dysfunctionality and the duration and stage of development. For instance, prolonged conflict can damage a child's neurochemistry, thereby making him or her anxiety-prone and insecure and affect his or her attachment with others. Likewise, in families where either or both of the parents have mental disorders, children too tend to develop both symptom disorders and personality disorders, may fail to develop healthy relations with significant others, and their education and career may be hampered. Children from dysfunctional families may lack empathy and sensitivity, show anxiety and aggression, stubbornness and truancy, and may develop anti-social behaviours. Their restricted friendships and relationships with outsiders may lead to isolation and loneliness. Children of abusive parents learn to be abusive and may indulge in intimate partner violence in their adulthood. Individuals from dysfunctional families tend to have a higher incidence of behavioural disorders.

Looking at the situation of children, macro-level data pose a grim picture and also point to the significance of social work practice with this social group of crucial importance. The infant mortality rate is 47 per 1,000 live births (Sample Registration System [SRS], 2011). Every second child in India is malnourished (National Family Health Survey, 2005–2006). Nearly 11.6 lakh infants die every year due to lack of immunization (Ministry of Health and Family Welfare, 2012). Gender disparity is stark in India. There are 914 girls for every 1,000 boys (Census, 2011). Girl children, in the age-group of one to four years, have 61 per cent higher rate of mortality than boys, and 56 per cent adolescent girls, aged between 15 and 19 years, are anaemic, in contrast to 30 per cent adolescent boys. Further, about 45 per cent girls in India are married off before they attain the marriageable age of 18 years (National Family Health Survey, 2005–2006), which vividly shows gender-based discriminatory treatment against females. Looking at the educational scenario, data from the Ministry of Statistics and Programme Implementation (2012) show that the net enrolment ratio at the upper primary level in government schools is merely 58.3 per cent and gross enrolment ratio at the secondary level is below 50 per cent. In addition, nearly 35 per cent children with disabilities remain out of elementary school (District Information System for Education [DISE], 2011–2012).

Moreover, Census 2011 estimates that there are 10.12 million child labourers in India aged between 5 and 14 years and about half of them are girls. The National Crime Records Bureau (2011) maintains that there has been an increase in child murders by over 25 per cent since 2000 in India.

Children born in Dalit families often face several survival constraints. The National Family Health Survey-III (2005–2006) brings out that 55 per cent of children younger than three years belonging to Scheduled Caste and Scheduled Tribe families are underweight, as compared to about 37 per cent of children from the general population. The NFHS data further show that the Under-5 Mortality Rate (U5MR) is 88.1 per cent for Schedule Caste and 95.7 per cent for Schedule Tribe children, against the national average of 59.2 per cent.

SCOPE OF SOCIAL WORK WITH FAMILIES

Among other things, in the present times, the role and functions of the family are declining. The Indian family system has been traditionally characterized by 'conformity' to family norms, values and practices. There has been a substantial dilution in these traditional normative roles and interaction patterns. The stability of familial relations is at risk more than ever before. Marital conflict, whether culminated in divorce or not, is on the rise. Though families are trying to cope with the changes and challenges encountered in the present socio-cultural milieu, several families find themselves in crisis as their old coping patterns fail to provide any help. There is therefore a vast scope of social work intervention at each stage of the family life cycle.

The following challenges require social work intervention at the independence stage or the pre-coupling stage of a family life cycle: unrealistic and heightened expectations from the prospective marriage partner on roles and relationship norms; sexual experimentation in clandestine manner—due to the 'culture of silence', and as a consequence, open communication on sexual matters being considered taboo, leading to spread of sexually transmitted diseases including HIV; unemployment, under-employment, financial constraints and poverty; and the normalization of gender-based violence and aggression.

Further, there may be temperamental incompatibility between couples—leading to conflicts, frictions, frustrations and stress. At the coupling stage, adjustment demands with spouse and in-laws, role confusion, role strain, dowry demands, job stress and inability to meet partner's and other family members' expectations are factors leading to disharmony in the family.

In the expansion stage of the family life cycle, parenting issues are a huge concern. When parents are authoritarian, the personality of child(ren) get suppressed, making them hostile and rebellious. In contrast, permissive parenting can be perceived by children as proof of lack of care, indifference and timidity of the parents, and consequently children become arrogant, hostile and stubborn. At this stage, parent–child conflicts may lead to familial disputes and dysfunction. In certain families, spousal conflicts aggravate susceptibility to parent–child conflicts, while in certain other families, conflicts between parent(s) and child(ren) are exclusive in nature. The reasons for conflicts in parent–child dyads are the differential value systems in the family, as well as societal expectations and norms as reflected through peers, schoolmates, mass media and the like, while communication patterns remain a cross-cutting variable.

In the last stage of family life cycle, that is, 'Stage of Contraction', couples become old and their children leave the household either for their career requirements or after marriage. The elderly too face a range of challenges in the contemporary world. They no longer enjoy the traditional ascribed status and so encounter 'rolelessness'. There is a sharp rise in crime against the aged, with the motive of depriving them of their property. Elder abuse, which was unheard of in traditional India, is also increasingly manifested in both rural and urban areas. Destitution and poverty too are adding to the vulnerabilities of older persons.

Families have porous boundaries. Members of the family may face problems at their respective workplaces, schools or other social systems they interact with, and these impact their family relations. The dynamic nature of family is such that it gets affected by the problems and challenges that arise in its interaction with various systems in its socio-cultural milieu. At the same time, problems arising within the family system also influence the interaction of its members with other systems. Several factors result in family crisis, which may be extrinsic or intrinsic or both. Extrinsic factors such as unemployment, poverty, limited accessibility to resources and services, natural (such as earthquakes, floods) and/or man-made calamities (such as accidents, terrorism and wars) may challenge the coping capacities of the family, thereby hampering its social functioning.

AREAS OF FAMILY INTERVENTION

Social work in family setting has a vast scope. Academicians and social scientists, engaged in family studies, have postulated models and modalities of family assessment so as to identify areas of family conflicts. Areas requiring interventions of family social workers are investigated by studying:

- authoritarian and regressive family norms that violate rights of individual family members;
- patterns of family interaction that have turned dysfunctional;
- problems in facilitating individual family members' developmental tasks and
- family ecology that entails interaction of family systems with other social systems in the larger socio-cultural milieu.

Though the causes and consequences of family disorganization are countless due to a high level of diversity and heterogeneity, some major challenges commonly encountered by families that require social work interventions can be identified. These are noted as follows:

1. Families having individual members facing abuse, exploitation and violence of the following kinds: child abuse, violence against women, elder abuse and abuse of the disabled;
2. Individual family members facing problems such as disability, chronic/terminal illness, addiction of substance abuse and the like;
3. Marital conflicts, disharmony and breakdown (reflected in divorce, death or separation);
4. Family deprivation manifested in destitution among children, adults and/or the aged;
5. Families that are affected by instability or imbalance in other systems, such as those facing political violence or environmental

disasters, or those forced to migrate, take refuge or otherwise uprooted;

6. Families that are in conflict with other systems due to unemployment, indebtedness, landlessness, lack of sufficient resources, inadequate or no housing and/or other issues and

7. Problems with bearing and rearing of children, such as infertility or unwed motherhood.

The family situations listed above are neither exhaustive nor mutually exclusive. These situations invariably affect familial interactions, the roles played by family members and the functioning of the family as a system. There may be detrimental effects on the well-being of family members, particularly on children, women and the elderly. Without timely intervention, in some extreme situations, the family system may even disintegrate, leading to vagrancy and destitution of vulnerable family members. Family social workers aim to restore social functioning and ensure family well-being, which entails a whole range of support services and programmes. The salient ones among these are mentioned in the following section.

FAMILY INTERVENTIONS

Families are dynamic institutions, and family problems, conflicts, crises and consequences are highly complex issues with intertwined causal and precipitating factors. The foremost task of family social workers is the assessment of the situation—the causes of family dysfunction and its impact on individual members. Assessment, if appropriately done, aids in designing effective interventions. Family assessment is carried out in a holistic manner, as part of which the social worker appraises the dyadic interactions between family members, communication patterns, family norms and values, and the perception of individual members about the conflict situations as well as their existing coping patterns.

Based on the assessment, social work interventions are designed at various levels. Programmes for awareness generation, linking families with needed resources and services, and for capacity building and training, are examples of interventions that are preventive in nature. In contrast, promotive initiatives include family enrichment programmes that cover imparting of appropriate knowledge and skills among members of families, so that they are able to carry out tasks and roles related to the different stages of the family life cycle in an efficient manner. Stress management, crises interventions and family therapy are planned at the ameliorative and curative levels, alongside the provision of services and goods for facilitating rehabilitation of families.

Family casework, family counselling, couple counselling, crisis intervention, legal aid, marital and family therapy are some of the methods and techniques employed by family social workers, and their differential usage depends upon the nature and types of problems encountered. Apart from assessment and implementation of intervention and services, social workers engage in monitoring and evaluation of these services and raising awareness in public about these services.

During family interventions, there may be specific work with and for children, women, men or elderly family members, but the assessment involves—and the focus is on—the family as a whole. Many times, dyadic relationships central to conflicts are considered as units for intervention.

The locale or settings of family social work are diverse and numerous. Community projects, family service centres, family planning agencies, family courts and so on are considered primary settings, while schools, colleges, health centres, hospitals, industries and such others are secondary settings.

SCOPE OF SOCIAL WORK WITH CHILDREN

It may be noted that children are highly dependent on nurturing and loving environments with adequate economic and physical resources. Childhood is critical for cognitive, emotional and physical development. Anything that goes wrong with children in any domain (physical, social or psychological) has far-reaching complications in their lives. Social workers engaged in the field of child welfare and development frequently make use of the United Nations Convention on the Rights of the Child (UNCRC), which India signed in 1991. The UNCRC has propounded four categories of basic rights—Right to Survival, Right to Development, Right to Protection and Right

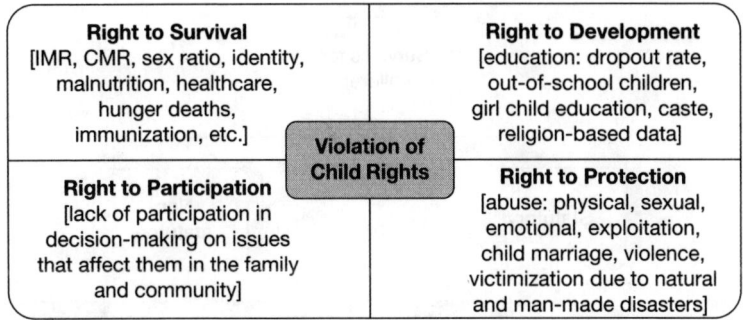

Right to Survival [IMR, CMR, sex ratio, identity, malnutrition, healthcare, hunger deaths, immunization, etc.]	Right to Development [education: dropout rate, out-of-school children, girl child education, caste, religion-based data]
Right to Participation [lack of participation in decision-making on issues that affect them in the family and community]	Right to Protection [abuse: physical, sexual, emotional, exploitation, child marriage, violence, victimization due to natural and man-made disasters]

Figure 2.1 *Violation of Child Rights*
Source: Author

to Participation. However, violations of these rights occur at rampant levels under each category (see Figure 2.1).

UNICEF (2016) has broadly categorized work under the following major themes:

- Child protection and social inclusion (adolescent development, child protection, children with disabilities, children in conflict areas, refugee children, social inclusion etc.);
- Child survival (early childhood development, health, HIV/AIDS, immunization, nutrition, water, sanitation and hygiene);
- Education (basic education, girl's education, learning for peace, out of school initiative, innovation for education);
- Gender equality.

Social work professionals and trainees in their fieldwork practice, using UNCRC framework, often work with children who are in need of protection and care. This includes children in vulnerable situations such as those living on and off streets, abused, abandoned, deserted, displaced, orphaned, homeless, trafficked, infected and/or affected with HIV/AIDS, working as child labourers, in labour bondage, and in conflict and disaster situations.

The multifaceted nature of problems faced by children and the even more complex structural problems makes social work practice

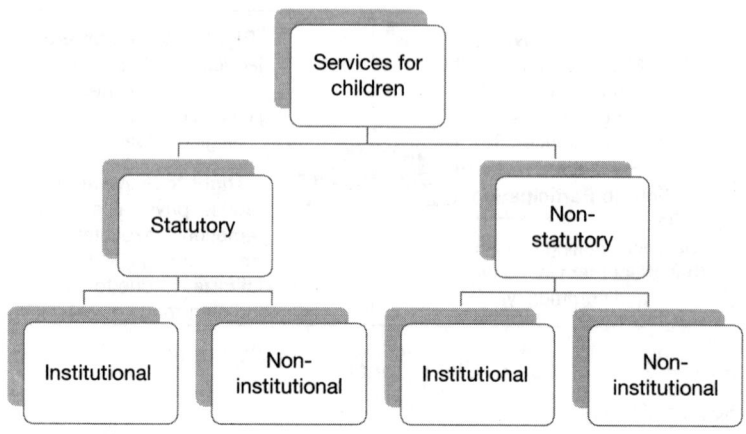

Figure 2.2 *Broad Categorization of Services for Children*
Source: Author

with children quite challenging. Social workers engage with other professionals across government and non-governmental agencies to develop policy and to design and deliver services for the care and protection of vulnerable and marginalized children.

Services for the children may be broadly divided into two categories—Statutory and non-statutory (see Figure 2.2). Statutory services are under the legislative frameworks for child protection, largely under the JJ Act system. The Integrated Child Protection Scheme has laid out an extensive range of services for children. Students of social work are largely placed in various children's homes, observation homes, child-lines, child welfare committees, and such other instruments of the JJ Act in their concurrent and block fieldwork training. Statutory services are further categorized into institutional and non-institutional ones. Trainee social workers are engaged in case work, group work, research and administrative work in institutional settings. They mainly work for repatriation and rehabilitation of children in these settings. A wide range of non-institutional services are there, such as sponsorship, adoption, foster care and after-care, to meet the varied needs of the children in need of care and protection.

Likewise, non-statutory services, mostly implemented by non-government organizations and other civil society organizations, cover a whole spectrum of needs and problems encountered by children. Under this category, non-institutional services in the areas of health, education, skill development, vocational training and awareness generation on significant topics are the common ones. Orphanages, residential programmes for children of prisoners, as well as HIV/AIDS affected and infected children and so on are the services under the non-statutory institutional category.

The fieldwork settings for social work with children are numerous. A fieldwork trainee or social work professional interacts with a child in various situations such as open settings—urban slums, resettlement colonies, villages; or in schools, non-formal education centres, hospitals, family counselling centres, de-addiction centres or child guidance centres; institutional settings—observation homes, special homes or children's homes; or on the streets, railway stations, traffic lights (child beggars), factories (child labourers) and many others.

LEARNING REQUIREMENTS IN FIELDWORK PRACTICUM

Certain salient leaning requirements for trainee social workers in a family setting as well as for working with children are enlisted as follows:

- Develop the ability to work in a conceptual framework to assess problems in the marital relationship and/or family functioning.
- Learn various skills and strategies to intervene in the family that needs professional help.
- Understand the dynamics of intimate relationships and the need to develop 'the smallest democracy at the heart of human society'.
- Understand families as social systems and the factors affecting family functioning.
- Acquire theoretical knowledge on child development, child psychology and behaviour problems among children.
- Develop communication skills (attitude and approach) for working with children, especially children in distress.
- Develop skills specific to working with families and children.
- Understand the policies, services and programmes for families and children.

- Acquire basic knowledge of casework and group work to get involved with children on individual and group basis.
- Learn various methods of working with children—creative/play way and so on.
- Learn counselling techniques for children, family members and elderly persons.
- Comprehend the rights of the child (constitutional safeguards and other laws related to the fieldwork setting).

POTENTIAL FIELDWORK ENGAGEMENTS

Social workers have been involved in ensuring child welfare since ages. There are several conventional roles of a social worker in child welfare settings which are relevant even in the present times, while some other roles have undergone change depending on change in approach in social work. Certain social workers' roles which have been found to be existing and emerging in CWCs and CCIs are as follows:

For case workers, their major responsibilities include conducting initial comprehensive assessment and preparing social information reports, doing on-going assessments, developing and amending plans for the child, record keeping and maintaining case files, linking available legal services to the child, preparing individual case plans and ensuring that every child's health, educational, developmental, emotional and recreational needs are met, identifying their family/kinship support system for repatriation, and conducting home visits for assessment and follow-up.

For counsellors, the major responsibilities include providing assistance to improve the social and psychological functioning of children. For foster care workers, the major tasks are registration of foster families, conducting home visits, periodic visits to check the progress of children placed in foster families and so on. Likewise, as adoption workers, social workers conduct home visits for preliminary assessment, check the background of prospective parents, carry out counselling, and facilitate adoption and post-placement adjustment.

As welfare officers, social workers are involved in effective delivery of services, supervision, conducting spot and home visits, restoration of children, taking children to child welfare committees, maintaining and updating databases of cases, preparing individual development plans for each child and conducting inspection visits to child care institutions. When child welfare workers are based in community settings, they identify cases of child abuse and neglect, locate informal support to strengthen and enhance family functioning, and conduct periodic home visits to check on the progress of the child.

Social workers advocate for resources and system reforms so as to improve services for children, youth and families.

There is now a growing interest, at least among policy makers, to explore alternatives to institutional care for children. Family-based care and protection of children are the emerging areas of intervention. Integrated services covering dimensions such as health, education, development, protection and rehabilitation are being promoted. Along with this, the services are designed in a manner that the delivery is at the community level rather than at institutions. Government and civil society partnerships are also being prompted in various areas such as advocacy and lobbying, counselling, training and development, research and documentation, running childcare institutions, and monitoring and evaluation for greater reach and efficacy.

Social workers also work for strengthening social systems for protection of child rights. These cover amendments in social welfare policies, adequate budget allocations and their public acknowledgement. They facilitate enforcement of legislations. They also ensure meaningful and active involvement of all stakeholders in strengthening the process of care and protection. They cater to the physical, educational, social, psychological and spiritual needs of children who are into the child protection system.

Social workers plan and intervene suitably for early identification of vulnerability, risk reduction and strengthening supportive and protective services. They also work on capacity building of the staff engaged in service delivery systems. They are actively involved in monitoring, evaluation and documenting the process of care and protection of children. Social workers are also involved with children in education, gender empowerment, disability and rehabilitation, community work, health and so on.

Social work professionals are engaged in assessment of the needs and problems of families and networking, referrals and provisions of resources and services to families in conflict with systems in larger social environment. The assessment of the family in terms of its norms, functioning, role relationships, decision-making and dynamics is important. Though pre-marital counselling is provided, its coverage and reach is limited. Family social workers are required to create awareness about such preventive services, along with designing programmes to prepare families about the anticipated challenges of the different stages of the family life cycle. This would substantially reduce maladjustment within the family (between various dyads) as well as between family and other social systems in the social environment. This would also result in successful and smooth transition of families from one stage of the family life cycle to another, thereby preventing stressful situations and avoiding conflicts. Social workers also have substantial roles in designing and implementing family enrichment programmes aimed to ensure the well-being of families.

BOTTLENECKS AND CHALLENGES IN FIELDWORK PRACTICE

The following are the prominent bottlenecks and challenges that are encountered in fieldwork practice in the area of social work with families and children.

At the Level of Social Work Education Department/Institution

Assessing family dynamics and identifying its dysfunctional aspects is a complex task that requires a specialized set of knowledge, skill and value bases. There are various models of assessment of family dynamics such as family-centred ecological social work, Circumplex model and McMaster model. These models offer comprehensive as well as complex designs of family assessment, where families are ranked as per varied degrees of dysfunctionality and functionality. The students at the post-graduation level learn about these models in the third semester, while they come across a wide range of issues affecting family functioning right in the first semester in their fieldwork practicum.

At the undergraduate level, classroom teaching–learning and field practice of these assessment models of family functioning are almost non-existent.

Moreover, family therapy and even family counselling are highly specialized areas of intervention, which require years of practice to hone the skills. Limited time in a semester system and the generic nature of the courses do not make it feasible for social work trainees to imbibe such skills and areas of expertise.

In addition, along with the theoretical knowledge given to the students in the classroom setting, the strategic handholding of the department or college supervisor is required for practicing family-centric social work in various fieldwork settings. However, in most social work educational institutions, 'social work with families and children' is an elective paper. It implies that faculty supervisors may not themselves be aware of specialized assessment models as well as skills and techniques of working with families. Student trainees are randomly allocated to faculty supervisors, who may or may not be well versed with technicalities related to family assessment and interventions. This hampers family-centred social work practice by trainees in their fieldwork. Also, there is dearth of indigenous literature on culturally competent social work practice with families and children.

At the Agency Level

The models mentioned above have wide applicability. However, most often the agency supervisors are not from the social work discipline and, in particular, not aware of skills and techniques of working with families.

The practice of models and techniques of family assessment and interventions is very helpful in identifying family strengths and weaknesses, family dynamics, assessing communication patterns, cohesiveness, adaptability and such other important areas of family functioning. However, it often demands huge time allocation and concerted efforts. Also, the agency may not be willing to offer a lot of time to the trainee to observe and respond to the needs and problems of one family. This is also true with regard to working with children. Child–centric counselling and the skills and techniques of working with children often remain a miniscule part of the curriculum, and there are limited opportunities available to student trainees to practise and hone the related skills in the fieldwork practicum. For instance, if the mandate of an agency is to provide non-formal education to children, the trainees are hardly able to work on parent–child relationships or on other familial issues.

A high level of heterogeneity is observed in family systems, which makes it difficult for the social work trainees to ascertain the patterns of communication and behaviours among the families within the limited time period of their fieldwork practice. It also poses difficulties in theorizing the assessment and interventions in the fieldwork settings.

At the Community Level

The cultural norms and values in India do not facilitate carving out the required space for family-centred social work practice. Approaching a social worker to resolve a family's internal conflicts is not culturally aligned. The vast majority of families, especially in rural areas, strongly believe that family matters are private and have no idea that 'outside help' can be an option.

As stated earlier, conformity to familial and societal values, norms and practices is a characteristic feature of Indian families. Though there are many positive aspects to it, denial of individual rights is a fallout, which is reflected mainly in restricted access to developmental opportunities to females. In juxtaposition, social work rests on the rights and justice approach. This makes the role of social workers in family assessment and intervention quite challenging, but at the same time very much needed, as it aims to build and ensure the 'smallest democracy at the heart of society'. At times, social work trainees encounter intra-psychic conflicts, as they have imbibed certain family values which may not coincide with the rights and justice-based values of the social work discipline.

Further, a social work trainee in the field interacts with children in some way or the other. It is necessary to develop a conceptual shift—from a standpoint where one only gets acquainted with the differential needs of children in various situations to one where the trainee social worker also realizes the need to uphold their rights and safeguard them from any kind of violations. However, the socio-cultural milieu of India does not offer a conducive environment for a rights-based approach, especially with regard to children. The family systems have strong conformity norms, as per which children are expected to be obedient and submissive to their parents. School systems also validate this conformity approach. In such a scenario, working as per a rights-based approach is challenging, especially when social work trainees themselves have imbibed the values of conformity to their elders.

CONCLUSION

The universal and primary institution of family is changing, structurally and functionally, so as to adapt to the requirements of the altering socio-cultural milieu. The joint, nuclear and alternative family patterns have brought about changes in the roles and functions that families perform or give up, which in turn has implications on family functioning. Consequently, the problems emerging in family systems are multi-dimensional and multi-layered, critically impacting the well-being of its members.

Malnutrition, hunger deaths, being out of school, lack of quality education, abuse (physical, mental or sexual), child marriage, lack of family protection, compulsion to work, labour bondage and trafficking are the stark realities faced by a huge proportion of children in India.

Since families have universal existence and the human life cycle coincides with the family life cycle, almost every issue addressed by social workers have causal and consequential linkages with families. This highly relevant area of social work practice offers a vast scope of intervention at the independence stage, coupling stage, expansion stage and contraction stage; at the preventive, ameliorative and rehabilitative levels; and also covering all aspects of issues amongst families not fitting into the normative format of the family life cycle design. Using the United Nations Conventions on the Rights of Children, violations of any of the four domains of child rights—right to survival, right to protection, right to development and right to participation—provide a wide scope for social work intervention with and for children.

Families and children have always been the target group for social work interventions. However, as a specialized area of study and practice, social work with families started gaining ground in the 1950s and thereafter. Since then, educators and practitioners have developed several models of assessment and intervention in family functioning and dynamics. In India, insufficient availability of indigenous social work literature and the mismatch between the socio-cultural norms and practices reflected in traditional family functioning and the rights-based social work approach pose hurdles to social work trainees while working with families and children in their fieldwork settings. Though there is universality of scope of work with families and children, social work practice with families and children has not emerged as a core subject or a specialized practice area in most of the social work educational institutions.

The social work profession enables people to live more cordially and successfully within their families and communities by helping them find solutions to their problems. Families and children are the crucial constituencies that social workers engage with, in their endeavour to promote positive social change, enhance well-being and bring about empowerment of people. Fieldwork is the backbone of social work education. Developing the required knowledge and competencies during the training of students in the area of families and children is of critical importance in the process of making them dextrous and efficient social work professionals.

REFERENCES

Brewer, E. J., Jr., McPherson, M., Magrab, P. R., & Hutchin, V. L. (1989). Family-centered, community-based, coordinated care for children with special health care needs. *Pediatrics, 83*, 1055–1060.

Desai, A. S. (1987). Development of social work education. In *Encyclopaedia of social work* (Vol. 1, pp. 208–218). Ministry of Welfare, Government of India.

Desai, M. (2010). *Ideologies and social work: Historical and contemporary analyses.* Rawat Publishers.

Desai, M. (2019). Debates, achievements and directions for indigenization of social work in Asia. Paper presented at the 25th Asia-Pacific joint regional social work conference, Bangalore, India, 17–20 September.

Dunst, C. J., Johanson, C., Trivette, C. M., & Hamby, D. (1991). Family-oriented early intervention policies and practices: Family-centered or not? *Exceptional Children, 58*, 115–126.

Dunst, C. J., Trivette, C. M., & Deal, A. (1994). *Supporting and strengthening families: Vol. 1. Methods, strategies and practices.* Brookline Books.

Hartman, A., & Laird, J. (1983). *Family-centered social work practice.* Free Press.

International Federation of Social Workers. (2019). Global definition of social work. Retrieved 3 January 2019 from https://www.ifsw.org/what-is-social-work/global-definition-of-social-work/.

Kulkarni, P. D. (1993). The Indigenous base of social work profession in India. *Indian Journal of Social Work, 54*(4), 555–565.

Manshardt, C. (1936). The Sir Dorabji Tata Graduate School of Social Work, Ceylon Men, July 1936. (Reprinted in *The Indian Journal of Social Work*, Education for Social Work, *XLVI*(1), April 1985)

Ministry of Health and Family Welfare. (2012). *Annual report 2011–12.* Department of Health and Family Welfare, MHFW, Government of India.

Ministry of Statistics and Programme Implementation. (2012). *Children in India 2012: A statistical appraisal.* Social Statistics Division, Central Statistics Office, Ministry of Statistics and Programme Implementation, Government of India.

National Crime Records Bureau. (2011). *Crime in India: 2011 statistics.* National Crime Records Bureau, Ministry of Home Affairs, Government of India.

Shelton, T. L., Jeppson, E. S., & Johnson, B. H. (1987). *Family-centered care for children with special health care needs.* Association for the Care of Children's Health.

UNICEF. (2016). *The state of the world's children 2016: A fair chance for every child.* UNICEF.

Chapter 3

Emergence and Development of Professional Social Work in Correctional Settings

Sanjoy Roy

INTRODUCTION

The criminal justice system all over the world consists of at least four major components, namely the police, judiciary, prosecution and correctional services (Roy, 2018). Each of these four components functions as a sub-system in an integrated manner with the other sub-systems to meet the overall objectives of the criminal justice system. In other words, correctional services are a specialized function of the criminal justice system. In general, the criminal justice system is defined as a system comprising government agencies endowed with legal authority, either under the Constitution or by law or under both, to enforce law, adjudicate crime, correct criminal conduct and punish those involved in the violation of law (Ahuja, 2000). Originally, the criminal justice system was an important function of society and was an instrument of social control. Every society identified some conduct of its members as socially approved behaviours and others as violative of social norms. It ensured adherence to the socially approved behaviours or social norms through various institutions such as family, school, religious institution and clan panchayat (Abraham, 2019). With the evolution of the modern nation-state, the criminal justice function of society was taken over by the state. Thus, today's criminal justice system is a modern replacement of old system of social control (Kashyap, 2016). One distinctive aspect of modern criminal justice system is that it has replaced the retributive justice system of earlier societies with the restorative justice system. This means that today's criminal justice system aims to prevent occurrence of crime, correct criminal tendencies of individuals, punish individuals who violate laws and rehabilitate perpetrators in society after due punishment, instead of causing proportionate harm to perpetrators in return, as was prevalent in the retributive justice system of earlier societies (Strang, 2002). Thus, the modern criminal justice system is a system of law enforcement with a view to provide a sense of security to the people and the state. *The American Heritage Dictionary* (2001), therefore, defines the criminal justice system as 'the system of law enforcement, the bar, the judiciary, corrections, and probation that is directly involved in the apprehension, prosecution, defense, sentencing, incarceration and supervision of those suspected of or charged with criminal offenses'.

The corrective function of the criminal justice system has been acquiring greater significance all over the world in the contemporary period due to change in the understanding of the purpose of the criminal justice system. Today, the criminal justice system all over the world places greater emphasis on correcting criminal behaviours than on punishing the criminals (David, 2002). This change in understanding has occurred with the recognition of every individual member of society as a productive social being and it is the responsibility of the state or the government to inculcate law-abiding attitudes in every individual. This notional change, no doubt, reflects one more advanced stage of human civilization. In pursuance of this changed view, correctional services are defined as an amalgamation of a variety of services, facilities or assistance that are given to the individuals who are in conflict with laws or those who have been convicted for violation of any law. These may include supervision, treatment, punishment, imprisonment, parole, probation, rehabilitation and so on (John et al., 2019). From this perspective, prisons are considered correctional institutions and law-enforcing persons as correctional officers.

Ever since the emergence of the prison system, the criminal justice system all over the world has been criticized for inhuman treatment of prisoners and its failure to transform prisoners into law-abiding individuals. This necessitated specialized training of prison officers in rendering correctional services to prisoners, among other forms of training. Since the main aim of social work education is to promote the welfare and development of people, liberation and empowerment of disadvantaged sections of society and upholding social justice and human rights for all (Ornellas et al., 2016), social work education found a more congenial place in the field of criminal justice or in the correctional settings than any other social science discipline. As a result, Correctional Social Work or Criminal Justice Social Work was started as a specialized subject within social work education in several universities (Sinha, 2019). The primary objectives of Correctional Social Work Education are as follows:

1. To provide psycho-social counselling and various types of behaviour modification therapies;
2. To help prison officers implement rehabilitation provisions properly;
3. To help offenders/criminals access various types of correctional services;
4. To provide empirical inputs for prison reforms and policy formations to address the problems and needs of criminals within the larger framework of the criminal justice system;
5. To work with groups and communities to eradicate the root causes of criminality; and
6. To help ensure a crime-free society and bring peace to the people.

EMERGENCE AND DEVELOPMENT OF PROFESSIONAL SOCIAL WORK IN CORRECTIONAL SETTINGS IN INDIA

In India, as like most other countries, social work was originally understood as charitable work done by individuals and organizations on humanitarian, philanthropical or religious grounds. It was only in the beginning of the 1930s that professional social work was started in correctional settings with the support of the Sir Dorabji Tata Trust

(SDTT). At that time, an American missionary named Dr Clifford Manshardt was carrying out a number of welfare services through an institution called Neighbourhood House for catering to the needs of children and adults of Nagpada area of Bombay Presidency. He soon realized the need of professional social workers and conducted a six-week training programme for this purpose. Later, he started a school for imparting social work education. Finally, in 1936, he upgraded Neighbourhood House into Sir Dorabji Tata Graduate School of Social Work (Sir Dorabji Tata Trust, 2011). This was later renamed the Tata Institute of Social Sciences (TISS).

Criminology and juvenile delinquency were specialized subjects among a range of subjects at TISS right from its inception. As early as 1952, TISS endeavoured to provide specialized training in correctional services to prison officers of various state governments and offered a six-month training programme for this purpose with the help of Ministry of Home Affairs, Government of India. The United Nations also assisted this training programme by providing two experts. Next year, in 1953, TISS created a separate department named Department of Criminology and Correctional Administration (CCA) for training purposes. Until the 1970s, a majority of candidates enrolled in the CCA Department were government officers. They mostly came from prison, social welfare and women and child development departments of various state governments. In the following years, many state governments developed their own training centres, which led to the declining enrolment of government officers at TISS for training purposes. Sanober Sahni was the first person from a non-government background who joined the CCA Department at TISS. She earned her PhD from this department on undertrial women prisoners. She later became a faculty at the CCA Department. In 1990, she started an action project called Prayas to provide legal and welfare services to undertrial prisoners of Mumbai Central Prison. Over the years, Prayas proved to be a successful initiative and many state governments started or sponsored similar projects for various categories of the prison population (Sir Dorabji Tata Trust, 2011).

The work of TISS is also commendable in the area of women and child welfare. As early as 1984, TISS set up the first Special Cell for Women and Children in the office of the Police Commissioner of

Mumbai to render various kinds of welfare services to women and children, and also to work to prevent various forms of violence against women and children. Gradually, the work reach of TISS expanded and it set up the second Special Cell for Women and Children in Dadar Police Station in 1988 and the third in Kandivali Police Station in 1994. In 2004, when TISS signed a Memorandum of Understanding with the United Nations Development Fund for Women (UNIFEM) and the Government of Maharashtra, the number of Special Cells for Women and Children witnessed a dramatic increase in the state. Looking at its importance, the Department of Women and Child Development, Government of Maharashtra took over the responsibility of Special Cells in the state in 2005. Later, with the support of the United Nations Development Programme (UNDP), the Government of India also started Special Cells for Women and Children in various police stations of Madhya Pradesh and Haryana (Ganesh, 2007; Ronald, 2011; Sir Dorabji Tata Trust, 2011). Over the years, the number of Special Cells for Women and Children have increased across the country. The main objective of these Special Cells is to work towards ensuring that society recognizes women as equal to men in all aspects of human life and children as the future human resource of the country.

MAJOR WORK AREAS OF CORRECTIONAL SETTING IN INDIA

Though there are a number of work areas in the correctional settings in India, it is proposed to discuss its five major work areas in this chapter. These are as follows:

1. Public interest litigation
2. Bail system
3. Prison system
4. Legal aid and services
5. Compensation to the victims of crime

Public Interest Litigation

Public interest litigation (PIL) emerged first in the United States around the 1960s as a part of the legal aid movement. It aimed at protecting the rights of the weaker sections of the society, namely women, children, persons with disability, ethnic minority and economically poor (Roy, 2018). In India, it emerged in 1979 when the then Chief Justice of the Supreme Court, P. N. Bhagwati, allowed the PIL provision for the first time in the case of *Hussainara Khatoon v. State of Bihar.* This provision allows that other than the aggrieved person or party, a spirited citizen or organization may also file a petition in the court on behalf of the aggrieved person or party to enforce the law of the land. The main idea was to empower the marginalized sections of society, who otherwise had limited access to justice due to several reasons (Sen, 2012). The introduction of the PIL system in the Indian judiciary truly made the courts the protectors of fundamental rights of the citizens and guardians of the Indian Constitution. However, it has been alleged in recent years that the courts sometimes encroach upon the jurisdictions of the legislature and the executive. This has created a tussle between the various organs of the state, namely the legislature, the executive and the judiciary.

Bail System

Bail in any judicial system refers to the provisional release of an accused from judicial custody in a criminal case in which the court is yet to pronounce its judgment. As the main objective of arrest is to ensure the presence of the accused before the court for delivery of justice, it is considered legally fair to grant bail to the accused if his or her presence is guaranteed in the court for trial without putting the accused in prison. There are three types of bail in India which a person can apply for. The first is *regular bail*, which is granted to a person who has already been arrested and kept in jail. The second is *anticipatory bail*, which is granted to a person by the court before his/her arrest by the police. The third is *interim bail*, which is granted to a person for a short period before the hearing of the case by the court for grant of regular or anticipatory bail (Shivi, 2018).

Prison System

Prisons are correction centres for reforming and rehabilitating criminals. In India, prisons are governed by the Prisons Act, 1894 and are managed by the state governments. The central government provides assistance to the state governments only in the management of prisons. This assistance may include improving security in prisons, repairing and renovating dilapidated prisons, modernizing prison infrastructure, creating good living conditions for prisoners, providing medical facilities, arranging special facilities for women prisoners, giving vocational training to prisoners and providing security training to prison personnel. There are currently eight types of prison in India—central jails, district jails, sub-jails, women jails, open jails, special jails (or high security jails), borstal schools (or youth detention centres) and other jails—which do not fall under the specified categories of jails mentioned above (Ministry of Home Affairs, 2003).

Legal Aid and Services

The Constitution of India provides for free legal aid and services to those persons who are unable to bear the cost of availing them due to economic and other reasons. It places obligation upon the state to ensure that the legal system operates on the principle of equal opportunities and no citizen is denied access to justice on any ground. It further states that it is the responsibility of the state to arrange free legal aid and services for those who cannot afford to access justice for some reason. The court, for the first time, pronounced in the case of *Hussainara Khatoon v. State of Bihar* (1979) that if any accused is unable to afford the legal services needed, then he should be given free legal aid by the state at its own cost. The legal aid and services usually given to an accused include: (a) employment of a lawyer for the defence of the accused, (b) payment of charges of legal experts involved in the case for the defence of the accused (c) payment of charges for filing the petition in the court; (d) payment of court and other processing fees and (e) payment of costs of paper work and for obtaining copies of judgments or any other documents (Mallikarjun, 2013).

Compensation to the Victims of Crime

The Constitution of India does not contain any specific provision for compensation to victims of crimes. However, the Directive Principles of State Policy lay down that it is the duty of the state to provide adequate compensation to victims or their dependents who have suffered loss, injury or harm due to the illegal activities of others or as a result of the crime (Dube, 2018). The compensation given to the victims of crime may take several forms. When the court imposes a fine upon the accused after he is found guilty of a crime, then the amount fined or a part of it may be given to the victim as compensation. In the case of death, the family of the victim is given compensation in the form of cash and reimbursement of medical expenses. For offences such as theft, cheating and criminal misappropriation, compensation is given to the victim by recovering the stolen goods from the culprit if possible. If recovery is not possible, then the estimated price of such goods is recovered and used to compensate the victim. In cases where the culprit is unidentified or non-traceable, but victim is identified and approachable, the victim is given due compensation for the loss or for enabling rehabilitation, either by the state or the concerned District Legal Services Authority (Pandey, 2017).

ROLES OF SOCIAL WORKERS IN CORRECTIONAL SETTINGS

Roy (2017) identified eight correctional institution types in which social workers can play an important role in reforming the criminal conduct of offenders and in proper management of these institutions. These eight institutions are prisons, observation homes, special homes, children homes, after-care organizations, protective homes for women, short-stay homes and beggar homes. In addition to these, there are other important correctional institutions, which include courts, probation and parole boards and borstal schools (Sikk, 1980). These institution types are depicted in Figure 3.1. As correctional officers, social workers work with the management staff of these institutions to provide various types of correctional services to the inmates and re-integrate them with their communities.

In correctional settings, social workers play a number of roles in various areas and stages of the correctional services delivery process. These roles of social workers along with their areas of intervention and the stages of the correctional service delivery process are presented in Figure 3.1. Raghavan (2013) argues that though social workers perform

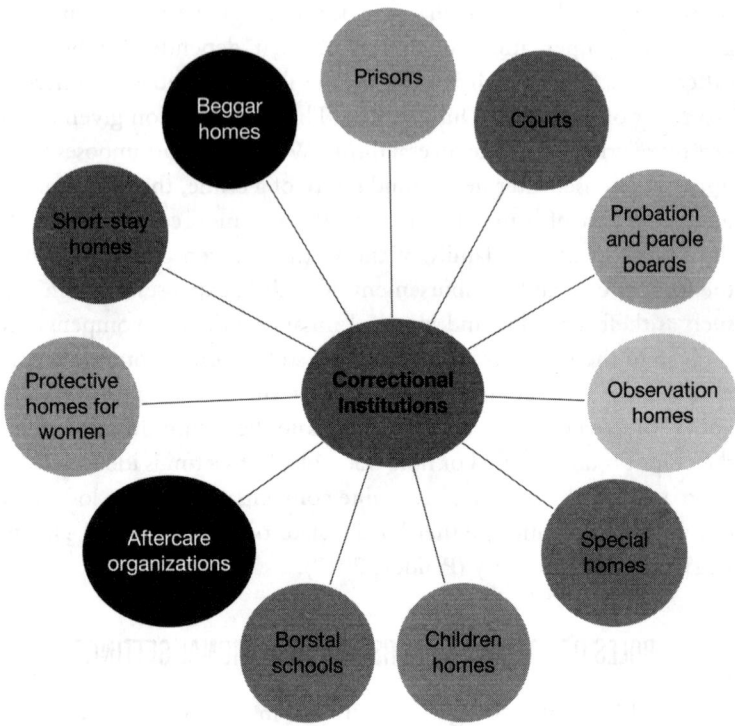

Figure 3.1 *Major Correctional Institution Types in India*
Source: Author

different roles in correctional settings, their ultimate aim is to make the offenders realize that they are as productive human beings as others are and can contribute to society to the fullest of their strength once they reform their behaviour, start acting in a socially appropriate manner and get released from jail. This realization of inherent strengths in offenders as persons is what is called the strength perspective in social work literature.

SKILLS REQUIRED IN CORRECTIONAL SETTINGS

Social workers working in the area of correctional services need to possess the following skills:

Table 3.1 *Different Roles of Social Workers in Correctional Settings*

Areas of Intervention for Social Workers	Different Roles Performed by Social Workers	Correctional Services Delivery Process
Rehabilitation of prisoners	Advocate Broker Rehabilitator	**Admission** ⇩
Family re-integration	Probation officer Parole officer Planner Activist	Imprisonment ⇩
Individual therapeutic intervention	Trainer Teacher Enabler Counsellor Therapist	Sentence ⇩ Re-union ⇩
Community involvement	Facilitator Mediator Catalyst Consultant Rapport builder Programmer Implementer	Pre-release ⇩
Crime prevention	Preventer Researcher Change agent	Release integration with family/community

Source: Author

1. *Rapport building skill:* When a social worker identifies a client to work with, he first needs to build rapport with the client, so that the client feels comfortable in sharing all information with him.
2. *Documentation skill:* The social worker must have the skills to maintain proper documentation of all information shared by the client with him.
3. *Presentation skill:* The social worker should be well versed in all aspects of effective presentation of the case of the client in front of the other experts who are involved in the treatment process of the client.

4. *Leadership skill:* The social worker should take the lead in taking forward the case of the client and mobilize resources for his treatment.
5. *Network building skill:* The social worker should be able to build social and institutional networks and utilize them for the treatment of the client.
6. *Negotiation skill:* The social worker should be skilled enough to initiate negotiations among different authorities who may be able to help in the treatment of the client.
7. *Coordination skill:* The social worker should have the ability to coordinate among different agencies, so that the services rendered by them to the client do not overlap.
8. *Motivational skill:* The social worker should know a variety of ways to motivate the client to continue his treatment in case he develops negative feelings or perceptions about it.
9. *Rehabilitative skill:* The social worker should be able to properly rehabilitate the client with his family, community and the society at large.
10. *Termination skill:* The social worker should be able to properly wind up the professional relationship between him and the client when the client's problem is completely solved.

PROFESSIONAL OBLIGATIONS OF SOCIAL WORKERS IN CORRECTIONAL SETTINGS

Social workers in correctional settings have to maintain the following professional obligations:

1. *Maintaining the privacy of sensitive information of clients:* The social worker should not disclose any sensitive or private information of the client with anyone except the professional experts who are involved in the process of treatment of the client. In some cases, prior consent should be sought from the client when his private information is shared with even the experts.
2. *Respecting the dignity and individuality of clients:* The social worker must respect the client as he is and not encroach upon his individuality. While presenting the case of the client before the

experts, the social worker should ensure that the client's dignity is not hurt and his individuality is respected.

3. *Respecting the client's right to self-determination:* The social worker should offer a number of alternatives for the treatment of the client and the client should be given the choice to select one of them, which he considers the most appropriate to treat his problem.

4. *Treating clients of different backgrounds alike:* The social worker must not discriminate against the clients of different backgrounds based on their religion, caste, class, race, gender, age, nationality and so on. He must view all clients as equals and treat them with equal respect.

5. *Upholding the integrity of law-enforcing officers:* The social worker should take every possible care to ensure that the law-enforcing officers' personal and professional integrity is not diluted and their honesty upheld.

6. *Devaluing crimes but not criminals:* The social worker should help eliminate crimes but not criminals. He should hold the view that crimes are the results of socio-structural inequalities prevalent in society and not of the biological conditions of some persons. He should also firmly believe that criminals can be reformed and rehabilitated in society as law-abiding citizens.

7. *Balancing between the needs of clients and public safety:* At times, the social worker may come across situations where the client's needs come into direct conflict with public safety and security. Such a situation often occurs in prison settings, where the client may consciously or unconsciously share highly confidential information (such as a plan to escape from the prison or a planned attack on the country by his cohorts) which may cause an immediate threat to public safety. In such cases, the social worker must breach his promise of confidentiality to the client and share such information with the concerned authority in the larger public interest.

CASE STUDIES

Social Case Work with an Economic Offender

The social caseworker recognizes the structural inequalities prevalent in each society, which enable some individuals to become rich and force many others (usually a large number of people) to live in abject poverty. Some of these poor people, over a period, turn into petty offenders who steal food and other items including money to survive. The social caseworker can identify one such offender and work with him to reform his behaviour. At the same time, he works with the government to introduce legislation to distribute ceiling surplus land to the landless poor (many of whom tend to become petty offenders in the course of a lifetime), so that structural inequalities are to some extent narrowed down or their effects on the lives of the poor are minimized. In this entire process, the social caseworker may use behaviour modification therapy for the petty offender, involve himself in the process of advocacy to secure the economic rights of the people, persuade the government to introduce legislation and so on.

Social Group Work with Alcoholics

The social group worker can identify, during his field visit, a group of alcoholics and start working with them. He may first try to build rapport with them and persuade them to accept him as one among them. He himself must also accept them as they are. He may then work towards helping them to modify their behaviour and change the perceptions of their family members as well as society towards them. In the process, he may realize that while some alcoholics show signs of significant change in their drinking habit, others do not. In such a case, the social group worker can work to enrol these no-changer alcoholics in de-addiction centres, where they are given advanced treatment and therapy. When these alcoholics are completely de-addicted, the social group worker reunites them with their family members and terminates his professional relationship with them.

Social Work with Communities

The social worker usually works with the communities to help them solve a variety of community-related problems. For example, if the majority of members of a community suffer from various types of diseases, the community social worker—with the consent and help of community members—can persuade doctors and health authorities of that area to organize a health camp in the community for free check-up of community members. In the same way, the community social worker works with the community for the rehabilitation of criminals, drug addicts, petty offenders, persons with deviant behaviour and so on.

CONCLUSION

Though the criminal justice system is a well-established institution, correctional services is a relatively new field under it. Since the underlying philosophy of social work is very close to the primary objectives behind rendering correctional services to the offenders, social work in correctional settings has emerged as a new area of study. As a result, many colleges and universities across the world offer social work degrees with specialization in correctional services. Such a course is often termed Correctional Social Work. With the continuously increasing rate of crimes (most of which are committed by juveniles) in society in the present times, the need of Correctional Social Work both as a specialization and an independent subject is continuously increasing. This opens an arena of opportunities for young students who find difficulty in pursuing law courses, but wish to work with prisoners in correctional settings without having much technical knowledge of law. This chapter is an attempt to impart concise understanding of what social work in correctional settings involves and what professional skills and expertise the students and professionals need to acquire during the course of their study or before entering actual practice.

REFERENCES

Abraham, M. F. (2019). *Contemporary sociology: An introduction to concepts and theories* (2nd ed.). Oxford University Press.

Ahuja, R. (2000). *Criminology*. Rawat Publications.

Bhagwat, P. N. (1979). *Hussainara Khatoon v. State of Bihar*. (Case study). https://www.legitquest.com/case/hussainara-khatoon-and-others-v-home-secretary-state-of-bihar-patna/3975

David, F. (2002). Prisoners as citizens. *British Journal of Community Justice, 1*(2), 11–20.

Dube, D. (2018). Victim compensation schemes in India: An analysis. *International Journal of Criminal Justice Sciences, 13*(2), 339–355.

Ganesh, I. M. (2007). *Next steps: Taking the special cell process ahead.* Tata Institute of Social Sciences.

John, V. J. S., Blount-Hill, K., Evans, D., Ayers, D., & Allard, S. (2019). Architecture and correctional services: A facilities approach to treatment. *The Prison Journal, 99*(6), 748–770.

Kashyap, S. C. (2016). *Our political system.* National Book Trust.

Mallikarjun, G. (2013). Legal aid in India and the judicial contribution. *NALSAR Law Review, 7*(1), 234–241.

Ministry of Home Affairs. (2003). *Model prison manual for the superintendence and management of prisoners in India.*

Ornellas, A., Spolander, G., & Engelbrecht, L. K. (2016). The global social work definition: Ontology, implications and challenges. *Journal of Social Work, 18*(2), 222–240.

Pandey, A. (2017). *Compensation of victim of crime in India.* https://blog.ipleaders.in/compensation-victim-crime-india

Raghavan, V. (2013). Social work intervention in criminal justice: Field-theory linkage. *Social Work and Social Development, 14*(1), 265–289.

Ronald, Y. (2011). Social work intervention with prisoners: The case of VARHAD in Maharashtra. *Rajagiri Journal of Social Development, 3*(1), 99–108.

Roy, S. (2017). Field work practice in correctional setting: Indian social work perspective. *Global Journal of Archaeology and Anthropology, 2*(1), 31–38.

Roy, S. (2018). Social work in a correctional setting in India. *Asia Pacific Journal of Advanced Business and Social Studies, 4*(2), 124–126.

Sen, S. (2012). *Public interest litigation in India: Implications for law and development.* Mahanirban Calcutta Research Group.

Shivi. (2018). *Meaning, concept and types of bail in India.* https://www.legistify.com/blogs/view_detail/meaning-concept-and-types-of-bail-in-india

Sikk, K. D. (1980). Professional social work in correctional institutions. *Indian Journal of Criminology, 8*(1), 55–61.

Sinha, R. (2019). Criminal justice social work education and practice in India: An analysis. *International Journal of Criminal Justice Sciences, 14*(1), 22–38.

Sir Dorabji Tata Trust. (2011). *Social work in India's criminal justice institutions: Need, experiences and challenges.* (Case Study 1). https://www.tatatrusts.org/upload/pdf/social-work-india-criminal-justice-institutions.pdf

Strang, H. (2002). *Repair or revenge: Victims and restorative justice.* Clarendon Press.

The American heritage dictionary of the English language. (2001). Fourth edition. Houghton Mifflin Harcourt.

PART 2

Major Practice Areas in Social Work

Chapter 4

Palliative Care
Emerging Field of Social Work Practice

Tushti Bhardwaj

INTRODUCTION TO PALLIATIVE CARE

Palliative care is an interdisciplinary approach to improve the well-being and quality of life of patients with incurable and deadly diseases by providing optimal pain and symptoms management as well as emotional, social and spiritual support since diagnosis of the disease until the last moment of life. Palliative care also involves offering care and support to the families to minimize their difficuties. The scope of palliative care also covers bereaved families after death of the patients. Thus, 'palliative care' is a patient- and family-centred approach with the main focus to add quality to the life of patients by minimizing their sufferings. Palliative care is generally available in case of serious and chronic illnesses such as cancer, HIV/AIDS, heart conditions, respiratory renal diseases and progressive neurological conditions such as multiple sclerosis.

The main aim of palliative care throughout the disease span is to attend to the physical, social, psychological and spiritual concerns of the patients as well as their families. It also aims to facilitate the patient's autonomy for decision-making by making information accessible to them. Although palliative care is an important component of end-of-life care, it is not limited to the last stages of life. It is important to understand that palliative care is appropriate at any stage of a serious illness irrespective of the patient's age and can be offered along with on-going treatment. The multidisciplinary teams in palliative care consist of physicians, nurses, psychologists, social workers, occupational therapists and physiotherapists and other professionals, who offer the best care and support to the patients and their family. Palliative care is offered through various settings such as hospitals, the patient's home, hospices and day care centres.

The World Health Organization (WHO) defines palliative care as 'an approach that improves quality of life of patients and their families facing life-threatening illness, through prevention and relief of suffering by means of early identification and impeccable assessment and treatment of pain and other problems, physical, psychosocial and spiritual' (WHO, 2017).

Thus, palliative care as per WHO guidelines includes pain relief and symptoms management. This approach neither quickens up nor delays death and considers dying as a normal process. Palliative care integrates emotional, social and spiritual aspects to help patients live an active life until death and ensure their quality of living. The bereaved families are also provided emotional and social support to help them cope up with the loss.

Palliative care is relevant even during the initial phases of disease, especially in case of chemotherapy or radiation therapy, which is known to aggravate distressing symptoms.

ORIGIN OF PALLIATIVE CARE

Palliatve care was orginated in England in 1948 by the efforts of Dame Cicely Saunders. She was a nurse by profession and began working with terminally ill and dying patients. The need of palliative care was felt due to increasing life expectancy coupled with the burden of life-threatening diseases. The movement graduallly reached the USA where specialized care for the dying was introduced in 1963. In 1967, the first hospice, namely St. Christopher Hospice, was founded in London for the care of terminally ill patients. This was a major landmark for the palliative care movement around the world. Palliative care speciality is relatively new to India. In the mid-1980s, with the efforts of committed health professionals, volunteers and support from international organizations, palliative care began in South India. Dr M. R. Rajagopal is considered the father of palliative care in India. His pioneering efforts led the way to the development of NGOs to offer palliative care services to the people. The efforts and advocacy by palliative care professionals in India gathered some support from the Indian government too. In 1984, the government introduced a few modifications in the National Cancer Control Programmes by making pain relief one of the basic services at the primary healthcare level. Further, in 2012, the Ministry of Health and Family Welfare of the Government of India nominated an expert group on palliative care, which submitted a proposal on the palliative care programme. On the basis of recommendations of this report, an effective palliative care note was introduced in the 12th five-year plan. However, unfortunately, no separate budget was allocated to the National Palliative Care Programme; however, palliative care was made a part of Mission Flexipool under the National Health Mission (NHM). It implies that the states/union territories can include proposals for palliative care in their model programme implementation plans for seeking financial support under NHM. For this programme, the central and state government share would be 60:40, but for the North East and hill areas, this contribution ratio would be 90:10.

APPROACHES TO PALLIATIVE CARE

Palliative care was traditionally offered when curative treatment no longer remained responsive. This approach demarcates curative and palliative care, represented graphically by a straight line suggesting that the later starts when the former finishes. However, gradually, the modern approach to palliative care is developed whereby curative treatment and palliative care run side by side through a diagonal relationship. In cases where high chances of curative treatment exist, the scope of palliative care is limited but never becomes non-existent. Unfortunately, due to limited resource and manpower, India is still using the traditional concept of palliative care which demarcates

Traditional approach

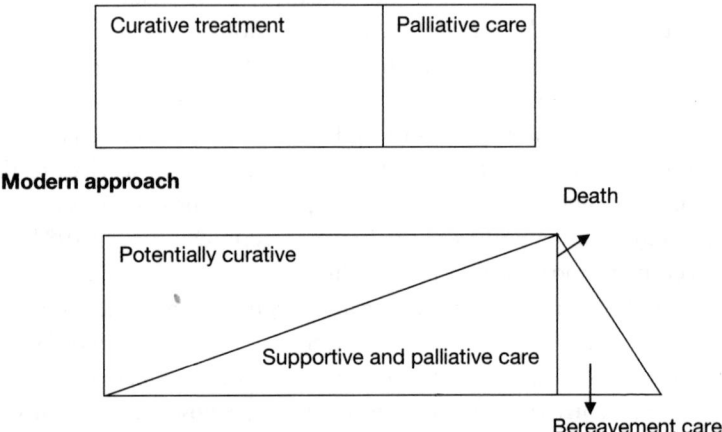

Figure 4.1 *Approaches to Palliative Care*
Source: Lynn & Adamson (2003)

curative and palliative care with a thin and straight line. However, we need to remember that the patients and families face myriad issues and concerns in case of life-threatening diseases such as cancer from the time of the diagnosis itself. These concerns need to be addressed to strengthen the quality of life of the patients and family as a whole. Thus, we need to give more emphasis to the modern concept, which recognizes the need of palliative care from the beginning of diagnosis and functioning alongside curative treatment in an inverse relationship. The provisions of palliative care in modern approach extend even beyond death, as bereavement care is necessary for the family and caregivers. Figure 4.1 presents the two approaches to palliative care (Lynn & Adamson, 2003).

MODELS AND AGENTS OF PALLIATIVE CARE IN INDIA

Palliative care does not have a uniform model for service delivery in India. The absence of a national-level policy on palliative care, inadequate recognition of the speciality and lack of required infrastructure and trained specialists contribute to the existence of

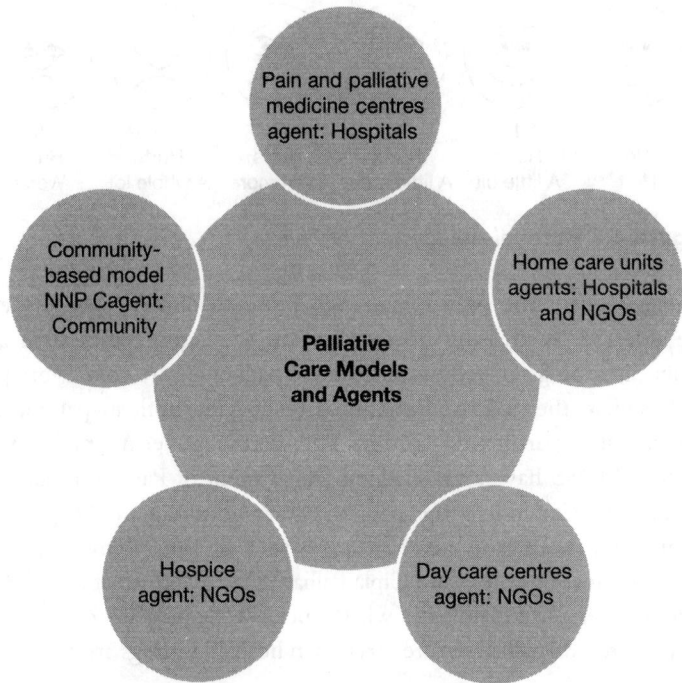

Figure 4.2 *Palliative Care Models*
Source: Author

various models of palliative care which offer care services through varied agents. Palliative care is offered through various models in India as shown in Figure 4.2. These models are as follows:

1. Pain and palliative medicine centres
2. Home care units
3. Day care centres
4. Hospice care
5. Community-based model

Pain and Palliative Medicine Centres

These are run by big hospitals (both government and private) to care for terminally ill patients (especially cancer patients), for whom pain

0	1	2	3	4	5
No	Hurts	Hurts	Hurts	Hurts	Hurts
Hurt	A little bit	A little more	Even more	A whole lot	Worst

Figure 4.3 *Pictorial Assessment of Pain*

management is the only remaining option to obtain relief. Patients are referred by treating doctors for the management of pain and other distressing symptoms. Since these palliative care centres are part of hospitals, they are well equipped to provide both in-patient and outpatient department facilities. The central government hospitals such as AIIMS have a full-fledged Department of Pain and Palliative Medicine to attend to the palliative care concerns of the patients. Similarly, private cancer care hospitals such as Tata Memorial, Rajiv Gandhi Cancer Institute and Cipla Palliative Care Centre offer palliative care services. The main roles which social work professionals need to play to provide palliative care services in hospital settings are as follows:

- Make an assessment of the pain severity and discomfort. Many a time, patients might not describe their discomfort or extent of pain. You may make use of a pictorial for assessment as presented in Figure 4.3.
- You need to be very careful to make assessment of the various factors contributing pain.
- Coordinate with the medical team for prescription and ensure timely administration of medicines.
- Help the patient to perform his daily routine of bathing, dressing and eating. Help him to sit and offer his routine prayers if he wishes so. This would make him feel closer to his normal health.

Home Care Units

Home care units run by hospitals and NGOs represent a widely prevalent model in India. Home care units of hospitals cater to their registered terminally ill patients, while NGOs provide palliative care services to all patients who need such care. Poor patients are a major group receiving palliative care services from NGOs, as they often cannot reach the big hospitals. A team of medical doctors, nurses, counsellors, psychologists and social workers manage this service by making home visits on a weekly basis or more frequently as required. They look after the patient's medical, nursing and psychosocial needs. In addition to providing care to the patient, the team also educates family members to care for basic medical and nursing needs of patients, as most patients at end-of-life stage need care round the clock. NGOs such as Can Support in Delhi and Pallium India in Kerala are leading organizations for providing home-based palliative care to patients free of cost. These organizations run their dedicated telephone helplines and networks with big government and private hospitals to identify patients who need palliative care. As a social worker, you need to play the role of a counsellor to keep the patient in positive spirit. You need to educate the family for the care needs of the patients. You must maintain regular contact with the treating team and inform them in case of any emergency.

Day Care Centres

Day care centres are run mainly by the NGOs, but a few private hospitals also offer day care services for their registered patients. Palliative day care centres are different from those day care units of the hospitals where curative treatment is provided without hospitalization. The day care centres for palliative patients offer emotional, social and spiritual support through art, craft, fun-time, yoga, meditation, music, nutritional and other recreational activities. Patients in day care centres are given learning opportunities to lead their day constructively with fun. Generally, day care centres are kept age specific, which means different age groups are not mixed together. This ensures homogeneity in the group and makes patients comfortable. Moreover, the needs of various age groups are different. For example, children generally like to play, but adults may like to engage in yoga or discussion. Thus, considering their requirement and comfort level, day care centres are better organized as per age group. It is important to remember that smaller groups (12–15 patients) are easier to manage. In case of bigger groups, additional group coordinators are required, so that individual attention can be paid to all the participants. The role of professional social workers in day care centres will include preparing weekly activity plans. Your activities have to be age appropriate and participatory to retain the interest of the patients. If you are planning to call a resource person for a particular session, do the necessary coordination beforehand. For example, if you are planning to call an expert on puppet making, complete all the communication in advance and ensure that your expert reaches the venue on time. While working in groups, you need to be careful about the individual needs of each patient. Many a time, a few patients hesitate to express themselves in the company of others. You need to give special attention to such persons, so that they do not remain left out. You need to plan the activities in a way that each patient gets the opportunity to express themselves. Keeping the attendance record of each session is very important for assessment of interventions. You must keep your patients informed about the next activity to elicit their maximum participation.

Hospice Care

Hospice care focuses on palliative care needs of the terminally ill patients in a residential set-up called hospice. The hospices are generally charitable centres which attend to a patient's physical symptoms and other concerns like social, spiritual and emotional needs at the end of life. Hospices provide care services to patients to make their last days of life as comfortable and content as possible. Hospice care is provided to those patients for whom curative treatment is no longer responsive and expected to live for less than 6 months for normal course of an illness. St. Christopher Hospice was the first modern hospice developed by Cicely Saunders in 1967 in London. In Delhi, Shanti Avedana follows similar principles of care. Recently, Ganga Prem Hospice was started on the same principles in Rishikesh. Any patient irrespective of socio-economic background is welcomed in the hospice. They are provided the best care services round the clock through trained nurses, doctors and social workers. In case of death, the families of the patients are informed about it immediately, so that the last rites can be conducted by the family. In case of unattended patients, the appropriate government authorities are informed and the proper procedures are conducted for the last rites. The role of social workers in hospices is very similar to that in hospital settings, but here you would encounter two major differences. First, your patients may be staying here for longer durations unlike hospitals, where stay is quite short and limited to a few days only. Second, unlike in the hospitals, patients here are not at the curative stages, but rather at the end stage of their lives. So, the patients here may be very sick, fragile or even immobile. Many a time, working in hospices may be emotionally draining, as witnessing death every day is a huge challenge. Thus, it is important that you become aware of your burnout potential and prepare yourself emotionally for this.

Community-based Model

Kerala developed a community-based model for palliative care called Neighbourhood Network in Palliative Care (NNPC), whereby community volunteers are trained to care for patients and their families. As per NNPC, the volunteers learn to identify the problems of chronically ill patients in their areas and provide them care and support through trained professionals. The NNPC involves community participation with the aim to empower communities to address health-related issues themselves. Under this programme, people who can spare some time on a weekly basis are enrolled in structured training programmes. On the successful completion of training and practice sessions, they are encouraged to work in groups to identify the needs of chronically ill patients in their areas and plan effective services under the supervision of trained professionals. They also follow up patients visited by palliative care professionals and look after their day-to-day care issues. The NNPC volunteers work as link between patients in community and professionals in institutions. Since this model draws its strength from community volunteers instead of professionals, it is cost-effective for a resource-poor and developing country such as India. The NNPC model of India is one of the lowest-cost palliative care interventions, which has been recognized by WHO as the best evidence-based model for low-income countries. Though the NNPC model has potential to offer lessons for initiating and managing palliative care programmes for countries with poor resources, this is not an alternative for professional services, as continuous evidence-based care and new therapies are needed for the continuous progress of palliative care speciality. In the community-based model of palliative care, your role will be to identify patients who need palliative care. You need to link these patients with your organization and register them for services. You may be required to make needs assessments of the patients. This will help you understand what kind of services these patients may require. If the patient is sick or has physical concerns, you must refer the case to a medical doctor in your team. If the patient is stressed, tense and has emotional concerns, you need to provide emotional support and counselling to the patient.

CURRENT STATE OF PALLIATIVE CARE IN INDIA

The provisions of palliative care services in India are still in initial stages. The palliative care services in our country are mainly for cancer patients and concentrated mainly to a few states. A large number of states in India are still without palliative care provisions (McDermott et al., 2008a), and only two states, namely Kerala and Maharashtra, have palliative care policy. The lack of a national palliative care policy is one of the main factors for the restricted growth of palliative care in India even after long years of rigorous efforts by professionals and volunteers. Moreover, India has uneven service provisions where one of the states at the southern end (Kerala) was nominated for the WHO model of community-based palliative care, but other states including the capital city have sporadic palliative care services (McDermott et al., 2008a). Although the government has increased the budget for cancer control, limited funds are granted to palliative care despite increasing needs of these services in our country.

A brief reflection on the literature highlights the existing state of palliative care in India. A study which was based on literature review, field visits and qualitative interviews with professionals revealed that palliative care services in India are mainly concentrated in urban areas except in the state of Kerala (McDermott et al., 2008b). The lack of specially trained professionals and specialized education programmes in medical and social science institutions also hinders the growth of palliative care in India. A research conducted with graduate medical interns reported lack of understanding and confidence in performing palliative care activities (Bharadwaj et al., 2007). Another study brought out that counselling and disease-related details offered by medical staff were inadequate and unsatisfactory to the patients, which reflected lack of knowledge and specialized skills among professionals (Gupta et al., 2007).

The demographic distribution of India also presents serious challenges to the development of specialized palliative care services in the country. The fast-changing population profile, inadequate disease and death registration systems, and the cultural beliefs of the people towards life-threatening diseases such as cancer, heart complications and HIV/AIDS further make it difficult to assess the exact palliative care needs. The growth of palliative care speciality is also hampered due to unavailability of opioids. Though, India is one of the world's leading suppliers of medical opium, our patients have to suffer excruciating pain due to restricted access to opioids (Mudur, 2012). Research suggests that to access palliative care services and pain relief facilities, people have to travel long distances (Butola, 2012). In light of such evidence, India needs to take up measures to promote education of professionals, increasing opioid availability and mobilizing government support.

RECOMMENDATIONS

India needs to develop national strategies for palliative care for country-wide coverage of the palliative care programme. The state of Kerala gives us invaluable learning lessons where palliative care was initially developed through voluntary efforts. Later, with support from advocacy groups, the government recognized the need and the state palliative care policy was framed. WHO suggests three essential foundation measures (Rajagopal & Twycross, 2010) for the development of palliative care, namely (a) educational programmes of professionals and awareness for policy makers, (b) drug availability and (c) government policy. Thus, pressure groups and service providers need to focus on these three areas, as they are currently very weak in the Indian context. The interdependent relationship between the three components is depicted in Figure 4.4.

As evidence suggests, due to lack of confidence and specialized skills among professionals (Bharadwaj et al., 2007; Gupta et al., 2007), India

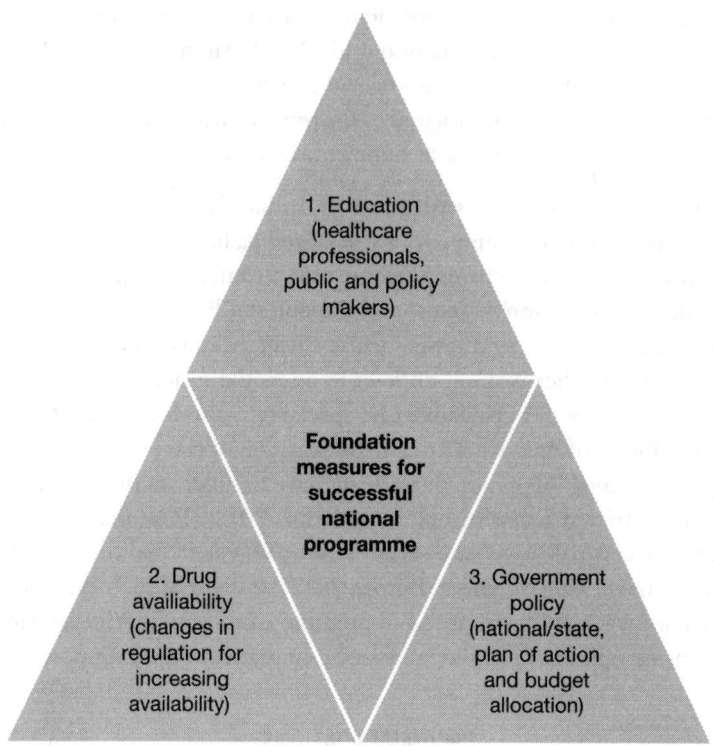

Figure 4.4 *Foundational Measures for a Successful National Programme*

Source: Rajagopal & Twycross (2010)

needs to invest more to train multidisciplinary professionals, since a well-performing, skilled workforce is the foundation base of an optimal palliative care structure. Currently, palliative care education in India is meant for medical and nursing professionals. However, we need to extend its scope to educate and train social workers and psychologists, so that a strong multidisciplinary team can be readied to serve patients. Palliative care education needs to be integrated with the undergraduate and postgraduate curricula.

The availability of opioids is a major concern for making palliative care accessible to all in India. The regulations governing use of opioids need a certain level of flexibility to ensure better accessibility to patients and thus help them avoid unnecessary long travel to procure their medicines. The recent amendments to the Narcotic Drugs and Psychotropic Substances Act in 2014 eased out the process of drug procurement and dispensation. It is now important to educate the ground-level practitioners for appropriate prescription of opioids.

Advocacy groups need to come forward to build up a National Council of Palliative Care, so that such a pressure group can influence policy makers. Such a national council, in tandem with Medical Council of India, can also ensure that only specifically trained volunteers and professionals provide services in order to maintain the quality of such services. India lacks a comprehensive database for causes of death, as death registration is yet not compulsory. India needs urgent and reliable quantification of causes of death. In addition, assessment of prevalence of symptoms for different diseases is required, so that appropriate interventions can be designed.

India also needs to foster understanding of palliative care needs among the general public, because people may not demand palliative care as they lack knowledge about it (Higginson et al., 2007; Koffman et al., 2007). Public awareness and building up of public opinion through community networks is required. Coordination and networking with media may work as the best tools for this. We also need to recognize the social character of health and illness. People need to be educated to view dying as a normal process of life and not as a failure of the medical profession. We also need to recognize the efforts of family caregivers and introduce mechanisms to support them such as care giving leave and tax benefit, as they cannot otherwise afford costly treatment.

Research is the base for growth of a profession, as indigenous literature and practice is required to strengthen any emerging field. Researchers in palliative care speciality may encounter challenges such as lack of expertise, problems in constructing RCTs, selection, recruitment, retention and lack of valid measurement tools. However, research-supporting policies from healthcare institutions and government will support the development of palliative care research in India.

SUMMARY

India lacks a uniform model of palliative care, which poses a debate whether palliative care is a speciality offered by multidisciplinary teams or just a basic care facility which can be provided by community volunteers (Gupta, 2004). Increasing population, poverty, vast geography, opioid unavailability, limited staff and lack of national policy for palliative care are a few major hurdles for the development of palliative care in India.

Despite all limitations, India just cannot ignore the concerns of populations at the end of their life. Palliative care is an urgent humanitarian need in the context of fast-changing demography and health issues. India needs to respond urgently to this change and develop models for wide coverage. Considering our multicultural society, our services have to be culturally appropriate, easily accessible to disadvantaged groups and focused on empowering communities.

REFERENCES

Bharadwaj, P., Vidyasagar, M. S., Kakria, A., & Tanvir Alam, U. A. (2007). Survey of palliative care concepts among medical students in India. *Journal of Palliative Medicine, 10*(3), 651–653.

Butola, S. (2012). They suffer in silence. *Journal of Pain & Palliative Care Pharmacotherapy, 26*(2), 167–169.

Gupta, H. (2004). How basic is palliative care? *International Journal of Palliative Nursing, 10*(12), 600–601.

Gupta, V., Kumar, S., Shukla, A., Kumar, S., & Kumar, S. (2007). End-of-life care of terminally ill geriatric cancer patients in northern India. *National Medical Journal of India, 20*(2), 74–77.

Higginson, J., Hart, S., Koffman, J., Selman, L., & Harding, R. (2007). Needs Assessments in Palliative Care: An Appraisal of Definitions and Approaches Used. *Journal of Pain and Symptom Management, 33*(5), 500–505.

Koffman, J., Burke, G., Dias, A., Raval, B., Byrne, J., Gonzales, J., & Daniels, C. (2007). Demographic factors and awareness of palliative care and related services. *Palliative Medicine, 21*(2), 145–153.

Lynn, J., & Adamson, D. M. (2003). *Living well at the end of life. Adapting health care to serious chronic illness in old age.* Washington.

McDermott, E., Selman, L., Wright, M., & Clark, D. (2008a). Hospice and palliative care development in India: A multimethod review of services and experiences. *Journal of Pain & Symptom Management, 35*(6), 583–593. https://doi.org/10.1016/j.jpainsymman.2007.07.012

McDermott, E., Selman, L., Wright, M., & Clark, D. (2008b). Hospice and palliative care development in India: A multimethod review of services and experiences. *Journal of Pain & Symptom Management, 35*(6), 583–593.

Mudur, G. (2012). Palliative care in India lags behind government initiatives. *British Medical Journal, 345*, e6845.

Rajagopal, M. R., & Twycross, R. (2010). Providing palliative care in resource-poor countries. In G. Hanks, N. I. Cherny, N. A. Christakis, M. Fallon, S. Kaasa & R. K. Portenoy (Eds.), *Oxford texatbook of palliative medicine*. Oxford University Press.

WHO. (2017). Palliative care. Retrieved 26 June 2017 from http://www.who.int/cancer/palliative/definition/en/

Chapter 5

Social Work and Counselling
Contemporary and Emerging Practice Areas

INTRODUCTION

Social work is known as a helping profession. In social work practice, the use of counselling skills is central for service delivery. Social work and counselling are not two completely separate entities; rather, the two professions have many components that are closely related to each other. Although they are separately rooted, they are also interdependent. The common concern of both is the well-being of the individual and society at large.

In the context of the well-being of the individuals and society, social workers are trained with professional knowledge and skills to deal with problems of individuals and their environment. The social work profession believes in the worth and dignity of individuals, and their right to seek assistance, self-determination and a secure state of well-being. Social workers use different methods to work with people. The primary methods include 'social case work', 'group work' and 'community organization'. In all these methods, social workers utilize their theoretical knowledge and various techniques to provide services. By utilizing theories of human behaviour and social systems, social workers plan for intervention to address the concerns of people, group and communities. Professional attitude, ethical conduct and principles of human rights and social justice are fundamental to social work (IASSW, 2014).

Since beginning of social work profession, working with individuals is central to social work and 'social case work' is considered the primary method of social work practice. Also, in other methods such as 'group work' and 'community organization', social workers get in contact with individuals, families and community and in all methods the counselling skills are required in direct or indirect ways. Booysen and Staniforth (2017) highlighted the role of counselling in social work, derived from the definition of the International Federation of Social Workers (IFSW), that defines social work practice as follows: 'Social work practice spans a range of activities including various forms of therapy and counselling, group work, and community work; policy formulation and analysis; and advocacy and political interventions' (IFSW, 2014). Thus, social work professionals use counselling under various methods of social work to deal with psychosocial problems of client system and to enhance his/ her problem-solving capacity.

SOCIAL WORK AND COUNSELLING

The global definition of social work guides social work professionals to work for promotion of social change, empowerment and liberation of people by adhering the principle of social justice and human rights. It is also guiding the professionals to create networks to engage people and institutional structures to address concerns of society and to enhance well-being for all (IFSW, 2014). Similarly, if we look at the definition of counselling, it is defined as a process of change by bringing new perspectives and goals to achieve. The American Counselling Association (ACA) 2004 defined professional counselling in view of principles of mental health, psychology and human development and application of these principles for interventions aimed at cognitive and behaviour change for overall wellness of the client system. In contrast, the 2010 version defined counselling by enhancing its scope and clearly pointing out empowerment of 'diverse individuals, families and groups' (ACA, 2010).

Both social work and counselling are theory-based professions; they utilize theoretical knowledge from social sciences, humanities and other disciplines to address the issues of client systems. Also, it is important to note that both social work and counselling emphasize the use of multicultural approach to address the issues of diverse individuals, groups and communities in specific regional context. It presents the liberal and flexible approach to professionals to practise and to protect the client identity, worth and dignity. At the same time, both social work and counselling set out clear norms for adherence to code of ethics and accountability in order to protect the rights of clients (ACA, Code of Ethics, 2014).

Professional social workers are trained to identify social issues and problems and to adopt a professional approach to address these problems by using different methods of social work. The social workers deal with different clients under various situations. Therefore, the major emphasis is always on building up professional relationships with the client and one of the core needs is to provide informed choices. It is also important to note that the ACA *code of ethics* (2014) highlights the role and responsibility of counsellors; this includes the establishment of professional relationships for providing services to diverse populations. This also guides professionals to build up professional attitude with comprehensive knowledge of the subject domain. The need to build up professional networking and consultations with allied professionals is also highlighted under the code of conduct for counselling provided by ACA.

Counselling is no more confined to a limited role; rather, there is a continuous expansion of counselling services, and counsellors play important roles in expanding welfare activities and advocacy for the overall well-being of the client. As we know, social work and counselling are interlinked with each other; thus, the knowledge of theoretical perspectives of both the subjects is important for professionals. Social work interventions primarily focus on bringing about change at individual levels, for which the knowledge of counselling theories and application of counselling skills are required.

As far as practice is concerned, traditionally social workers perform counselling roles in mental health settings through the use of counselling skills for undertaking psychosocial assessment and providing direct services. Supportive counselling skills are still central to work with children and their families in many government and non-government agencies. However, in any social and local context the social workers offer services primarily within the agency setting and its framework. These agencies offer services to individuals, groups and communities under various domains such as family and child welfare, physical and mental health, justice and legal rights protection, crisis and disaster, and conflict and violence. Along with traditional practice areas, new areas of practice also emerged. Thus, the scope of social work practice and counselling is not static; rather, it is continuously evolving with growth and development of society.

CONTEMPORARY AND EMERGING PRACTICE AREAS OF COUNSELLING

Social workers contribute through various methods and skills, which they learn through academic learning, continuous supervision and fieldwork practice. Counselling is a skill-based technique and is professionally used by social workers to work with different clients. Broadly, it includes assessment of problems, developing new perspectives, setting goals for change, evaluation and follow-up. Counsellors and clients work together in this process of change and create empowering environments to achieve specific goals. If we locate the current practice of counselling in the Indian context, it is spread over different specialized fields. These specialized fields are gaining importance with increase in public awareness and acceptance of their utility by governments, people and communities.

In India, the scope of counselling practice is huge. The area of counselling is very wide and cannot be defined in a limited practice setting and specific time frame. With social and economic growth and consequent development and advancement of society, different complex issues are emerging. These advancements at one end have resulted in growth and development of societies and individuals, but at another end have affected them with complex personal and social issues. People are exposed to different psychological issues and conflicts. Sometimes people face difficulties to cope with fast and changing societal realities, and feel stressed and frustrated in such a competitive atmosphere. In such a situation, the social workers directly deal with individuals and different personalities and provide services to such people by using various counselling methods. All social work processes—interviewing, assessment, planning, interventions and evaluation—take place in the context of meeting people with their worries and life crises. In counselling, the social worker deals with complex relationships and personal and family problems, for example, marital disputes, domestic violence and parent–child conflicts. Many social workers specialize in serving a particular population or work in a specific counselling service setting/agency such as HIV/AIDS, substance abuse and alcoholism, cancer, disability, rape and sexual abuse, mental health problems, natural disaster, and war and conflict. Social workers get many different opportunities to engage themselves through counselling.

In the present context in India, counselling in some specialized areas is legally mandatory in government institutions. Counselling is in practice in many social work areas such as mental illness or psychological disorders, HIV/AIDS, domestic violence and dowry, divorce and family dispute, rape and sexual abuse, school education and special needs, children in conflict with law and in need of protection, human conflicts and disaster management. Other than government institutional efforts to provide counselling for marginalized and vulnerable people, the non-governmental organizations also provide specialized and generic services to the people who are in need. Sometimes these services are integrated with government programmes and policies and at other times, they also exist independently.

Healing and wellness are culturally embedded in Indian cultural system. The age-old techniques such as meditation, self-reflection and energizing the inner core are central to Indian ancient wellness philosophy. The area of exploration of counselling systems, from ancient to contemporary, is huge. Today, a mixed approach is used by many institutions in order to get the best out of existing service delivery mechanisms. The social work trainee in the fieldwork practice setting is expected to learn all these service delivery mechanisms, and the various government and non-government sectors' approach towards counselling services, along with identification of emerging areas of practice. With such a vast area of practice, social workers are required to gain insights through theoretical understanding of complex situations and issues. They need to work on themselves to create professional competence to generate sensitivity and to remove prejudices. Also, in order to practise counselling, knowledge of skills of counselling is a must to develop professional attitudes for dealing with diverse clients.

COUNSELLING AND APPLICATION OF PSYCHOSOCIAL APPROACHES

Counselling is a process and a therapeutic communication between counsellor and client. It is a professional relationship based on the need of the client to resolve the personal or social issue or problem affecting their life and well-being. The aim of counselling is to assist the client in dealing with their problems by adopting professional approaches. The British Association for Counselling (BAC, 1986) highlighted the use of skills and principles of the counselling for optimum use of self. Though counselling service is need based, it can be of use in various developmental issues such as crisis and problem-solving, self-awareness, decision-making, identification of inner dilemmas and improving social relationships. Malcolm Hill et al. (1990) also pointed out that counselling aimed at empowerment of client system to bring about change through use of self and professional services. With more clarity on working model and expected outcome of counselling, American Counseling Association (ACA 2010) defined the professional counselling as empowering professional relationship to address concerns of diverse populations.

In this context, social workers may be required to deliver counselling services. For that, they have to learn and adopt the approaches that are being used in counselling to help individuals and groups to deal with their specific problems (Sharf, 2011). Traditionally, the counsellors utilize the subject knowledge of psychology in order to understand human beings, their psychosocial growth, family and social environment and individual responses. Through classroom learning, the social work trainees get insights and knowledge of these important approaches in a systematic manner. Richard Nelson-Jones (2012) wrote on the existing literature on theoretical approaches of psychology that can be used in counselling, as per which the four main schools are psychodynamic school, humanistic–existential school, cognitive behaviour school and postmodern school. There are differences and similarities between all counselling and therapy schools. Nelson-Jones (2012) has given the explanation of these four counselling and therapy schools. (A brief introduction to these schools is given in Box 5.1.)

Box 5.1 *Counselling and Therapy Schools and Theoretical Approaches*

S. No	Important Counselling and Therapy Schools	Theoretical Approaches and Originator
1	The psychodynamic school: It is focused on mental energy, structure and consciousness of the mind. Unconsciousness affects individual functions and behaviour. The aim of this therapy is to bring knowledge of the unconscious and enhancement of conscious ability to control the functions and behaviour. There are many techniques suggested by this school, such as dream analysis, working through transference and counter transference and so on.	Classical psychoa-nalysis: Sigmund Freud (1856–1939) Analytical therapy: Carl Jung (1875–1961)
2.	The humanistic-existential school: It is focused on the principle of humanism, a value system that holds the belief that every human being has the potential and capability to enhance his/her potential. Self-actualization, reflection and use of existence are helpful in having experience of the inner feelings and enhancement of capabilities for better relation-ship with self and others.	Person-centred therapy: Carl Rogers (1902–1987) Gestalt therapy: Fritz Perls (1893–1970) Transactional analysis: Eric Berne (1910–1970) Reality therapy: William Glasser (1925– 2013) Existential therapy: Irvin Yalom (1931–) and Rollo May (1909–1994) Logotherapy: Viktor Frankl (1905–1997)

S. No	Important Counselling and Therapy Schools	Theoretical Approaches and Originator
3.	The cognitive behaviour school: It emphasizes thinking patterns, cognitive self, belief system and responses. This school concentrates more on behaviour change with identification of pattern of thoughts and cognitive images of the client system. Developing new perspectives and setting goals for change are major interventions suggested by this school.	Behaviour therapy: Ivan Pavlov (1849–1936), B. F. Skinner (1904–1990), Joseph Wolpe (1915–1997) Rational emotive behaviour therapy: Albert Ellis (1913–2007) Cognitive therapy: Aaron Beck (1921–) Multimodel therapy: Arnold Lazarus (1932–2013)
4.	The postmodern school: This school highlights the importance of 'social constructionist viewpoint', the process of developing views on self and the outer world in the context of existence is the main area of intervention with client. The use of the cognitive process in order to use past to control the present, identification of thoughts and feelings about people, and interpretations are important in bringing about change through professional interventions.	Solution-focused therapy: Steve de Shazer (1940–2005) and Insoo Kim Berg (1934–2007) Narrative therapy: Michael White (1948–2008) and David Epston (1944–)

Source: Nelson-Jones (2012)

The basic purpose of having knowledge of psychotherapy and approaches to counselling is to gain theoretical understanding of psychological problems of a client in a given situation and his/her context. About the application of these theoretical approaches, Cooper and McLeod (2007) explained that different approaches can be used for different clients at different point of time. We can learn from this explanation that it is a matter of choice and theoretical position of a professional to choose either a single approach or multiple approaches to deal with the case or client at different points of time.

Further, for professional application of this theoretical knowledge with the clients in a practice setting, the counsellor must adhere to the ethical guidelines of the professional discipline. Therefore, professional social workers and counsellors are expected to work under codes of ethics of their professional discipline. All social work trainees must understand the professional boundaries of their practice. It is not to be doubted that these approaches are helpful in gaining understanding of the client's psychosocial problems and their situations. However, the practice of therapies is subject to adherence to the codes of ethical practice under the given ethical and legal framework of the academic discipline.

If social work trainees aim to enter the field of counselling services, they need to know the basic concepts of the psychological approaches in order to gain knowledge about human personalities, behaviour and actions. These approaches help counsellors to gain insights into the issues of clients and to assist them to find the appropriate meaning of their thoughts, emotions and behaviour and their impact on their life. Also, in the process of counselling, these approaches are helpful in developing new perspectives and enhance problem-solving capacity of individuals. If a social worker acquires such knowledge, he/she would be in a position to help clients to make informed choices about the therapies offered to them and to provide information on what approach might be most helpful to them. Thus, it is expected at the fieldwork setting that the social work trainees learn about the theoretical basis of psychological approaches and the appropriate use of these approaches in practice settings in different counselling situations.

COUNSELLING AND PROFESSIONAL RELATIONSHIP

The counsellor is a person who through his/her professional knowledge and skills works with individuals/clients to make them use their potential to resolve their life problems or issues. The professional relationship between counsellor and client is the first requirement to start the counselling process. The professional relationship is based on qualities and competence of counsellors. The counsellor is required to possess certain good qualities to deliver the services in a professional manner. These qualities are interpersonal skills, knowledge or awareness, empathetic connection, ability to work with specific approaches, therapeutic communication, genuineness, consistency and stability. Through the application of professional skills and use of professional self, the counsellor makes efforts to establish professional relationship, bring new insights and facilitate change in the best interest of the client.

All human beings have certain basic needs such as survival, love and belonging, power, freedom and autonomy (Glasser, 1998). Clients' unmet needs create problems in their life and they feel sad, angry, dissatisfied, frustrated and so on. Sometimes due to these unmet needs the individuals may encounter crises in their life. With the help of counselling services, the clients can achieve more control on their lives by utilizing therapeutic relationships that exist between them and their counsellors. Thus, in counselling it is important to have a trustworthy and genuine relationship between counsellor and client. The relationship of counsellor and client is of a special kind, in which the client needs to be understood—not only in a superficial sense, but also in a deeper sense to make contact with their internal experiences. Rogers emphasized that the relationship between counsellor and client is a source of healing and is therapeutic in nature, consisting of three basic elements: congruence, unconditional positive regard and empathy. The counsellor should provide an atmosphere of genuine care and concern rather than a 'job-oriented role' (Miller, 2012).

Counsellors should take reasonable steps to seek peer supervision to evaluate their efficacy as counsellors. The profession demands interdisciplinary consultations and teamwork. By drawing on the perspectives, values and experiences of the counselling profession and those of the colleagues from other disciplines, counsellors with professional knowledge and resources contribute to decisions that affect the well-being of clients.

PROFESSIONAL COMPETENCE AND USE OF SELF IN COUNSELLING

To become a competent counsellor, social work trainees must learn to adopt standard professional approaches to work with different clients. BACP, Ethical Framework (2012) recognized the importance of professional attitude and guided counsellors to use self-awareness for working with clients with non-discriminatory approach. The self-awareness and cognitive understanding that trainees are expected to have involves one's value system and relational processes. The counsellor needs to be aware of his/her thoughts, feelings, beliefs, behaviour, values and attitudes and the importance of these in the development of individual personality. The trainee should have reflections on one's perceptions and experiences. The knowledge of these factors is important to build up genuine and therapeutic relationships with clients, which is a prerequisite of effective counselling.

Along with application of approaches (theoretical knowledge) and skills of counselling, self-awareness is an integral component of the counselling service delivery system. In any given context, the counsellor is required to work with the client as per the principle of acceptance and non-judgmental attitude. This can only be done with accurate understanding of clients' situation and empathizing with the client. In order to help the client to understand his/her situation and problems and to motivate the client to take decisions, counsellors should be in a state of self-awareness. This would help counsellors to be in neutral positive regard towards the client and his/her structural context. To know the structural context of the client, knowledge of all possible life situations and the individual and social positioning of the client is required. Some of the structural areas of exploration would be the social and cultural context, age and pathology, gender, sexuality, family, community, religion, faith and the geographical and regional context. The important issue is that counselling should be done as per the multicultural framework, in order to serve a range of clients or people having different psychosocial problems in their specific contexts.

Also, self-awareness involves having knowledge of one's own personality, including their strengths, weaknesses, thoughts, beliefs, motivation, attitudes, emotions and feelings. Self-awareness allows us to understand other persons' perceptions, how they perceive us, our thoughts and our attitudinal responses to them. When a counsellor attends multicultural clients, it is important to work on self-awareness and to be in self-reflection continuously, in order to come out of individual biases and to deliver the services with professional attitude.

The counselling job requires cognitive flexibility and an understanding of how one's own beliefs, values and attitudes can influence the counselling process adversely in direct and indirect ways. The counsellor needs to be aware of his/her biases, so as to control his/her emotions in counselling that client. Social work professionals are expected to work under an ethical framework of practice. BACP (2016) provides an ethical framework to be followed by counsellors, which emphasizes fundamental values and commitment towards clients and professional service delivery. In this practice, the framework focus is on respecting dignity and worth of individuals, to build up effective relationship, and to accept diverse culture of clients for empowerment. The facilitation and extension of professional services should be aimed at empowering clients to get relief from sufferings through use of self. The protection and well-being of client should be integral part of professional services.

SUPERVISION AND APPLICATION OF COUNSELLING SKILLS

Through theoretical orientation, the social work trainees learn the skills of counselling. They are expected to learn the importance of building a trusting relationship with the client, and to bring clarification about the professional nature of the counsellor/client relationship. The counsellor must create enabling and confidential environment for the clients to allow the client to discuss his/her issues or problems without any barrier or hesitation. Under designated supervision, the trainees must gain knowledge of the counselling process and the setting of enabling environment, which is very important in order to facilitate the clients to explore their thoughts and feelings in a safe and confidential manner.

In the professional capacity of social work trainees, it is very important to believe in the principles and to learn skills of counselling to deal with the clients. The principles of counselling are important to follow for the trainees in professional relationships. Some of the important principles are accepting the client as a unique individual, keeping a non-judgmental attitude, maintaining confidentiality and upholding the client's right to self-determination. The professional relationship is based on principle of working together, therefore understanding on the use of 'controlled emotional behaviour' and 'use of authority' is crucial in counselling practice.

Some of the general skills that can be applied in all counselling sessions while dealing with the clients include putting clients at ease, allowing clients to ventilate, forming a professional relationship and building trust, and developing an understanding towards client problems/challenges/difficulties. All this can be done through micro skills such as attending, active listening, empathy, focusing, reflection, questioning, paraphrasing interpretation and summarizing. These skills would help social work trainees in conducting field analysis, reality orientation, constructive utilization of guilt feeling and facilitating change in behaviour of client.

Social work as an academic discipline has two components, which are important to complete the professional requirements of the social work degree. These are attainment of theoretical knowledge of the subject and practical learning through fieldwork practicum. Thus, the professional social worker must be competent in understanding the client situation in a social context and in the application of micro skills in dealing with clients, which are both important in human service professions. The social work educators have the responsibility for providing theoretical knowledge to social work trainees and for developing their perspectives on the principles of social justice and human rights in local and global context. This process of education requires space and opportunity to the social work trainees for application of theoretical learning in the fieldwork placement setting or agency. It is to be done through continuous mentoring and supervision of social work trainees by their fieldwork supervisors or faculty. The fieldwork practice placement component under social work education is important not only for exposure of social realities, but also to practise micro skills that require dealing with individuals, to conduct field inquiries and assessment, to apply problem-solving and networking skills and so on.

In the fieldwork practice setting, to enhance their professional competence, trainees are expected to work under the regular supervision of the agency supervisor. They have to learn the theoretical bases of social issues and specialized areas of practice, and also to generate understanding on the professional approach of social work for interventions. Through theoretical knowledge on contemporary issues and challenges in the field, they have to develop their insights for critical analysis of theoretical contemporary issues and challenges. With this learning, it is expected from the trainee to gain first-hand knowledge from these practice settings or agencies. For this, the important requirement of the social work educational institutions is to explore the settings or agency where trainees can apply his/her theoretical knowledge and understanding. This is important for developing a professional approach for intervention in a systematic and planned manner within the assigned period.

The trainees should be oriented that social work interventions and use of counselling skills are always subject to capacity to use professional authority; therefore, knowledge of professional limitations is important in context of practice. For this, trainees are expected to utilize their supervisory inputs and feedback provided under supervisory arrangements made by the agency/practice setting.

Trainees learn their professional responsibilities and duties under the continuous guidance and supervision of the academic supervisor. In a fieldwork practice setting, the social work trainees are expected to explore the opportunities to use classroom learning and to utilize the learned skills in order to gain confidence in dealing with clients in a professional manner. He/she should learn to reflect on personal biases, attitudes, thoughts and perceptions and should learn to use oneself with professional approach in the counselling profession. The trainee must learn the importance of the use of a professional approach and process in counselling, how to identify the problem and create a plan of action to deal with issues or find ways of coping.

The trainees learn the use of appropriate authority and approaches under different formats to work together with the client. The social work trainee under the concurrent fieldwork placement and supervisor guidance learns to be culturally sensitive. Under supervisory guidance, the social work trainees are expected to develop the ability to maintain confidentiality, keep positive unconditional regard, self-awareness and a non-judgmental, caring and empathetic attitude towards their client. Also, trainees work on enhancing knowledge, updating the information about the subject and raising awareness of practice learning resources. Also, students or trainees are supposed to learn the process and skills of professional documentation, communication and to achieve the set goals and targets as per their fieldwork term planning. At the end of the term, the trainee's fieldwork is evaluated and feedback is provided by the supervisor. The fieldwork evaluation in social work is conducted under standard parameters of educational institutions. In general, the fieldwork evaluation parameters include the assessment of the trainee's planned work, conceptualization of issues/problems, application of theoretical knowledge, identification of marginalized and vulnerable sections of population, commitment for protection of human rights and social justice, values and attitudes, skills and knowledge, commitment, consistency, discipline, transparency, assessment of limitations, identification of core areas of intervention, application of learned methods and techniques, networking, referrals and alliances, follow-up and use of supervisory inputs, future areas of improvement, follow-up of timeline and completion of practice hours and so on.

In order to understand client concerns, the field practice setting and agency is important in providing the insights of subject reality to the trainee and facilitating the creation of the atmosphere where the trainees can identify their qualities and strengths to utilize them for adopting the professional skills of counselling. In present context, social work educational institutions in India are recognizing the need of counselling services under larger domain of social work intervention.

DISCUSSION AND CONCLUSION

In conclusion, we can say that the social work profession is a helping profession and it is aimed at bringing about micro and macro changes for the welfare of the individuals of diverse backgrounds and the society at large. In context of attainment of this aim, the professional relationship in social work and counselling practice becomes more important. Social work interventions primarily focus on bringing change at individual level, and to practise social work, the knowledge of counselling theories and the application of skills are not only useful, but also an important requirement. Counselling approaches help social workers to understand the psychosocial determinants of human personality and behaviour. In view of the increased complexity in human life and its relation to larger social issues, social work intervention is important. It can be done with sound knowledge of the cultural context, theoretical understanding of human personality and behaviour, interpersonal relationships and complexities, social and political environment and so on. Counselling and social work share that academic relationship which provides theoretical understanding of human beings and society and the legitimacy to use counselling skills in the social work practice areas. This requires competence and accountability on the part of professionals in order to protect the rights of the individuals, group and communities. Advocacy and social action for protection of human rights and social justice are also recommended for social work interventions.

The scope of understanding of counselling as a subject is not restricted only to the postgraduate degree of social work, but is also open for professional social workers to seek specialization further to enhance their subject knowledge and to practise counselling independently in multicultural settings. The subject has scope to utilize mixed methods and to generate new approaches through research and practise according to need and suitability to the psychosocial context of the client. The social work profession's objective is to create sensitivity and commitment among the professionals to work for society at large. The knowledge of counselling as a subject helps social workers to adopt the professional approach to deal with psychosocial issues of human beings. The primary objective of social work and counselling is to facilitate the clients with scientific knowledge and methods. This is to explore and improve their potential and empower them, by adopting the principles of human rights and social justice, and to bring about social change, for the overall well-being of human society.

REFERENCES

American Counseling Association (ACA). (2004). *Definition of counselling.* https://www.counseling.org/news/updates/2004/07/26/definition-of-professional-counseling#:~:text=The%20Practice%20of%20Professional%20 Counseling,development%2C%20as%20well%20as%20pathology

ACA. (2010). *20/20: Consensus definition of counselling*. https://www.counseling. org/about-us/about-aca/20-20-a-vision-for-the-future-of-counseling/ consensus-definition-of-counseling

ACA. (2014). *Code of ethics*. https://www.counseling.org/resources/aca-code-of-ethics.pdf

BACP. (2016). *Ethical framework for counseling profession*. https://www.bacp.co.uk/ media/2176/bacp-ethical-framework-for-the-counselling-professions.pdf

BACP Ethical Framework. (2012). https://www.bacp.co.uk/media/3103/bacp-ethical-framework-for-the-counselling-professions-2018.pdf

Booysen, P., & Staniforth, B. (2017). Counselling in social work: A legitimate role? *Aotearoa New Zealand Social Work, 29*(1). https://doi.org/10.11157/ anzswj-vol29iss1id214

British Association for Counselling (BAC). (1986). *Definition of counselling*. https://www.ccpa-accp.ca/wp-content/uploads/2015/05/NOE.What-is-Counselling-A-Search-for-a-Definition.pdf

Cooper, M., & McLeod, J. (2007). A pluralistic framework for counselling and psychotherapy: Implications for research. *Counselling and Psychotherapy Research, 7*(3), 135–143. https://pdfs.semanticscholar.org/14bd/35761e4817b1b9fabf6 f6cd64841bf18b783.pdf

Glasser, W. (1998). *Choice theory and the new reality therapy*. https://www. coursehero.com/file/6647366/Choice-Theory-Reality-Therapy-Chapter/

Hill, M., Ford, J., & Meadows, F. (1990). The place of counselling in social work. *Practice, 4*(3), 156–172. http://dx.doi.org/10.1080/09503159008416892

IASSW. (2014). Global definition of the social work profession. http://cdn.ifsw. org/assets/ifsw_94359-2.pdf

International Federation of Social Workers (IFSW). (2014). Definition of social work. http://ifsw.org/get-involved/global-definition-of-social-work/

Miller, A. (2012). *Instructor's manual on Carl Rogers on person-centered therapy*. https:// www.psychotherapy.net/data/uploads/5110340dadcda.pdf

Nelson-Jones, R. (2012). *Theory and practice of counselling and therapy* (Chapter 1, pp. 5–7). Sage Publications.

Seabury, B. A., Seabury, B. H., & Garvin, C. D. (2011). *Foundations of interpersonal practice in social work promoting competence in generalist practice* (3rd ed., pp. 44–45). Sage Publications.

Sharf, R. S. (2011). *Theories of psychotherapy and counselling: Concepts and cases*. Publisher Brooks Cole.

Chapter 6

Social Intervention through Social Enterprises
A Sustainable Approach to Social Work

Preeti Jha

INTRODUCTION

Social work as a profession has evolved in phases. From philanthropy to volunteering to professional social work guided under code of ethics, the profession has transformed over the last decade. However, it lacked the respectability of a profession for quite long. The declining welfare state, expanding magnitude of poverty, increasing inequality, ethnic conflicts, human rights violations, depletion of natural resources and family disintegration resulting in destitution are all serious concerns for social work (Alphonse, 2008). Increased demands for social work professionals in various fields indicate that the long due recognition to the profession has finally started coming along. Social work interventions are practised in many fields. The professional social worker dwells into areas of child rights, human rights, women empowerment, environment conservation, sustainable development and so on. The role of social work is crucial in upholding the rights of people who have been rendered powerless and marginal (Alphonse, 2008). Social work practice is most relevant when it caters to social justice, democracy and human rights.

Social work is practised through many ways. The most common is through the functioning of not-for-profit (NFP) organizations. These organizations have boomed in such large numbers that terms such as non-government and NFP has become synonyms. The past decade has seen the emergence of social enterprises (SEs). SEs provide a sustainable model to the social work profession. The entrepreneurs of these SEs may not be from the field of professional social work, but the vision, mission, belief and values of the organization have been similar to the ethos of professional social work development. The chapter will highlight SEs as a sustainable method for social interventions. This chapter will also discuss how social entrepreneurs practise the values of social work in their organization. The chapter shall provide a case study of a prominent SE in India with international reputation and how its work is creating intervention through the mirroring business model. Hence, SEs give a social dimension to business, making it self-sustaining by following social work principles.

SOCIAL WORK AS A PROFESSION IN INDIA

Social work as a vocation started with the establishment of Sir Dorabji Tata Graduate School of Social work, which later came to be known as Tata Institute of Social Work in 1936. The medical social work was undertaken by the institution by 1946. The Delhi University established Department of Social Work in 1946. The next two decades saw social work institutions in different central and state universities. Mukundrao (1969) mentions that America has influenced the shaping up of social work curriculum more than the need of the state at a practical level. The initial design of social work in professional sphere was inspired by the 'beliefs and convictions of an elite group who were impressed by the American model of professional training for social work' (Mukundrao, 1969).

Professional social work has various attributes. Professional mentoring of the social work approach has been offered by many government and private universities. The bases of these teachings are in accordance with the social work values and ethics laid by the International Federation of Social Work. Interestingly, SEs have not yet found place in the prescribed curriculum. Instead, there are management institutions that have started training young individuals in social entrepreneurship. However, if we look at the values and principles of the SEs, they are much in accord with the values and principles of professional social work. Hence, in the long run, SEs may become the more sustainable mode of practicing social work.

Mary Alphonse (2008) stressed upon the requirement of community-based practices in India. This needs to be more fully realized by addressing the areas of health, nutrition, employment, literacy, welfare and governance issues with the advent of international forces that create increasing disparity. In addition, at the macro level, social work practitioners also need to be more attentive to international migration and the social and economic integration of immigrants and refugees. The spread of international corporate ownership of resources means that social workers must also attend to the land rights of indigenous peoples, promote moderation in the use of natural resources, fight against dehumanizing technological advances and provide solidarity through networks. The increasing marginalization of groups of people makes concerns such as gender rights, conflicts between ethnic and cultural identities and nationhood central issues in social work (Alphonse, 2008). These practices are also at the heart of social entrepreneurial activities. SEs, and more so, the hybrid enterprises which have the core values of enterprise as well as NFP organizations, tend to cater to issues of empowering women, earning livelihood, creating employment, improving health, protecting the environment, addressing social exclusion, supporting agriculture and allied activities, promoting education, addressing and supporting financial inclusion and so on. They create employment within the organization and engage the community, making it self-sufficient.

EMERGENCE OF SOCIAL ENTERPRISES

The past decade saw a rise in the growth of SEs. SEs do not have a single definition. Bielefeld (2009) suggested that the term 'social enterprise' can be applied to non-profit, for-profit and government activities. SEs can be defined under a distinct category, since they have business goals and social goals simultaneously (Mathew, 2008). The social aspect of the organizational goals makes it different from a corporation. An SE may be for-profit as well as NFP. The organization that will be discussed in detail incorporates a model that makes the organization self-sustainable. Yet, it considers itself to be an NFP organization because the organizational goals are not measured in terms of profit but in terms of numbers of lives affected. SEs have essentially a sustainable approach. The term 'enterprise' itself has a commercial connotation to it. Mathew (2008) further adds that SEs have profit maximization as one among the core objectives, though they find a business case from the sustainability angle. SEs are 'not-for-profit'; but they are not 'non-profit' entities either. These are dynamic enterprises with a social purpose. They are based on the 'triple bottom line' principle, that is, economic viability, environmental sustainability and social responsibility. They are not 'charities', but are enterprises in the strict sense of the term (Mathew, 2008).

The term 'sustainability' simply implies an ability of a profession or an organization to sustain itself. The development sector is not audited in terms of financial profits and losses but on the lives it impacts. As stated previously, many organizations come under the umbrella of development sectors. These could be non-profit organizations, think tanks, SEs—both for-profit and non-profit, hybrid organizations and so on. Any organization in the development sector is expected to impact maximum number of people by uplifting their conditions. In India, the development sector relies heavily on funds. These funds are derived from corporate organizations, individual contribution, crowd funding and so on. The term 'business model' was used first with reference to electronic commerce (Balan & Balan, 2015). The business model emphasizes on the ability of an organization to create value and develop sustainable advantage (Balan & Balan, 2015), enact commercial opportunities (George & Bock, 2011), make money and create a pipeline for recurring profits (Stewart & Zhao, 2000). SEs are more business centric in their approach compared to non-governmental organizations (NGOs). The deliverables are clearly defined. In many organizations, the product becomes important. These products can range from a simple sanitary napkin made from old clothes to organic clothing. The strategies used for attracting investors or bringing the product to the market are similar to what is followed in corporate organizations. Therefore, an SE provides a more business–centric model of social work. The ideas are not dependent on donations, but invite investors. These SEs also have a long-term sustainability, not only for the community needs that they fulfil, but also in generating employment for many people.

REGISTERING SOCIAL ENTERPRISES

SEs lack a definite legal framework catering specifically to their structure and operation. There is no separate act under which SEs can be registered. Currently, the SEs for profit can be registered under sole proprietorship, partnership, limited liability partnership, private firm and cooperative under the Companies Act, 2013. NFP SEs are registered under the Indian Trusts Act (1882), section 25 of Companies Act (1956) and state society registration acts. Satar (2016) states that legal provisions have their own limitations. He states, 'While the traditional non-profit organisational model enables the firms to get tax and foreign donation benefits under the Income Tax Act (1961) and Foreign Contribution Regulation Act (2010) respectively, the legal structure simultaneously makes them to raise funds continuously.' Therefore, it is difficult to recruit top talents or invest in infrastructure and technology. This results in transition from non-profit to for-profit or sustainable framework.

HOW SOCIAL ENTERPRISES FOLLOW VALUES OF SOCIAL WORK PROFESSION

The core values of social work are identified in service of humankind, social justice, recognizing the dignity and worth of a person, importance of human relationships, integrity, competence and human rights. SEs function in a way that all the core values defined above are exercised through organizational activities. Bisman (2004) stressed that the 'primary focus of a profession such as social work is not defining and explaining, which are objectives of the social sciences…, but caring and changing'. She further added that the essence of social work is in achieving social justice. The skills are not exclusive to the social work profession. Many people employed in development sectors are not professional social workers. There have been many overlapping skills, for example, relationship building, therapy and case management. Psychology majors are also often counsellors. Similarly, there are multiple disciplines stepping for professional social workers. What makes them stand out is achieving social justice through their course of work. Therefore, the curriculum of social work borrows from other disciplines such as social systems, human behaviour, political systems, legal systems and so on. However, it is the application of knowledge within the framework of social work skills that defines the role of a professional social worker. It is the application of knowledge and skills towards moral ends that imbues the profession with meaning and defines the role of the social worker (Bisman, 2004). The primary goal of a social worker is to help people in need and to address social problems. SEs also function to fulfil these needs of society. The approach is not philanthropic, but a self-sustainable one.

The British Report of Social Enterprises, 'The State of Social Enterprise in India, 2016', states that social impact and entrepreneurship are part of Indian culture. The entrepreneurial environment was set by cooperative and community-owned business models such as Amul and Fabindia since the 1950s. Ashoka, the global sport organization, introduced the term 'social entrepreneur' in 1981. Domestic and international investors and support organizations began to grow widely. All of these are in coherence with the definition of social work. Hence, interventions in the field impact majorly, and this impact sustains for a long period. SEs in India are emerging very strongly. The report by British Council further suggested that there might be more than 2 million organizations in the country in the embryonic stage. Most of the SEs studied by British Council have started in 2010 or later. The report surveyed 258 organizations, of which 24 per cent were led by women.

The report further testifies that there has been a tremendous growth in entrepreneurial activities in the development sector since the last decade as the ideas and business plans have been more innovative. The entrepreneurs in SEs have come up with more sustainable avenues due to the environment of growing awareness, training and workshops and institutional support for social entrepreneurs. This institutional support has provided 'direct, indirect, financial, and advisory assistance to social enterprises' (British Council, 2016).

SEs receive support through various funding agencies. Similar to the start-up model, many agencies invest or sponsor the development initiatives. As per the report by British Council (2016), incubators for SEs, such as UnLtd India and Villgro, support the entrepreneurs at seed stage and early stage to create an impact within the envisioned sphere. Villgro supports the SE ecosystems in tier II and tier III cities through its 'unconventional' initiative. These incubators support SEs by providing access to funding, mentoring, conducting workshops and training, refining business models and innovations, and providing research support to measure impact.

More than 50 per cent of the SEs, surveyed by the British Council Report (2016), have operations in the skills development sector. These enterprises have focused on providing relevant skills training to producers, artisans, and unskilled/semi-skilled labourers. Other sectors which emerged for these enterprises are education, agriculture, fisheries, dairy, financial services, energy and clean technology and healthcare. In South India, the clean energy sector is most dominant with 75 per cent of activity. The survey shows that affordable housing, water and sanitation, eco-tourism and forestry and environment are on the lower side of the ladder of SE activity in India. Only 5 per cent of the SEs surveyed work in the affordable housing sector. Governance, cultural development, disaster risk reduction, social gaming and networking have also featured in the social entrepreneurial framework. Therefore, with the similar ethos and values, SEs essentially work as per the principles of social work.

GOONJ: A CASE STUDY

Goonj is an internationally recognized Indian NGO. It is a hybrid organization working on the model of SE as well as an NGO. It was started in 1999. The founder of the organization, awarded with many national and international accolades, believes that the basic human need has been ignored by the state as well as any other NGO and that is clothing. He got inspiration from the people he closely encountered while doing internship in field of mass communication. After working as a freelancer in a few organizations, he left to start this NGO, which basically started by collecting unused clothes and other materials from urban people and providing it to the needy. Today, the NGO carries out a number of campaigns running successfully in 22 states.

The organization is located in a residential area of Delhi, which was the earlier residence of the founder. As an MPhil study states (Jha 2016), there are 11 branch offices in different states from where the organization has been actively working in 21 regions. The head office is in Delhi along with the biggest processing unit (where goods are made for sale) and many collection centres in every zone of Delhi. In Delhi, the workforce comprises around 100 employees at the processing unit, most of them being women from nearby communities. The employees at the head office are further divided into departments such as campaigning, marketing, administrative, human resources (HR) and processing unit care. The organization has 205 formal employees.

The founder, Mr Anshu Gupta, started this organization in 1999 with the help of a few like-minded people. He has a professional degree in mass communication and has experience of working with the corporates. The need of the organization was realized while he was engaged as an intern with a corporate. He found that the most basic issue for living, that is, clothing, is invisible and needs to be addressed. He also realized that donations for disaster relief are often the discards by urban areas and are not according to the culture of the area. Hence, he envisioned an organization with the concept of dignified giving. The core value of this SE is human dignity. Although the founder has no formal education in social work, the organizational goals have inherent values practised in social work settings.

The belief of the founder is translated in the vision, mission and goal of the organization. These are reflected in his public speeches, press releases and at various other platforms. First, he believes that the state has devised enough programmes and policies for the development of people. The role of the organization is to aid to these policies and work with government. An example of this belief is his school-to-school initiative, which encourages students of the urban elite schools to donate the uniforms, schoolbooks, shoes and stationeries for underprivileged children in the rural areas. The second belief of the founder is that people in cities have benefitted from the subsidies provided by the state. The fees of government schools and colleges, public transport and government aids are subsidized, and hence it is an inherent responsibility of the citizen to take care of the needs of the fellow citizens. Third, he practises what he propagates at personal and organizational levels. For example, the organization uses furniture which is donated and not bought. The employees are very proud to showcase this. The organization stresses working as a cohesive team to reach the goals. Fourth, the founder also believes that his ideas should not be limited to his organization. These should be replicated by all. Those should become a 'virus' which spreads, as mentioned repeatedly in his keynotes. The founder and his organization have won many national and international awards and accolades for the work undertaken by them.

There are six key members at Delhi head office, who head various divisions. Out of six core members, only one is a professional social worker but she works as an administrative in-charge and not in the campaign department. The employees who are part of active fieldwork have different educational background. Zeal, passion and longevity in the organization are the different desired traits to become a core team member. These core members head teams of particular departments. The leader keeps travelling to the branch offices and diffuses organizational culture at the regional level.

Vision, Mission and Goals of the Organization

The vision of the organization is to address clothing as a basic need, which deserves a place on the development agenda. Clothing, as basic as it sounds, remains unaddressed in the pyramid of need seen by development agencies. News records will show the number of deaths reported every winter in the North Indian zones where winters are unbearable. This recognition of clothes as needs comes with an asterisk mark that these needs shall not be fulfilled by the discard of urban household. In the name of charity, people in urban sectors 'donate' their old clothes without thinking if it is suitable for the receiver or not. It also aims to constructively revive rural volunteerism and strengthen it to solve their own needs, digging deep into the knowledge base of the villages. The organization has tried to maximize its reach amongst masses in the most backward of villages, as well as metropolitan cities with the same effect. Third, it wants to create a parallel economy that would be trash-based and not cash-based.

The organization aims to grow as an idea. The founder says that the idea of the organization has to be picked and replicated worldwide. The idea of charity has to be busted as the cities discard their useless material and not 'donate' them. Therefore, the dignity of the receiver is kept above the pride of the donor. The material is to be understood as an instrument of highlighting the issues of basic needs. The material shall bring communities together and actualize their power as a community and facilitate infrastructural changes in rural areas. The mission of the organization is to 'involve rural wisdom in bringing together solutions for problems in infrastructure'.[1]

The goal of the organization is to address very basic needs of the society, that is, clothing. Clothing as a need is understood only in the times of disaster, when clothes are donated without understanding the culture of the region. However, the organization has turned the piece of waste cloth into suitable and dignified piece of clothing. The clothes are sorted, rectified, marked into appropriate sizes and are distributed as per the climatic conditions and cultural need of the people. The organization does not only work in the time of disaster, but also when communities work towards creating resources, for example, the cleaning of the Dal Lake or constructing a bridge. Second, it wishes to work towards menstrual hygiene. Third, the organization aims to make people aware of their basic rights. Finally, it wants to move the surplus of the urban area to rural for fulfilling the pressing needs of the community. The campaigns are designed to meet the goals of the organization.

The Organizational Structure

The organizational structure is very simple to understand. The organization has few basic premises. First, the organization does not follow any hierarchy. There are no designations for employees in the organization. Therefore, the founder has retained his title as founder, and the others are addressed as team members. The governing body has

---

[1] https://goonj.org/

five members, including the founder and his wife. There are six core team members who are specially mentioned on the website. These people have more than 10 years of experience with the organization. The departments are not acknowledged formally. Roles are not clearly defined. Employees of a department are encouraged to take up tasks in other departments as well to have an exposure of all kinds of work. Interns and volunteers also form a very strong part of the organizational structure. The work of interns is formally assigned and closely monitored. The interns can choose the campaign in which they are interested to work. In association with a close team member, they work equally as employees in terms of the accountability they have to the organization. The interns are regularly motivated by Mr Gupta himself. Being a Ramon Magsaysay award winner, TED speaker and having many more feathers to his cap, Mr Gupta serves to be a major inspiration to these budding students of all fields. Interestingly, interns at Goonj are not only from social work profession but also from management, including aspiring MBAs; engineering; law; development studies and other professions. Social work education has specific courses teaching women empowerment, community development, upliftment of the poor and marginalized, use of traditional wisdom, mobilizing resources, engaging urban and rural youth in resource generation and so on. The major work of Goonj encompasses all that. If only SEs can be accepted as a legitimate social work area, the scope of practice will be increased manifold.

Goonj is a hybrid organization. On the one hand, it functions as an NGO, while on the other hand it has a processing unit that manufactures different products for urban population and generates revenue for the organization. The raw material for the products comes from collection camps and contributions by people. There is no fundraising department nor are these fundraising targets, which otherwise are crucial for NGOs. The self-sustainable model of the organization makes it fall under the category of SE rather than NGO. Apart from the formal offices, they also have dropping centres in all the states where people donate the material they wish to. The material is collected from these dropping centres and sent to the processing unit of that state. In Delhi, for example, there are 20 dropping centres which cover the National Capital Region as well. These dropping centres are run by volunteers of the organization. The organization has a strict

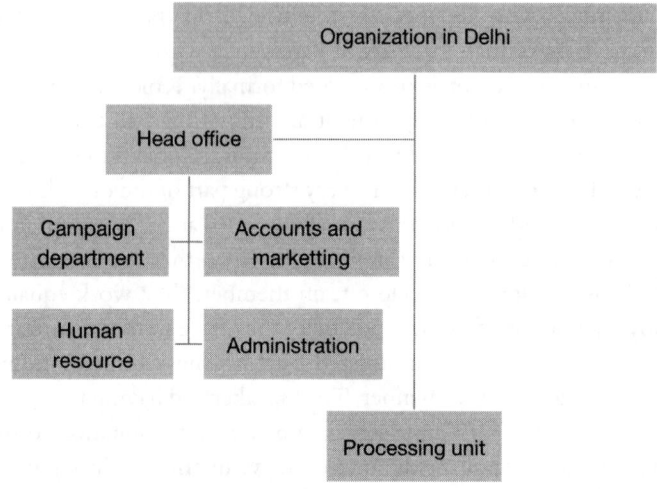

Figure 6.1 *Structure of the Organization*
Source: Author

guideline for what can and cannot be donated. The organizational structure can be understood through Figure 6.1.

The organization is functioning through three models: charity model, barter model and self-sustaining model. Under the charity model, the organization devises programmes that focus on distributing the material in the underprivileged areas. The material is taken from the urban discard and modified into a product suitable for distribution. The charity model provides material during disasters. Under the barter model, the organization gives a designed kit to people who work as part of the community initiative, for example, building a broken bridge or cleaning of a river. The organization believes that products distributed for free are taken for granted and hence a 'reward' perspective to the kit would add more meaning to the initiative. Even when organization distributes products to children in school, the organization encourages children to cut nails or wash hands. The third model is the sustainability model. The SE unit helps to economically sustain the NGO unit of the organization. The products are designed for the corporate and urban population. The brand is created by the organization to give

Figure 6.2 *Models Followed in the Organization*
Source: Author

satisfaction to the buyer of contributing towards a cause. Apart from the various products of daily use, the most important product devised by the organization is sanitary napkin. An entire programme was created around this product, which addresses the issue of menstrual taboos and importance of hygiene. The diagram in Figure 6.2 would show the models used by the organization.

Networking with Other Organizations

The organization has been working with 250 NGOs in the areas where it is functional. Local NGOs help the organization to perform a need analysis and provide resources. These NGOs address the other employees during the annual meet. Campaigns are designed in partnership with the NGOs. Corporates also tie up with the organization and donate material on a daily basis. The organization also networks with media for attracting contributions. Currently, there are campaigns with radio stations and international clothing companies which collaborate with the organization to widen the objectives.

Employees at the Organization

The organization has more than 200 employees. These include workers at the processing unit as well as the employees at the head offices and regional offices. Apart from these employees, there are interns from all disciplines ranging from engineering to MBA. The organization has defined HR policies for all employees. Employees at the processing centre form a strong part of the organization. They come from nearby communities and are paid according to the skills they possess. Those in need of work but do not have skills are given tasks such as sorting of clothes and are gradually taught to stitch and make products. There are different policies for employees in the processing unit. They are aided financially and provided support. In case of emergency, for example, a disaster situation, they can even work from home by making products at home. Only at the processing unit does the organization hire part-time workers who work from home by collecting raw material and making products. The women at the processing unit design the products such as bags, folders, slings, laptop bags and many more things, without any help or outside assistance. The idea is to explore the indigenous talent and design of these women who produce beautiful products from cultural knowledge.

Projects and Campaigns at the Organization

At present, there are five major projects on which the organization is working. These projects are:

1. *Clothes for work initiative:* Under this programme, the organization encourages rural participation in social development activities. For instance, the employees created awareness and organized a cleanliness drive for people in Kashmir to clean the Dal Lake. A total of 300 people participated, who were given a kit which consisted of clothes for men, women and children, *sujnis* (sujnis is the traditional cloth quilt of rural India layered with tattered and shredded pieces of clothes stitched together. It is also used as a quilt in winter and as a mattress during summer season.) and packets of sanitary napkins. Similar activities such as building roads, bridges and public platforms have been conducted in other regions as well.

2. *School-to-school initiative*: This programme addresses the educational needs of thousands of remote and resource-starved village schools or slum schools, by channelizing the under-utilized material of Delhi's affluent schools, not as a thing to distribute but as a tool to bring about comprehensive behaviour change in the recipients and contributors.

3. *Menstrual hygiene programme*: This programme is their most crucial programme and has brought many awards and recognition. The organization makes sanitary napkins from shreds of cotton clothes that cannot be converted into any other material. These shreds are cut into similar size and are folded to give a shape of sanitary pad. Besides, the organization designs undergarments to support these napkins. The campaign team conducts awareness sessions amongst rural village or urban slums for menstrual hygiene. These sessions are conducted by both men and women.

4. *Disaster relief programmes*: The organization works in the disaster-struck areas for relief and rehabilitation. It provides material such as food, clothing, blankets and other basic necessities.

5. *Fundraising programmes*: Although the organization does not have any fundraising targets, but it has programmes for collecting material from the urban spaces. These programmes are known as collection camps. The volunteers associated with the organization also maintain dropping centre at their residence where people come and donate to the organization. These donations can vary from clothes, utensils, books, old uniforms to even newspapers which are sold by the organization to raise funds. The organization claims that not even stapler pins are wasted. Products not having any use are sold to scrap dealers.

6. Apart from the material collection, the organization holds book sales and material sales. Festivals are the most crucial time of the year when it ties up with different corporate organizations for setting up stalls. People also give monetary contributions. One interesting programme asks the donor to maintain a piggybank. Every month many people deposit these piggybanks in different centres of the region. The donors also channelize the gifts and money received during birthdays, weddings or other celebrations, by requesting guests to donate to the organization rather to bring gifts for the host.

Goonj sets an example of what SEs are capable of and the future of social work. Recent studies have shown millions of NGOs are emerging. A recent study by TOI claimed that there are more than 3 million NGOs functioning currently. Yet the impact of these large number of NGOs is not seen. The philanthropic model of social work is not sufficient. The idea that 'social work is about enabling a person to help themselves' is truly realized in the ethos of SEs.

SOCIAL ENTERPRISE: A SELF-SUSTAINABLE MODEL

SEs are truly the future in the development sector. The simple fact that they are sustainable, provide employment, values and dignity of the community, enabling rather than providing makes SEs a lucrative choice for practicing social work. Higher corruption in the NFP sector and raising of funds without full realization for the community, the invisible field contributes to the doom of the NGO sector. A recent CBI report stated that more than 3 million NGOs are functioning in the country. This report highlighted the discrepancies in the developing sector. It states that not even 10 per cent of the NGOs comply with the requirement of running the organization, such as submitting balance sheets and income–expenditure statements with the Registrar of Societies. Fewer than one per cent have submitted financial statements. Almost all the states in India have poor status in filing legal papers for the organization. No audits, no assessments and no records have become the norm of the NGO sector. The report highlights state of Kerala has not filed for any details for NGOs, as the state law has not made it mandatory. Similarly, Maharashtra and West Bengal have only around 7 per cent of NGOs which have been filing such details. Therefore, the NGO sector leaves a huge gap for discrepancies to creep in.

The SEs have scope for giving a better life, not only to the beneficiaries but also to their employees. Vijay Padaki (2007) discusses stress, burnout and exploitation in the NFP sector. He states there are certain ethical issues faced by employees in the development sector. This ethical dilemma is about acknowledging and rewarding their employees. Should the organization reward with the funds it has achieved through donations? When an organization relies upon external source of funding, then promotions and rewards for its employees take a backseat. Thus, the high remunerations for people in the development sector call for justification in public view. The second issue is the ratio of the budget spent in the occupational cost to what reaches the people.

Rewards are considered to be 'not required' in the NGO sector. Often the questions arises: Is the intention of the employee is to have 'benefits' or to 'serve purpose' towards the poor and destitute. Therefore, the achievements are never monetarily acknowledged. The increments are also bare minimum. However, the international organizations often provide incentives to the fundraisers. This is similar to the for-profit industry where the sales division receives biggest incentives. The baseline is who brings the money? The sustainable approach to social work treats employees as assets. The contribution of employees in spreading the impact and their job roles shall be rewarded. If the SEs are self-sustaining, they will be able to create attractive rewards for the employees, which is absolutely absent in the development sector.

There is a need for acknowledgement of the requirement and facilitation of process of enabling a young professional force in SE. If there are institutional support providing professional skills, it should be mandatory for organizations to provide growth and recognition within social development sector as well. Ultimately, young professionals look towards their counterpart. In India, social work is not a licensed profession yet. The word is used loosely wherever there is charity and philanthropy involved. However, there is a need to define the line and give social workers their recognition and due. For that, social work as a profession has to open its arms to SEs as part of the mission of developing the ethos and values of professional social work.

CONCLUSION: SOCIAL ENTERPRISE AS A NEED OF THE HOUR

The aim of the chapter is to underline the emergence of SE in the landscape of the development sector. As the British Council study stated, the NGOs are blooming very rapidly. This has led to massive discrepancies and corruption in the NFP sector. Through a case study, this chapter stated that it is very crucial for any organization to be self-sustaining in the long run. SEs as a model, whether for profit or NFP, will help social work take the leap from philanthropic activity to a professional sector. Hybrid organizations such as Goonj are perfect examples of an organization working for the welfare of people in the development spectrum, yet be self-sustaining. The development sector in India has many cracks. A few of the issues which dominantly impact the development sector in India include a lack of defined boundaries of development organizations, lack of professional social workers, lack of adequate institutions imparting the practical vocation of social work, unaccountability in funding, lack of legal registrations of organizations, fudging of annual reports and data and lack of customized legal frameworks defining different institutions under development sectors. Therefore, a model which not only helps them to be self-reliant, but also creates a better workspace for the employees is required.

REFERENCES

Alphonse, M. (2008). International social work practice: The exchange experience in India. *Canadian Social Work Review, 25*(2), 215–221.

Balan-Vnuk, E., & Balan, P. (2015). Business model innovation in nonprofit social enterprises. In Göran Roos & Allan O'Connorn (Eds.), *Integrating innovation*. University of Adelaide Press.

Bielefeld, W. (2009). Issues in social enterprise and social entrepreneurship. *Journal of Public Affairs Education, 15*(1), 69–86.

Bisman, C. (2004). Social work values: The moral core of the profession. *The British Journal of Social Work, 34*(1), 109–123.

British Council. (2016). *The state of social enterprise in India.* https://www.britishcouncil.org/sites/default/files/bc-report-ch4-india-digital_0.pdf

Durkheim, E. (1938). *The rules of sociological method* (8th ed.). University of Chicago Press.

G, Gerard., Bock, Adam Jay. (2000). The Business Model in Practice and its Implications for Entrepreneurship Research. *Entrepreneurship Theory and Practice, 35*(1), 83–111. http://dx.doi.org/10.1111/j.1540-6520.2010.00424.x

Jha, P. (2016). *Organisational culture in not for profit enterprise: A case study.* Unpublished M Phil Dissertation, University of Delhi.

Mahapatra, D. (2014, February 23). India witnessing NGO boom. *Times of India.* https://timesofindia.indiatimes.com/india/India-witnessing-NGO-boom-there-is-1-for-every-600-people/articleshow/30871406.cms

Mathew, P. M. (2008). Social enterprises in the competitive era. *Economic and Political Weekly, 43*(38), 22–24.

Mukundrao, K. (1969). Cultural variants and social work practice in India. *Journal of Education for Social Work, 5*(1), 69–79.

Nair, H. (2015, September 19). 90 per cent of NGOs do not file annual statement: CBI to SC. *India Today.* https://www.indiatoday.in/india/story/90-per-cent-of-ngos-do-not-file-annual-statement-cbi-to-sc-263703-2015-09-19

Padaki, V. (2007). The human organisation: Challenges in NGOs and development programmes. *Development in Practice, 17*(1), 65–77.

Satar, M. S. (2016). A policy framework for social entrepreneurship in India. *IOSR Journal of Business and Management, 18*(9), 30–43.

Stewart, D.W., Q, Zhao. (2000). Internet marketing, business models, and public policy. *Journal of Public Policy, 19*(2), 287–296.

Chapter 7

Environment, Climate Change and Social Work
Imperatives for Practice

Neera Agnimitra

INTRODUCTION

Human beings are in the midst of the most challenging times, where the ongoing environmental decimation has put us on the brink of an existential crisis, together with the rest of our natural world. The global crisis caused by the ongoing environmental degradation, climate change and depreciation in the natural resources has created a monumental challenge to the survival and well-being of the human race. Environmental changes, whether in the realm of the global or the local, are largely anthropogenic, having stemmed from irrational human activities and excessive human interference in the natural environment.

Despite the overwhelming presence of problems in the earth's ecological domain, there has been relatively little cognition of the true nature and extent of the changes and the impact that these could potentially have on human well-being and on the survival of all other life on Earth. The seriousness of the environment contingency has been acknowledged only in a more recent context, leading to a concerted response by global actors, governments, civil society and citizens. The 'in-the-face' crisis emanating from the unremitting climate change and the immense devastation triggered by frequent 'natural' disasters has underscored the need for urgent and collective action to halt the menacing threat of an even more severe environmental catastrophe across the world.

Environment being a multidisciplinary and interdisciplinary domain, interest and response to the physical and social aspects of environmental problems have captured the attention of the natural, behavioural and social sciences. The dimensions of the deep and intricate consequentiality of environmental well-being and human well-being are increasingly being revealed by an ever-expanding body of empirical research across disciplines. With its committed stance towards the augmentation of human welfare, it has become imperative for the social work profession to also take up the environmental agenda and draw out a distinct response to the current ecological predicament, which has severe and multiple ramifications for the entirety of the living world, including human beings. It is high time that the erstwhile perspective of focusing entirely on the 'social' environment within the 'person-in-environment' approach, so revered by social work and social workers, undergoes a concerted change to include the 'natural' environment within its ambit. There is an undoubted and urgent need to acknowledge the essence of the two-way, symbiotic interface between human beings and their environment. Only such an integrated consciousness and thrust shall enable the profession to configure for itself a meaningful functional niche in addressing the critical environmental concerns and adopt a more visible role in restoring the symbiotic *prakriti–manav* (environment–human) relationship.

THE ENVIRONMENTAL JUSTICE MANDATE OF SOCIAL WORK

It is increasingly being realized that environmental justice concerns are core to any discourse and action to support social justice. Right from its inception, social work has rightly demonstrated a notable thrust on a spectrum of social justice concerns stemming from privileges and deprivations based on wealth, ethnicity, caste, religion, region, gender and (dis)ability. However, it is noteworthy that even in a context where a significant proportion of the world's population subsists on environmental resources, attention on the glaring inequities arising from differential ecological benefits and burdens has been found lacking in social work discourse.

As environmental benefits are primarily accessed by members of privileged nations and groups, the prevalence of an 'environmental apartheid' has emerged as a critical social justice and human rights concern. In context of the fact that this environmental apartheid is deemed to encompass the differential ability and access of environmental privileges among the countries of the developed and developing world (or the so-called Global North and Global South), Cannan (2000) had focused attention on the need for community development to create an urgent sense of cognition among the developed countries that their privileged life and living had forever been premised on an ever-increasing degradation of the environment in the poor and developing countries. Hillman (2002) also iterated that the most severe impacts of unbridled consumption and waste generation in the Global North were not confined to its territory, but these, in fact, impinged most disproportionately on the countries of the Global South. As the North continues to engage in the throes of a 'throw-away culture', the South continues to be exploited for its raw materials and cheap labour, made possible by its weak environmental policies.

This realization that the worst negative impact of the environmental problems is thrust disproportionately on the individuals and communities that are the poorest and the most marginalized, both within nation states and across the globe, substantiates the contention that the crisis is indeed grounded in serious concerns with respect to environmental justice and social justice. In the case of the industrialized nations of the North, groups which subsist on the margins are either subtly coerced or forced by circumstances to live and work in the more polluted and threatened environs. In the context of the developing nations, a significant proportion of the natural resource-dependent population is consistently stripped of its traditional rights to natural resources and therefore transform into migrants, who have little option but to dwell in unsafe and decimated habitats and adopt hazardous occupations. In either case, issues of social justice permeate environmental spaces, both physically and metaphorically.

While the rich and the privileged have the wherewithal to insulate themselves against the worst environmental fallouts of unsustainable living, people living in poverty are not only deprived of resources, but also lack the competency to recognize and respond to the enormity of the threat that the ongoing environmental decimation poses for them, thereby becoming susceptible to natural and man-made disasters of all hues. This makes environmental privilege/deprivation a social justice and human rights concern, within which Muldoon (2006) requisitions a proactive role to be played by the social work fraternity in rallying around issues and discourses in the domain of equitable distribution of environmental resources. Social workers are also expected to campaign for equitable, rational and prudent consumption norms; environment friendly and accountable systems of waste management, and the right to safe, clean and conducive environs for all people. Muldoon also recognizes the challenges inherent in fulfilling this intent, in that it would necessarily entail a curtailment of consumption by the rich and the over-resourced, in order that the poor can have their equitable share of environmental benefits, and therefore encourages community organizers to contribute to the integration of this perspective by including environmental privilege and difference in discussions in the realm of global or local community.

That the impact of environmental decimation is not gender-equal or gender-neutral is also a well-established fact, and much has been written about it. According to Bell (2016), women experience environmental injustice that is distributional, procedural and substantive in nature. Owing to the 'entwined and entrenched capitalist and patriarchal processes', they not only lack access to environmental resources, but also carry an inequitable burden of environmental degradation, and yet get to exercise little control over environmental decision-making (Bell, 2016). Mies and Shiva (1993) in their iconic book titled *Ecofeminism* iterate that science and technology are not gender-neutral. Both nature and women experience domination, displacement and exploitation under patriarchy and capitalism. However, despite this reality, there is discerning evidence to show that women and their collectives have been at the forefront of myriad environmental movements and action initiatives across the world, as also within the Indian landscape. Mies and Shiva assert that women's participation in environmental action has been directly and indirectly representative of their resistance to the capital intensive and profit-centric dominant development paradigm, which is also patriarchal in essence. As against the primacy of commercially determined commodification of nature, women underscore an alternative narrative woven around the subsistence-based household economy. The ecofeminist perspective is therefore integrally grounded in an analysis of power politics that permeates decisions affecting the environment, and confirms the imperatives of assuming a gendered lens within environmental justice debates and action initiatives (Bell, 2016).

In effect, as a profession claiming to work towards enhancing people's well-being, the acknowledgement of the critical link between the social work mandate and environmental justice concerns emerges as fundamental to social work practice in all locales. Given the urgency of the context, social work can no longer afford to sideline the centrality of environmental issues and mediation therein. Given its humanistic commitment and social justice and human rights-centric framework, social work must proclaim its deep stake in the environmental well-being of people across the spectrum, and most specially for the ones facing dire consequences of the impending ecological crisis. In a milieu where climate change and natural disasters are increasingly tending to exacerbate the plight of the already impoverished and marginalized people, social work does have an overwhelming professional obligation to amalgamate environmental justice concerns within its social justice mandate.

THE TRAJECTORY OF SOCIAL WORK RESPONSE

Based on a historical review of literature, Coates and Gray (2012) drew attention to three strands within the environmental engagement of social workers. These were (a) the 1970s, which were characterized by initial pioneering work by social workers to conceptualize the significance of environmental issues, (b) late 1980s and early 1990s, wherein social work interest in environmental issues showed an upswing, and the same was accompanied by a call for social work response, and (c) more recent articulation for the importance of incorporating the natural environment and environmental social work within the ambit of professional practice (Coates & Gray, 2012).

Despite the long-standing emphasis of social work practice to operate within the confines of the person-in-environment framework, which in turn remained grounded in the significance of understanding the individual and individual behaviour in context of the environment in which the individual was placed, social work continued to remain preoccupied with the 'social' environment for a significant span of time. The role and impact of the natural environment on human functioning remained outside its sphere of cognisance (Besthorn, 2003; Rotabi, 2007). Due to this neglect of the natural or physical environment, environmental social work remained a marginalized domain within social work practice, and social work remained largely focused on maintaining a sustained negotiation with social problems, without much reflection on the core and foundational assumptions underlying practice (Coates, 2003).

Reflecting on the growth of ecosocial work, Jef Peeters (2011) highlighted the perspective of Närhi and Matthies (2001). According to the latter, there ordained two dominant and divergent standpoints as far as early thinking with regard to the role that environment played in human welfare was concerned. While one standpoint was represented through the work of Mary Richmond, the other could be attributed to Jane Addams. While Richmond dwelt on the social dimensions of the environment within the person-in-environment perspective, and iterated the significance of social relationships, social interaction and social networks as core to human functioning, for Addams, the focus was on 'community work and urban environment', and on the inclusion of the physical and built environment, and social services in the depiction of the living environment. As far as both perspectives were concerned, the ongoing relevance of the ecological approach or the ecosocial approach, which acknowledged a connection between social problems, their solutions and the environment, remained all-pervasive. Based on the writings of authors such as Pinkus and Minahan (1973) and subsequently others such as Germain and Gitterman (1980), Peeters (2011) traced the subsequent growth of the ecosocial tradition in social work by highlighting the application of the systems approach and thinking from within social sciences to social work in the 1970s. Though this approach did not preclude the natural environment, Peeters observed that nature appeared as a peripheral entity in the classical person-in-environment approach, and therefore this approach did not provide an adequate basis for fostering strong bonds between environmental contingencies and social work practice. On similar lines, and as a corollary to exploring the temporal context for the neglect of the natural and physical environment in defining 'mainstream' social work practice, Zapf (2010) also underscored the serious constraints associated with focusing on social environment within the social work 'foundational metaphor' of person in environment. He strongly articulated the need to move beyond it, in order to address the critical environmental concerns of the twenty-first century. The passive response of the profession to connect and engage with environmental concerns and action was further documented by many authors in succession (Besthorn, 1997; Coates, 2003; Zapf, 2009, 2010).

Apart from the ecosystems approach, Närhi (2004) also drew attention to another perspective on ecological social work, which was referred to as 'the eco-critical approach' by Närhi and Matthies (2001). Based on the work of a group of social work academicians such as Berger and Kelly (1993) and Hoff and Nutt (1994) among others, and named thus on account of its critical orientation with regard to the prevalent development perspectives, this approach consolidated a cognition of significance of the environmental issues and the seriousness of the emerging environmental crisis. As awareness about the criticality of the ecological issues diversified from the 1970s onwards, ecological discussions started gaining ground in academic and public forums. All in all, the eco-critical approach emanated from the prevailing justification for environmental action within the context of the sustainable development discourse. This approach supports ecological sustainability coupled with social sustainability-based social work interventions (Matthies, 1987, 1990; Narhi, 2004).

The discourse to encourage the profession to reposition itself with regard to its erstwhile *environmental* innocuousness further grew in the 1990s. Berger and Kelly (1993) advocated that the ecological model of social work should be expanded to incorporate all ecosystems, including social and natural or biological, and should also acknowledge the role that human beings play within them. The 'person-in-environment' approach was re-envisioned and expanded ... beyond the 'social' (Besthorn, 1997; Hoff & McNutt, 1994). Emphasizing the need to expand the professional horizons of social work, Berger and Kelly (1993) evolved an environmental doctrine comprising of 12 essentials. These were centred around the interconnectedness of systems and the embeddedness of humans within the larger cosmology; respect for nature and the value of ecological niches of life forms; significance of equity in share of natural resources and social work support for policies supporting sustainable resource use; the responsibility of the profession to promote the integrity of the natural ecosystems; and social workers' obligations to foster ecologically sustainable lifestyles. Berger (1995) postulated the notion of 'Habitat Destruction Syndrome'. According to him, despite warnings, human beings continued to indulge in environmentally damaging activities, which are deemed to ultimately herald the self-destruction of the human race. He appealed for concerted individual and collective action partaken by social workers to arrest this prophesized eventuality. Proposing a spectrum of social work interventions, Berger highlighted the need for involvement in 'environmental activism' to reverse the habitat destruction syndrome. Soon after, Park (1996) stressed on the need for a determined response from the social work fraternity to promote a healthy environment that could sustain human life and well-being. Highlighting the role of environmental strains and stressors in undermining human well-being, he advised clinical social workers to configure these within their diagnoses and interventions.

In the early 1990s, the *National Association of Social Workers* (*NASW*) *Journal of Social Work* came out with a series of four articles which extended an appeal to social workers to include the physical environment in their professional ambit. Hoff and Polack (1993) highlighted the social ramifications of the global environmental predicament and its implications for professional practice. Hoff and McNutt (1994) explicated the uncontestable and resolute links between human welfare and environmental well-being, and the urgency for the profession to move beyond the oft-repeated confines of 'individual well-being' and 'social welfare' to evolve newer approaches to protect and sustain environmental well-being. Coates (2003) also iterated the critical choice that the profession needed to make between following the traditional and dysfunctional social order and transforming itself in order to strive towards creating an equitable and sustainable environmental and social context. Based on articles in the 1990s and the early years of the present century, such as those by Besthorn and McMillan (2002), Hillman (2002), Hoff (1994), Ife (1997), Marlow and Van Rooyen (2001) and Park (1996), Jones (2010) argued that there existed tenable connections between the generally accepted social mandate of social work and the environmental agenda. He supported the need for placing the natural and social environment, and the human–environment relationship at the core of both theory building and the evolving practice context of social work.

In the new millennium, a noteworthy development was the upholding of the imperatives for adding 'environment' to the professional mandate of social work by the notable social work professional organizations. In 2000, the NASW articulated that 'protecting people and the natural environment through sustainable development is arguably the fullest realization of the person-in-environment perspective' (NASW, 2000, p. 105). It emphasized the affinity between the concept of sustainable development and the person-in-environment paradigm as the basis for the application of macro-level professional social work interventions for the redressal of environmental problems. In a similar vein, the International Federation of Social Workers (IFSW) in 2004 appealed to the social work fraternity to take cognizance of the significance of the natural and man-made environment for the realm of the social environment, in order to augment the environmental obligations within social work engagement. Additionally, the need to collaborate with other professionals and community groups to enhance knowledge, skills and strategies to foster a healthy environment and create greater visibility of environmental concerns in social work education was also made explicit.

Zapf (2010) evolved the notion of 'people as place', which again projected the inseparable links between humans and their natural world, as also the critical connection between human welfare and environmental well-being. This notion conveyed a sense of unity and wholeness between the two entities, wherein neither was the environment a passive canvas for human endeavours, nor were humans inconsequential participants in the natural environment. He contended that the erstwhile models of practice were no longer adequate for coping with contemporary challenges such as climate change, and that time was rife to transcend the erstwhile person-in-environment perspective to incorporate a newer understanding of people as their surroundings. Zapf also metamorphosed the idea of 'living well in place', by assimilating social and environmental justice, human rights and environmental prerogatives, and human responsibilities and environmental obligations.

Another strong proponent of environmentalism, Dewane (2011) described the social work profession as being premised on the bedrock of social justice. Espousing the environmental justice premise, she stressed the role of social work education in provisioning the learners an opportunity to explore the interconnection between social work and environmental action. She also advocated for more community-focused action regarding environmental policy and exhorted an urgent need for 'Conservation Social Work' to step in as a cohesive and universal approach to deal with the interplay between human beings and nature, with the ultimate aim of augmenting the well-being of nature and all life forms within it.

While highlighting the justification for sustainable development to emerge as a viable arena for social work engagement, Peeters (2011) elaborated on a normative harmony between social work and sustainable development, in that, both focused on the notions of well-being, equality, human rights and participation, and thereby portended immense scope for mutual reinforcement. He advocated for the extension of social work ambit to include environmental concerns, as also issues pertaining to ecological justice; equity in the access and distribution of environmental privileges; a critique of consumerist modes of living; a concern for quality of living and an overall core thrust on the natural environment as the basis for the continued well-being of people. He presented a very comprehensive perspective for social work contribution in the realm of participatory research, multi-level collaborative action, social capital and resilience building, ecosocial interventions, social economy and social enterprises, advocacy with governments, and coalitions with social movements, in order to respond to the contingencies of the contemporary socio-ecological crisis confronting humankind.

In their classic book *Environmental Social Work,* editors Gray et al. (2012) provisioned an overview of the more recent ecological discourse and engagement of social work with an environmental action in order to analyse the course of action adopted by environmental social work, and also to gauge the level of social work response to the prevailing environmental issues. In their concluding chapter, the editors called for 'a new paradigm' relating to an altered worldview incorporating a 'quantum shift in consciousness' and 'a new framework that required a transformation from anthropocentrism to ecocentrism, from mechanistic to organic understandings of Earth, from dualism to holism, and from linear to organic determinants of change' (Gray et al., 2012, p.. 304). The editors also appealed to social workers and other professionals to shed their professional isolation and work cohesively to counter the grave challenges stemming from global warming and climate change, destruction of natural resources, toxic materials production and waste disposal, pollution, species extinction, natural disasters, sustainable development and food security domains. They contended that given the ongoing threat of global warming, there would be significant alterations in the sociopolitical, economic and physical environments in which social workers practised, and the nature of work that they would be expected to perform in order to mitigate the negative consequences of such a change, and help people to adapt to the altered contexts. In the preface of the same book, Doherty recommended that social workers take on the role of attending to the combined natural and human-made disasters; and assume work in the field of environmental health, both physical and psychosocial. He advocated breaking down of the artificial barriers between 'environmental issues', 'human health issues' and 'social equity issues' to work towards an expanded ecological vision or a 'shared' vision (p. xx).

The latest and perhaps the most influential in the series of environment social work crusaders is Dominelli, who has emerged as the most avid proponent of 'Green Social Work'. Dominelli (2012) has been very forthright in asserting the nature and extent of the negative fallouts of the global environmental crisis on human well-being. She has also been very lucid in highlighting that while environmental privileges were appropriated by the rich and the privileged, the worst negative ramifications of environmental decimation disproportionately accrued on the poor and marginalized populations. She defined 'Green Social Work' most comprehensively and holistically to incorporate that practice which configures the relationships between and among people, as also between people and the plant and animal world. It also looks at the interface between environmental contingencies and human behaviour, and how these impact the well-being of people and the planet Earth. The practice advocates for a core transformation in peoples' own conceptualizations about their society, and the canvas of their relationships, in order to address the diverse forms of structural inequality, and also to foster interdependencies and equity in the distribution of natural resources. It envisions the reformation of all such forces which inflict a negative impact on the marginalized groups, and seeks such changes in policy as shall enhance the well-being of people and the planet in all times. Thus, in visualizing Green Social Work, Dominelli has essentially enlarged the frontiers of social work practice and expanded the mandate of the social worker to intervene in key environmental issues of the times—environmental degradation, industrial pollution, overconsumption by a few, climate change, migrations caused by natural disasters and conflicts over water, land and clean air—in essence all that comprises a holistic 'green' agenda, rooted in the interdependency of all constituents of the planet.

ENVIRONMENT IN SOCIAL WORK LITERATURE: A REVIEW

The author has attempted to glean the erstwhile response of social work to the prevailing ecological crisis by locating some evidence within the theoretical discourse and practice parameters. This has been accomplished by assessing a few pre-existing reviews of literature that had been undertaken by the social work fraternity.

Premised on a review of social work journals, Jones (2010) highlighted that there was a shortage of literature exemplifying the linkages between the natural environment and social work. He also observed that in the realm of social work education, there existed very few courses which depicted the relationship between the social and environmental dimensions, both within the theory and practice of social work. He expressed concern that even with strong evidence to prove the escalating impact of environmental degradation on human well-being, and the recognition of discernible links between environmental justice and social justice, social work has been a passive claimant in seeking a role in mitigating the contingency of the situation.

A *Concept analysis of environmental social work* by Ramsay and Boddy (2017) also suggested that despite the strong justification for social work to perform a proactive role in the environmental context, many notable authors writing in contemporary times drew attention to the relative absence of the social work profession in contemporary environmental domain. They speculated that this may be on account of the involvement of the profession in an 'individualistic, materialistic, anthropocentric, clinical, modernist paradigm' (Ramsay & Boddy, 2017, p. 69). They did acknowledge that a professional change had been noticed in the last 15 years as publications had tripled twice and students of social work desired more knowledge for engaging with the environmental realm. The analysis further suggested that while the mandate to engage in environmental discourse and action was evident, not much had been attempted by way of practice, probably due to a diffused understanding about 'environmental social work'.

A review by Mason et al. (2017) was undertaken in the more recent context of 2017 to examine the status of social work research, which was centred on environmental issues, and was published in peer-reviewed journals over a 30-year period. This exercise revealed that social work research on global environmental change had accelerated in the recent context. While about one-third of the studies focused on hurricanes and typhoons in a limited regional context, others highlighted problems, causes and impacts, and yet others depicted the formal and informal responses and interventions of people. However, the review revealed that many studies lacked the 'rigorous outcomes measurement', thereby curtailing evidence for social work practice or policy. Thus, apart from enhancing the evidence base for interventions, the review recommended the generation of more research to understand the vulnerability issues and capacities of the marginalized groups exposed to environmental calamities in order to identify intervention strategies. The authors reiterated the implications of the global environmental change on social justice and human rights, and mandated a concerted focus on topics such as energy, water, food security, land-use changes and community mobilization.

Cumby (2016) shared that a general search for social work literature on the contemporaneously significant theme of 'climate change' revealed almost negligible results. However, an online literature search yielded better results, in terms of revealing published academic papers, online articles and books by social workers, who wanted to focus on issues and concerns within the environmental domain. The author highlighted a dearth of research studies by social workers and less than desirable involvement of social work in climate change-related environmental issues. Ritchie (2010) in his work on the significance of the natural environment for social work practice acknowledged finding only a few social work studies that related to the natural environment. Further, he found almost no mention of 'natural environment' in the many textbooks and general references pertaining to social work. Additionally, many contemporaneous social work theories also did not explicitly engage with natural environment within their frames.

Still more recently, Krings et al. (2018) undertook an analysis of social work articles published in English in peer-reviewed journals between the years 1991 and 2015. The analysis was intended to assess the relative share of environmental themes in the overall social work publications per year. The review found that work in the realm of environmental social work formed a miniscule 0.7 per cent of the total articles in the year 1991 and 0.4 per cent in 2004. This figure touched 2.4 per cent in the year 2013. On the whole, publications in this domain showed an increase from 1991 to 2015. However, as per the authors, one-third of the published work focused on natural disasters or environmental contingencies, and there also existed a 'geographically based scholarship' confined within three distinct nations.

The author of this chapter also undertook a small review of the theses listed by the 56 Departments of Social Work in India that were registered on Shodhganga, which constitutes a dedicated platform to make doctoral research work accessible to the academic community through the open access mode. She found that in the time frame between 1998 and

2018, only 35 studies falling under the domain of environmental social work were available on this platform. Notwithstanding some gaps in registration, the analysis still points to the fact that within the broader domain of social work education and research in India, environmental social work is indeed located at the periphery.

SOCIAL WORK EDUCATION AND ENVIRONMENTAL CONSCIOUSNESS

Gray et al. (2012) acknowledged that in the Australian context, 'social work education's engagement with an expanded ecological perspective has been generally piecemeal and often peripheral' (p. 217). Androff et al. (2017) also iterated that while environment-centric issues based on sustainability and rights were being registered in the practice context, they remained undermined in social work education. A literature review of articles focusing on environmental justice in social work education, which included 37 publications (from the early 1990s to 2016) led Beltrán et al. (2016) to posit that while the publications highlighted the links between environmental and social justice issues, none of them projected a need for the environmental justice discourse to get integrated within the realm of the social justice curricula in social work. The authors propositioned the desirability of incorporating environmental justice component in all courses within social work curricula, and most certainly press for its integration in specific social work courses, such as those that teach power, oppression and diversity. The review highlighted the recommendation that education in social work must permit student learners to understand and analyse the dominant notions and the ground context that leads to the sustenance of inequality, oppression and exploitation. It must also facilitate the educators to proffer space to the students to self-reflect and engage in work that enhanced the assimilation of personal and political associations, as both of these options led to the development of ecological consciousness among learners. The authors quoted Jones (2010) to bring to fore the prescription for 'a new paradigm in social work education based in transformative learning' (p. 73). In all, the review forwarded the contributions of several social work educators to propose incorporation of environmental issues and environmental sustainability in diverse courses within the ambit of social work education, thereby highlighting the need for a better understanding and critical reflection for enhancing ecological consciousness among social work students.

Further, professional associations such as the NASW have also advocated for the furtherance of social work education at diverse levels and have proposed the inclusion of relevant and contemporaneous themes pertaining to the integration of the 'social' and the 'ecological' in social work discourse, such as 'habitat destruction, chemical contamination, environmental racism, environmental justice, and sustainability' (NASW, 2008, p. 10). This has been deemed crucial for social work education and practice to establish a dynamic connect with justice, both environmental and social. In asserting thus, the professional association rightly emphasized the imperatives for enhancing the knowledge and competency base of social work students and practitioners with regard to issues of justice that prevail at the diverse sites of engagement of social workers. Besthorn (2012) strengthened this professional resolve when by linking the national and international policy statements and codes of ethics of diverse professional associations of social work such as the IFSW, NASW and British Association of Social Workers and others, he reflected the increasing proclivity of the social work profession to link social justice and environmental justice.

As far as the context of India is concerned, a review of the syllabi of 14 established schools of social work offering postgraduate social work educational programmes was undertaken by the author in 2019. The review revealed that four schools did not have any core, elective or even an optional course on 'environment' in their programmes. While five schools opted for courses on environment or disaster management, as elective or optional or as interdisciplinary domains, one school offered a specialization paper on environment and disaster management. The other set of five schools offered core papers on environment and/or disaster management. Note that courses on 'disaster management' have been more common, leading one to contend that disaster contingencies being experienced commonly; there has been a greater cognition among social work educators about the significance of managing them. The participation of social workers in disaster management initiatives in the country, as also the guidelines by the state to create awareness about disasters and their management has also contributed to this trend.

Among the schools that offered specialization domains, Green Social Work or Environmental Social Work had not been considered. In the context of the country, professional associations of the social work fraternity are yet to proactively support the inclusion of environmental social work as an integral component of social work education and training.

Under the prevailing context, the three possible pathways to diffuse an ecological orientation to social work education as have been propositioned by Gray et al. (2013) emerge as most significant. These are: 'A focus on adding ecological content into existing curriculum; to seek to "embed" material on ecology and sustainability; and endeavour to transform the entire curriculum to reflect a holistic ecological orientation' (p. 217). According to them, an ecologically transformative approach would necessarily entail 'significant shifts in content and pedagogy of social work programs' (p. 220). Development of ecoliteracy, importance of including indigenous perspectives and ways of knowing, exploration of spirituality in shaping the human–nature relationship; and the centrality of a critical approach to education have been projected as key dimensions of an expanded ecosocial approach to social work education. In a comprehensive analysis, the authors posit:

> Using ecology as an overarching thematic lens, and ecological justice as a serious concern, social work education has an opportunity to identify key ecological concepts and ecocentric values that can act as the foundation from which the knowledge, values and skills for professional practice might be developed (Gray et al., 2013, p. 226).

HOLISTIC GREEN AGENDA FOR SOCIAL WORK

Given their commitment to the development and well-being of vulnerable and marginalized groups and their connection with people across the spectrum, social workers can assume a key role in generating the critical environmental awareness among individuals, groups and communities. Assisting people to understand that environment is the bedrock of human existence, and that development and environmental conservation should not be perceived as antithetical but as aligned entities, emerges as a core professional obligation for social workers.

Environmental education that links the resource and energy-intensive lifestyles of the current generation with the emergent environmental catastrophes, and which illustrates the impact of unsustainable behaviours and practices in escalating environmental decimation and climate change, needs to be creatively delivered so as to augur the much-needed attitudinal and behavioural changes required to break the ongoing environmental impasse. As development professionals working in multiple domains, social workers can also integrate an environmental orientation and thrust into the wider developmental discourse and action, thereby creating a wider ethos for holistic and sustainable development.

Further, the need to partake an active role in building solidarities and alliances for environmental action was never more urgent than it is in the present context. Most struggles for environmental justice and action remain weak, invisible or localized, as they do not garner the requisite support and mobilization by communities of change agents. Such change agents have the wherewithal to bring them to suitable platforms, where the voices of the aggrieved can be heard and where their causes can translate into concrete agenda for purposive action. With their foundational knowledge of working with groups and communities and their engagement with the core domain of social action and movements, social workers are most advantageously positioned for consolidating strong and effective networks and coalitions for grassroots action. These may include natural resource-based user groups and associations, stakeholder groups, indigenous people's groups and other community-based organizations. The professional training imparted to social workers imbues them with the essential skills required for conscientizing and mobilizing people around local and regional issues; building and sustaining people's organizations; and skilling aggrieved communities to organize, plan, act, lobby, agitate and press for suitable action. By virtue of their training in advocacy and campaigns, social workers can help bring localized issues centre stage and create wider public interest and discourse around them. Active immersion in advocacy, networking and coalition building for spearheading effective and stringent environmental legislations, policies and programmes, and creating valid grounds for the insertion of environmental agenda in the electoral manifestos of political parties are the other mandated roles for the social work community.

By virtue of their work with a diversity of constituencies experiencing environmental deprivation, discrimination and marginalization, social workers can play key roles in upholding the rights of the environmental refugees and victims of disasters, both natural and man-made. Community-based disaster risk management and disaster management needs to translate into the everyday lives of hazard-prone and vulnerable communities. The social work community needs to stake a claim in this largely neglected domain.

Judicial activism has played a monumental role in safeguarding the environment and it can most certainly be a favoured means for concerted and urgent action for environmental well-being, if used purposefully by social workers. Facilitating the resurgence of contextual and indigenous environmental literature and the revival of traditional wisdom and practices is yet another realm of work that can have immense value in fostering environmental sustainability and preserving life.

The case of Kerala Sastra Sahitya Parishad (KSSP) as a people's movement can be cited here to substantiate the role that a social movement can play in ushering in mass mobilization for environmental action. Essentially a People's Science Movement, the KSSP was founded in 1962 to popularize science and scientific attitude among people. KSSP was involved in upholding models for sustainable and equitable development, campaigning for decentralized planning, undertaking a diversity of field experiments in local-level planning, empowering the grassroots communities through participatory research and creating people's collectives for participatory democracy. One of the primary objectives of the Parishad has been to raise the environmental awareness of the people through campaigns in order to popularize sound environmental attitudes and practice. This focus on environment was borne out of KSSP's commitment to sustainable development.

Hailed as an exemplar grassroots movement in India, the KSSP continued to engage with an array of the environmental activities including protection of forests, proactive campaigns against pollution by chemical industries, generation of environmental awareness with regard to faulty land-use patterns and protection of biodiversity and ecologically fragile zones, among others. In all of these, it popularized a holistic and sustainable perspective to environment. The Parishad facilitated people to develop an indigenous understanding of their natural and social environments and undertake a contextual analysis of their environmental concerns, with a view to harnessing popular participation. Inputs by experts helped people to envision environmentally conducive and technically and economically feasible solutions. Additionally, the movement focused on generating popular awareness about the prevailing anti-people and anti-environmental policies, and endorsing the value of indigenous culture and practices.

Beginning with campaigns against water and air pollution by the Gwalior Rayons factory in the Chaliyar River basin to many other anti-pollution struggles in various parts of Kerala, such as those within the Velloor Newsprint factory and the Titanium factories in Trivandrum and Chavara, and Moti Chemicals in Cannanore, KSSP was able to consolidate widespread popular consciousness and action in this regard. The approach entailed a combination of direct action backed by scientific research, technological assessment and legal action. The struggles were long drawn out and led people to becoming aware of the multiple challenges of confronting capitalist conglomerations. Yet, the participation of people in struggles such as these also made them reject the assumption that environmental degradation was an inevitable and inherent offshoot of the development process.

The Silent Valley debate was the most publicized environmental struggle fielded by the KSSP. Backed by a sound technological, economic and sociopolitical assessment by a multidisciplinary team of activists, and other scientific reports, KSSP strove to protect the Silent Valley, which was not only one of the oldest and the largest continuous forest stretches in the Western Ghats, but also one that was the richest in terms of biodiversity. Based on the fact that the project in question had the potential to benefit the local people through the provision of energy, irrigation, jobs and overall development prospects, KSSP realized that the resistance movement could not succeed without the mass participation of people. The subsequent mass campaign launched by KSSP was indeed inspirational in terms of its duration, scale and intensity. Besides legal action, a plethora of meetings, marches, lectures, seminars, exhibitions and theatrical performances were organized. Lobbying with political leaders, bureaucrats and academicians was undertaken, and media was optimally utilized to create mass awareness and widespread support for saving the Silent Valley ecosystem. The movement aroused significant national and international interest, and well-known scientists and scientific organizations offered unilateral support. All of this finally led the Central Government to withdraw the sanction for the project in 1983, thereby culminating in one of the most successful ecological movements in history, and one that has offered multiple insights for social workers engaged in grassroots action.

The work of KSSP illustrates the role that ecological struggles can play in social mobilization, social change and purposeful transformation. Creating popular consciousness about the importance of natural resources and the imperatives of protecting them as critical stakeholders emerged as the key to successful action. The use of indigenous forms of communication such as the *jatha* (traditionally, a long march usually aimed at spreading a message), which had been inherited from the sociopolitical movements of the past, was instrumental in generating large-scale public sentiment. This incorporated short plays, group songs and a variety of folk art forms. Often a *jatha* spread over several days would travel through the districts and would be accompanied by *padyatras* (foot marches), mass signature campaigns, *dharnas* (a form of a sitting protest), lectures and seminars. Over a period, these campaigns led to the creation of large-scale awareness regarding the importance of forests and the imperatives of protecting them. The work of KSSP is also significant in contextual terms, because of the immense support that it provisioned for the traditional fishing community in Kerala, which had been fighting a losing battle against the ecologically disastrous practice of mechanized trawling. In all, the multiple success stories in the portfolio of this people's movement continue to offer immense learning to human service professionals.

CONCLUSION

From the time when the profession of social work was less intent to integrate an environmental focus to the present context, social work has traversed many milestones. From its time-hallowed tradition of acknowledging the significance of people in their social environment, to the acceptance of the central role of the natural environment, social work has made a discerning shift. The growing global ecological movement and the emergence of a diversity of perspectives from social work educators and practitioners have contributed to the envisioning of this paradigm shift. However, a meaningful integration of the environmental thrust still requires committed engagement. As a human service profession that prides itself on social justice and human rights as its foundational principles, social work must take significant strides to include environmentalism in its scope of professional education and practice. It must mandatorily transcend from an 'anthropocentric' orientation and thrust to an 'ecocentric' one. Students of social work must be supported to engage in a critical discussion about the inextricable links between environment, environmental justice and human rights. The fraternity must coalesce to identify and establish an ongoing dialogue and evolve viable responses to the looming environmental crisis that confronts humanity and all life on the planet today.

REFERENCES

Androff, D., Fike, C., & Rorke, J. (2017). Greening social work education: Teaching environmental rights and sustainability in community practice. *Journal of Social Work Education, 53*(3), 399–413.

Bell, K. (2016). Bread and roses: A gender perspective on environmental justice and public health. *International Journal of Environmental Research and Public Health, 13*(10), 1005.

Beltrán, R., Hacker, A., & Begun, S. (2016). Environmental justice is a social justice issue: Incorporating environmental justice into social work practice curricula. *Journal of Social Work Education, 52*(4), 493–502. https://doi.org/10.1080/10437797.2016.1215277

Berger, R. (1995). Habitat destruction syndrome. *Social Work, 40*(4), 441–443. https://www.jstor.org/stable/23718376

Berger, R., & Kelly, J. (1993). Social work in the ecological crisis. *Social Work, 38*, 521–526.

Besthorn, F. H. (1997). *Reconceptualizing social work's person-in-environment perspective: Explorations in radical environmental thought.* PhD Dissertation, University of Kansas, UMI Microfilm.

Besthorn, F. H. (2003). Radical ecologisms: Insights for educating social workers in ecological activism and social justice. *Critical Social Work: An Interdisciplinary Journal Dedicated to Social Justice, 3*, 66–106.

Besthorn, F. H. (2012). Deep ecology's contributions to social work: A ten-year retrospective. *International Journal of Social Welfare, 21*(3), 248–259.

Besthorn, F., & McMillen, D. (2002). The oppression of women and nature: Ecofeminism as a framework for an expanded ecological social work. *Families in Society, 83*, 221–232.

Cannan, C. (2000). The environmental crisis, greens and community development. *Community Development Journal, 35*(4), 365–376.

Coates, J. (2003). *Ecology and social work: Toward a new paradigm.* Fernwood Publishing.

Coates, J., & Gray, M. (2012). The environment and social work: An overview and introduction. *International Journal of Social Welfare, 21*, 230–238. http://dx.doi.org/10.1111/j.1468-2397.2011.00851.x

Cumby, T. (2016). Climate change and social work: Our roles and barriers to action. *Theses and dissertations (comprehensive)*, 1828. https://scholars.wlu.ca/etd/1828

Dewane, C. J. (2011). Environmentalism and social work: The ultimate social justice issue. *Social Work Today, 11*(5), 20.

Dominelli, L. (2012). *Green social work: From environmental crises to environmental justice.* Polity.

Germain, C., & Gitterman, A. (1980). *The life model of social work practice.* Columbia University Press.

Gray, M., Coates, J., & Hetherington, T. (Eds.). (2012). *Environmental social work.* Routledge.

Hillman, M. (2002). Environmental justice: A crucial link between environmentalism and community development? *Community Development Journal, 37*(4), 349–360.

Hoff, M. (1994). Environmental foundations of social welfare: Theoretical resources. In M. Hoff & J. McNutt (Eds.), *The global environmental crisis: Implications for social welfare and social work* (pp. 12–35). Avebury.

Hoff, M., & McNutt, J. (Eds.). (1994). *The global environmental crisis: Implications for social welfare and social work.* Ashgate Publishing.

Hoff, M., & Polack, R. (1993). Social dimensions of the environmental crisis: Challenges for social work. *Social Work, 38*, 204–211.

Ife, J. (1997). *Community development: Creating community alternatives—vision, analysis and practice.* Longman.

IFSW. (2004). International policy statement on globalization and the environment (approved by IFSW 2004). http://www.ifsw.org

Jones, P. (2010). Responding to the ecological crisis: Transformative pathways for social work education. *Journal of Social Work Education, 46*(1), 67–84.

Krings, A., Victor, B., Mathias, J., & Perron, B. E. (2018). Environmental social work in the disciplinary literature, 1991–2015. *International Social Work, 63*(3), 275–290.

Marlow, C., & Rooyen, C. V. (2001). How green is the environment in social work? *International Social Work, 44*(2).Mary, N. L. (2008). *Social work in a sustainable world.* Lyceum.

Mason, L. R., Shires, M. K., Arwood, C., & Borst, A. (2017). Social work research and global environmental change. *Journal of the Society for Social Work and Research, 8*(4), 645–672. Matthies, A.-L. (1987). Ekologinensosiaalityö [Ecological social work]. *Sosiaaliviesti, 2*, 32–37.

Matthies, A.-L. (1990). Kapinastamuutoksenmalliksi: Vaihtoehtoinensosiaalityö Suomessa [From a rebellion to a model for change: Alternative social work in Finland]. Helsinki, Finland: HankijaJaä. https://www.researchgate. net/publication/230485576_The_place_of_social_work_in_sustainable_ development_Towards_ecosocial_practice

Mies, M., & Shiva, V. (1993). *Ecofeminism*. Fernwood Publications.

Muldoon, A. (2006). Environmental efforts: The next challenge for social work. *Critical Social Work, 7*(2), 1–7.

Narhi, K., & Matthies, A. (2001). What is the ecological (self-)consciousness of social work? In A. Matthies, K. Narhi, & D. Ward (Eds.), *The eco-social approach in social work*. soPhi.

Närhi, K. (2004). Kati. *The eco-social approach in Social Work and the Challenges to the Expertise of Social Work*, p. 104. University of Jyväskylä.

National Association of Social Workers (NASW). (2000). *Social work speaks: NASW policy statements*. NASW Press.

NASW. (2008). *Social Work Speaks: NASW Policy Statements Environmental policy*. In Social Work Speaks: NASW Policy Statements. National Association of Social Workers. https://www.researchgate.net/publication/266022641_ Environmental_Policy

Park, K. M., (1996). The person is ecological: Environmentalism of social work. *Social Work, 41*(3), 320–323.

Peeters, J. (2011). The place of social work in sustainable development: Towards ecosocial practice. *International Journal of Social Welfare, 21*(3), 287–298. https:// doi.org/10.1111/j.1468-2397.2011.00856.x

Pincus, A., & Minahan, A. (1973). *Social work practice: Model and method*. Peacock.

Pulla, V. (2013). Critical essay: Environmentalism and social work. *Rural Society, 22*(3), 263–268.

Ramsay, S., & Boddy, J. (2017). Environmental social work: A concept analysis. *The British Journal of Social Work, 47*(1), 68–86. https://doi.org/10.1093/ bjsw/bcw078

Ritchie, J. D. (2010). The relevance of the natural environment to social work: A comparison of fields that consider the natural environment in social problems: A project based upon an independent investigation. Theses, Dissertations, and Projects. 492. https://scholarworks.smith.edu/theses/492

Rotabi K. (2007). Ecological theory origin from natural to social science or vice versa? A brief conceptual history for social work. *Advances in Social Work, 8*(1), 113–129.

Zapf, M. K. (2009). *Social work and the environment: Understanding people and place*. Canadian Scholars' Press.

Zapf, M. K. (2010). Social work and the environment: Understanding people and place. *Critical Social Work, 11*(3), 30–46.

Chapter 8

Social Work and Terrorism

Basem Youssief Mohamed ELmoazen

INTRODUCTION

The phenomenon of terrorism confronts many contemporary societies at different levels of development. Of course, the magnitude of this phenomenon differs from one society to another. In some societies, this phenomenon has reached a high degree of complexity and spread, while in some other societies it has not reached a similar level of seriousness. The affected communities are determined to develop themselves even as they suffer from the dangers of terrorism, and so there is an urgent need to effectively confront these dangers.

Terrorism is one of the most serious crimes practised in modern societies. It not only threatens the security of states but also undermines their economic and social stability and various other aspects, resulting in the loss of human life and property and the deprivation of the rights of individuals to security by creating fear and panic among members of society. It is being increasingly recognized that this phenomenon is becoming increasingly prevalent across the world and cannot be associated exclusively with any particular community or group.

Since the beginning of the 1990s, terrorist crime has become a complex global phenomenon, a type of crime that transcends space and time between states, both in their effects and consequences. The planning and implementation of measures against terrorism are being carried out by all societies in varying degrees and forms. The political and socio-economic differences between various societies are the real causes and the existence of effective mechanisms and methods to deal with this phenomenon and reduce its risks are the most important factors in determining its impact (Shoaib, 2004).

Terrorism is, therefore, one of the most serious problems of the present century, if not the most dangerous of all (Aqeel, 2004). Social work is one of those professions that deal with various social problems, and contributes to solving them and even preventing them, in order to build a strong cohesive society. When we look at the previous studies done in this regard, these are of the following kinds: (a) studies dealing with terrorism prevention and treatment of its root causes (Al-Buraq, 1987), (b) studies on the impact of transformations in the international regime dealing with terrorism (Al-Shamrani, 2002), (c) studies on the role of media in dealing with terrorism (Taleb, 2004), (d) studies on the measures of preventive action against terrorism and its applications and (e) studies on the screening procedures for the scene of terrorist events (Al-Massaad, 2006). However, despite the importance of the role of the social work profession in tackling terrorism, research on this phenomenon is very scarce.

PROFESSIONAL PRACTICE OF SOCIAL WORK

Professional practice is a set of methods, means and skills based on a variety of knowledge derived from the theoretical background of social work and applied by social workers to assist the population of different age groups or class affiliations through community institutions. Ibrahim Marei defines it as 'the use of specialized techniques that can be trained and transferred to individuals through learning and structured training to equip them with the skills of practitioners in order to help them carry out their social responsibilities' (Marei, 1996, p. 43), and as a 'direct, knowledge-oriented and valuable intervention that adopts scientific methods and skills to achieve the goals on specifics' (Robert, 1998, p. 289). Professional practice is also known as 'the forms and methods of professional intervention and the resulting actions and measures through which the identification of the problems, attitudes, clients, business tasks and responsibilities, whether at the individual, collective or community level, and of the necessary requirements, resources and capabilities can be carried out' (Khalifa, 1987, p. 77). The concept of professional practice refers to 'the range of methods, techniques and skills based on a variety of knowledge derived from social work that is used and implemented by social workers' (Meyer, 1987).

THE CONCEPT OF TERRORISM

Terrorism is a type of political violence that includes the intentional targeting of civilians and distinguishes between direct victims and the audience that it wants to affect. In this sense, terrorism includes three factors: political violence or violent action aimed at delivering a political message, the deliberate targeting of civilians (Kushner, 2003). A terrorist act is notoriously troublesome to outline, partly as a result of the way the term has evolved, and partly as a result of it being designed.

Extremists take a coercive approach to individuals within international societies, and it is recognized that terrorism has no goal and no religion, just as it does not adhere to a law and violates everything that respects humanity and religions, and it also lacks the common goals between extremist parties. Terrorism is a language: a source of the triple verb 'terror', which means fear, dismay and terror, for terrorism is intimidation and intimidation. According to the definition in the criminal law, terrorism is any action or act that inflicts violence on individuals, robs the blessing of security and safety from community life in a country, creates an atmosphere of tension and fear, and its goal is political and offensive to a particular religious community, or the goal is ideological, and harms the lives of individuals and their installations, and these acts of violence are considered illegal war violations, and these terrorist groups impose their own laws that are criminal and adopt similar tactics.

DEFINITION OF TERRORISM

It has been difficult to develop a comprehensive and holistic definition of terrorism (Attalla, 2004). Terrorism can be said to be the illegal intimidation of individuals or groups. The US State Department has also defined terrorism as the threat or use of violence to achieve political objectives by individuals or groups, whether acting in the interest of or against governmental or official authority (Al-Hadidi, 2000). The Glossary of Social Sciences defines terrorism as 'Spreading terror that provokes fear and dismay in the way that a group, organization or party has achieved its goals through the use of violence' (Badawi, 1974). Terrorism is also defined in the Arab Convention on the Suppression of Terrorism as 'Any demonstration or danger of viciousness, whatever its inspiration or reason, that is completed in the execution of an individual or aggregate criminal endeavor intended to threaten or scare individuals by hurting them or jeopardizing their lives, freedoms or security or damaging the environment' (Houari, 2002). The United Nations defines as terrorism 'Serious acts of violence by an individual or group with intent to threaten persons' (Al-Shalawi, 2004).

MANIFESTATIONS OF TERRORISM

Terrorism in all its forms is inhuman and immoral and condemns individuals, groups and communities to great suffering (Attalla, 2004). Moreover, the illegal intimidation of individuals, groups or states in fact shows more than a manifestation of the phenomenon: there is sensory terrorism, moral terrorism, internal and external terrorism and terrorism as an individual issue. Terrorism is classified into three types: individual terrorism, organized and unregulated collective terrorism.

THEORIES AND SCIENTIFIC MODELS INTERPRETING TERRORISM

There are a lot of theories through which the intellectual deviation leading to terrorism can be interpreted. Functional theory shows that terrorist behaviour leads to the disruption of relationships and social structures and induces chaos and damage to the system, while the theory of conflict equates terrorism to the redistribution of unjust wealth and power in society —the permanent conflict between those who have power and wealth and those who do not. The interactive theory showed that many acts of terrorism were due to the way the offender was treated when convicted of crimes of lower intensity earlier in their lives (Al-Yousef, 2006; Khawaldeh, 2005).

Social Construction Theory (Robert Merton)

This aims to uncover the impact of social construction pressures on people in society, and the degree to which the individual adapts to sociocultural requirements, so that compliance leads to deviant behaviour. This theory is based on the following three pillars:

1. The aspirations or goals that individuals receive and believe in through the culture in which they live;
2. The social norms that govern the progress of individuals in realizing their aspirations;
3. The institutional means by which society prepares its members through all its institutions to achieve their goals and aspirations.

Differential Mixing Theory

This aims to explain how criminal behaviour is transmitted by learning from others. The basic hypotheses underlying this theory are as follows:

1. Criminal conduct is an uninherited behaviour acquired by the human being by learning.
2. A person learns criminal conduct by interacting with other persons.
3. Such conduct occurs in the context of primary relationships of an intimate personal nature and other friendly relationships.
4. Learning involves the art of committing a crime and the special direction of motivation, tendency, disposition and justification of conduct.
5. A person is deviating when he or she privileges opinions favouring the violation of laws over those in favour of non-infringement. This is the principle of differential relationship; it refers to both criminal thinking and resistance to such thinking.
6. The learning of such behaviour can occur through both criminal and anti-crime models.

7. Although criminal behaviour is an expression of public needs and values, such needs do not explain this behaviour because non-criminal conduct is also an expression of the same needs and values.

Strentz (1981) made a classification of fearmongers with respect to their principal actions: pioneer, go-getter and visionary. The contrary methodology is likewise a social learning model proposing that fearmongering is a consequence of social impacts and particular learning encounters that invalidate supportive character attributes or conduct inclinations. These are a couple of models clarifying psychological oppressors' conduct that do not disregard individual and situational components of such a crime. Absence of hypothetical foundation infers that no broad hypothesis of intimidation has been grown, nonetheless. M. Crenshaw (1995) proposes that concerning pressure a general hypothesis of conditions is beyond the realm of imagination as a definitive call to constrain or not to force relies upon the judgment of shifted political forces. In any case, scholarly writing investigates a couple of hypotheses that might be custom-made to dissect the improvement of intimidation. Fearon's (1995) exchange hypothesis of war proposes that contention narratives, arrangements of quieting and restraint have an impact over the long haul on compulsion. It asserts that popularity-based and stable states give the data and actuate the trust that transforms intimidation into authentic dispute. Lake's (2002) dissident's scrape hypothesis of contradiction shows that the contention narratives, quieting and restraint impact compulsion by invigorating adjustment inside the force differentials of contention heroes. Absolutist states, and states founded by world associations, produce the political shakiness that drives a number of these to attempt to shift the balance of power in their own favour by releasing state viciousness and coercion of the opposition.

CAUSES LEADING TO TERRORISM

Al-Baz (2002) states that terrorism has many international and domestic causes and is the result of political oppression, widespread unemployment, economic crises, lack of democracy, the entrenchment of misconceptions due to non-religious ideas, social and psychological illnesses, and the media's role in the growth of the phenomenon. Attalla (2004) also points out that terrorism has two kinds of motives: personal motives and environmental motives. While these factors at different levels may lead to criminal conduct in general, terrorism due to sectarian strife and committed by people of young age has specificity with respect to these factors, since at least some of these factors, not necessarily all of them, may feed the inclination towards terrorism in some people or strengthen their terrorist tendencies. Terrorism is not due to one single factor but the combination of many factors (Attalla, 2004).

Sharif (2002) also points out that ignorance of the principles of religion is the most important cause of individual terrorism. According to Al-Omoush (2001), there are many social causes of terrorism: neglect, emptiness, unemployment, destructive ideas, political frustration and misguidance by influential people. Absence of scientific temper, religious repression, rampant social evils and negative-minded companions are other factors (Al-Zahrani, 2004).

Another classification suggests that terrorism has a number of reasons and motives:

Psychological Causes of Terrorism

1. *Frustration*: One of the reasons for going out against the system and the established habits and traditions is frustration and the feeling of disappointment in obtaining one's rights. Many Arab countries have marginalized the role of social groups in general and have not cared for them. Many people have been tortured, killed, displaced and prevented from expressing their freedom of opinion and expression. This is the main reason behind the violent factionalism and the angry reactions in the form of terrorism and embracing of destructive ideas (Al-Zahrani, 2004).
2. The individual may acquire the psychological qualities of the surrounding environment, whether in the family or in the community; every defect in that environment is reflected in the behaviour of the individual and ultimately becomes part of his/her

psychological make-up. The failure of family life is one of the most important causes leading to the delinquency of individuals and the acquisition of destructive behaviours.

3. The cause of violence and extremism may be the failure of the education system, which in healthy form acts like a safety valve in the social control process, combating any potential for intellectual and moral delinquency of the individual and any feelings of inferiority and lack of acceptance by society. This may result in a motive for the person to prove his ability through other avenues, especially easy ways to prove oneself even if these lead to the commission of terrorist crimes.

That is why we often find that most of the people who are enrolled in terrorist movements are people who have not succeeded in achieving their life aims through regular, peaceful means, those with low-status professions and others who have a sense of inferiority, and who are all seeking to prove themselves or achieve their personal ambitions without any consideration for the consequences of their actions (Matroudi, 2008).

4. One of the reasons for the recourse to terrorism in some young people is failure in scientific or professional careers, other functional aspects or negative emotional experiences. Such people seek to find in these misguided sects what they think will cover their failures and restore their success.

Social Causes Leading to Terrorism

1. One of the reasons for the emergence of misguided ideas is the contradiction in people's experiences—between what they hear and what they see in society—which leads to misconceptions and confusion of ideas about how to deal with things in such a situation.

2. In the face of the disintegration of society and its lack of cohesion, the person does not feel that society could feel responsible for him or care for him and others. This leads to the desire to solve problems, if necessary, through violent means.

3. A state of emptiness of existence, often characteristic of unemployed or otherwise disengaged people, is fertile ground for developing

destructive thoughts and extremism that are difficult to uproot from a person's mind (Al-Zahrani, 2004).

Economic Reasons

1. If political terrorism is one of the most common, most virulent, most dangerous and deadliest forms of terrorism, there are economic reasons for its accumulation. This is because the individual's economic condition is one of the main factors in maintaining his/her psychological stability. When an individual's income is variable and uncertain, his dissatisfaction due to this may turn into hatred towards society. This frustration creates consequences such as feelings of non-affiliation and the renunciation of a sense of national responsibility, and often is accompanied by a sense of vengeance. This sentiment may be invested in by some tendentious and discouraged people, who then devote their ability to improve their own economic situation without looking at the consequent evils and the damage this is bound to cause.

2. The prevalence of unemployment is a social disease, and a society where unemployment is high and increasing opens its doors to the dangers of terrorism, crime, drugs, assault, robbery and so on. Failure to obtain full civic rights and lack of access to employment generates general discontent.

Educational Reasons Leading to Terrorism

1. The lack of role models and sincere advice from religious and other influential figures leads to confusion, disintegration, decadence and underdevelopment.
2. The absence of high-quality and focused education deprives individuals of the chance to imbibe positive values.
3. The lack or absence of true faith-based education based on the foundations and strong underpinnings of religion, understanding of the public interest and the need for prevention of existing and emergent evils, and the lack of awareness of history and the lessons of time leads to rootlessness and propensity to adopt thinking bereft of ethics and a sense of responsibility.

CLASSIFICATIONS OF TERRORISM

There are different classifications of terrorism. The Department of Executive Aid within the United States worked to establish the National Consultative Committee on Criminal Justice Standards and Objectives. It developed a classification of terrorism into six common categories:

1. *Civil unrest*: Collective violence that interferes with peace, security and the traditional functioning of society.
2. *Political terrorism*: Violent criminal behaviour designed to create fear within the community for political purposes.
3. *Non-political terrorism*: Geared towards political institutions and created for producing a high degree of anxiety for them; however, the top objective is individual or aggregate increase rather than the achievement of a political goal.
4. *Quasi-psychological oppression*: Exercises corresponding to the commission of violations of brutality. It is not the reason to instigate dread inside the quick casualty; in any case, the semi-psychological oppressor utilizes the modalities and strategies of the genuine fearmonger and delivers comparative results and responses.
5. *Restricted political fearmongering*: Demonstrations of psychological warfare that are submitted for philosophical or political intentions, however, that do not fill in as a conjunctive crusade to catch political force in the state.
6. *Official/state demonstration of fearmongering*: This identifies with countries whose rulers depend upon misuse and mistreatment that reach almost psychological oppression like extents.

Chime (1975) ordered this as follows: endemic dread, endorsed fear and volunteer fear. The last one is part into structure, faithfulness-based, useful, provocative, cunning and representative dread. The first far-reaching and complete classification is that of I. M. Antonian (1998): political, state, strict, narrow-minded, criminal, patriot, military, optimistic and guerrilla demonstrations of fearmongering. Combs (2000) isolated present-day demonstrations of fear-based oppression into six principal divisions based on the motivation behind organization, target and plan of action: mass terror, sanctioned terror, dynastic murder, random terror, focused random terror and revolutionary tactical terror.

EFFECTS OF TERRORISM

The negative effects of terrorism are many: the destruction of the economy, the negative psychological effects, the destabilization of security, the orphaning of the children, the widowhood of women, the disbursement of state resources to enhance security, the people wailing on the streets, the destruction of the nation's assets and infrastructure, collapse of support for charitable associations (Al-Zahrani, 2008), wasting the energies of the nation's youth and the loss of selfhood and development of depressive feelings (Al-Zahrani, 2004).

WAYS TO CONFRONT TERRORISM

Terrorism is a word that carries within it the meaning of relativity (Ismail, 2010, p. 7). Since terrorism is inherently a complex phenomenon and is not due to a particular reason, it is imperative for all societies to come together in the face of this danger, which threatens the security of communities. Al-Qahtani's study in Saudi Arabia confirmed, for example, that the Islamic media, represented by Friday sermons and religious seminars in mosques and Islamic events, is more effective in addressing people than the regular media (Al-Qahtani, 2006, p. 14), in addition to the role of the institutions of socialization, in the face of terrorism. On the role of the family, one study emphasized the importance of family, community and school impact. This is in addition to the role of educational institutions in establishing the right curriculum, upholding its constants and promoting a culture of dialogue and acceptance of other opinions.

MOST IMPORTANT PROFESSIONAL STRATEGIES AGAINST TERRORISM

1. *Communication strategy*: This strategy is exercised when it is important to facilitate communication between beneficiaries and

decision-makers in order to clarify the problems they suffer from or the services they need (Abdullatif & Abdulkhaliq, 1999, p. 232). This strategy is used to create a common connection with community associations and government institutions in the local society, as well as businessmen and leaders in society, to deal with terrorism and confront it.

2. *Change of direction strategy:* The data of this strategy can be used to change the attitudes of young people towards volunteering in the service of those who have been exposed to terrorist problems, as well as to contribute to joint action and cooperation between and among the various organizations, in order to achieve an end to terrorism.

3. *Capacity-building strategy:* This is a modern strategy designed to train individuals to increase their knowledge, in particular, of the needs and problems of those who have been exposed to terrorist operations, what resources and possibilities are available and to help them increase their expertise. The strategy focuses on managing and implementing awareness-raising and advocacy campaigns and developing the technical skills of such people in countering terrorism, so that they may achieve continuity in this area (Zayton, 2000, p. 109).

4. *Strategy of solidarity:* This strategy relies on the use of available resources to overcome the problems of terrorism, whether for victims or their families, and can be employed within the framework of the available community organizations, whether governmental or private, to help the specialists choose the strategies that enable the community to deal with the phenomenon (Sadiq, 2001, p. 296).

5. *Education strategy:* This strategy aims to achieve change by raising people's awareness of the issues that concern them, and assumes that people are able to participate effectively in society but lack awareness. This strategy is used to increase community awareness and develop attitudes towards participation. Volunteers are placed in the service of individuals who are exposed to terrorist operations, in order to achieve their goals and the goals of society at the same time.

MOST IMPORTANT PROFESSIONAL TECHNIQUES AGAINST TERRORISM

1. *Collective discussion technique*: This is used with all members of society, the families of victims and those injured as a result of terrorist operations, in order to support the sharing of experiences between them and the institutions of society, so as to encourage them and convince them of the importance of assisting those who have been subjected to terrorism and to teach and equip them with the skills to deal with present and past experiences and inquire about their concerns.

2. *Open communication technique*: This aims at the optimum investment of all the efforts and possibilities available to achieve the objectives for which the strategy was employed, such as contacting officials of the relevant institutions, whether other NGOs or popular leaders, or religious leaders and businessmen, or experts and specialists in the field of counter-terrorism, and the families of those affected by such terrorist acts, and to benefit from their experience in dealing with situations, and to help the families face their difficulties, which otherwise cause inability to continue with their lives optimally.

3. *Exchange of views technique*: It is used to exchange opinions with specialists and officials on matters related to the operational procedures for counter-terrorism, as well as the design of the content of the training and care programmes that must be provided to the volunteers or the injured and their families.

4. *Teaching technique*: This tactic focuses on providing accurate information and choosing available alternatives, so that satisfactory solutions can be reached for parties. This tactic can be used with the injured and their families as they need information and help on how to interpret the information received, how to overcome obstacles and avoid the difficult periods they are exposed to.

ROLE OF SOCIAL WORKERS IN DEALING WITH TERRORISM

Around the globe, over an assortment of watched settings, government assistance experts are grappling with an inexorably pervasive social issue—the peril of social help clients changing into administration abusers. Our social equity and rights-based methodology, along with our involvement with working with helpless individuals and grouch networks, implies government assistance has an urgent commitment to give to this space. The risk of rough political direction is a trouble that everybody in different regions of government assistance work—mental advising, kid assurance, criminal equity and aptitude advancement—could need to address. What is clear is that a great deal of enquiry must be made concerning the role of social work in this space.

Not all cases would require legal mediation; social assistance clients and families would appreciate an essentially network-based methodology. Altogether, and as proved through recorded cases, thorough appraisal and mediation should be our aides for ethically solid government assistance work. It is, moreover, important to recognize the role of the media in overstating hazard, along these lines impacting the worldview in which we work. While there is a hazard to our national and worldwide networks from demonstrations of psychological oppression and rough political direction, we have to ceaselessly address presumptions, generalizations and legends enveloping this issue. We should be politically mindful, prepared to take part in exchange, see how our work is affected by different variables and furthermore the job we can play in impacting others. We should be sure about what government assistance work offers as well as our impediments.

COMMITMENTS OF SOCIAL WORK IN THE FIGHT AGAINST TERRORISM

Social equity esteems and human rights: These ought to support our watch decisions and decisions.

Early community involvement and engagement: This is essential to help people in extreme situations. Our stress should be on serving families and people instead of observing or on the other hand commenting about them. By mediating at prior stages, the risk should be made low enough to encourage keen connections that stay away from over-accentuation on trust deficiencies. By consolidating essentially network-driven and family-based methodologies, new courses of action can be offered by legal administrations and network or third-party teams operating alongside.

Multi-agency operations: Many institutions have several different relationships with other institutions, some of which are related to health services and some others related to police services. These interlinkages must be expanded and used by cooperating with these partner institutions and different communities and exchanging any relevant information in this regard. This ensures that all institutions can perform their roles effectively, based on an assessment of whether or not a person or group of persons is vulnerable to the prospect of being drawn into terrorism.

Support: As social assistance clients open up concerning their encounters, social workers can encourage discourse concerning the social messages that people are presented to concerning war, the barbarities of war, social disparities, governmental issues, ethnicity, character and financial conditions and different issues (Itzhaky & York, 2005).

Another example showing the role of social workers in different sites (Fraidlin & Rabin, 2006) is as follows:

1. The casualty reception of a hospital is where terror victims are brought in and initial medical treatment designed to stabilize their condition is provided. The principal task for the social worker is establishing contact between the victims and their families, facilitating help for all victims and responding to the victim's specific needs.
2. The information centre headquarters is where knowledge processing is done, ensuring that the government is given a full list of each of the known and unidentified casualties from all the hospitals.
3. Phone data are given to families by methods for crisis telephone number given to the media. The social worker must compose crisis telephone lines and PCs, giving sufficient reaction in any event, when there are exclusively dark and equivocal data, to manage the guests in a satisfactory and thoughtful way, and offer the guest with elective helpline numbers in case he or she needs further information.

4. The task of furnishing information to the families and providing support to the victim by locating his or her relatives is also carried out by the social worker.

5. The social worker also locates the unidentified casualties, by joining data from the clinic stay with the information given by the families. This can be an extremely horrible encounter as commonly the casualties are either dead or severely injured.

6. Conversations are carried out with the casualties in a bid to urge them to talk, and here they are given the chance to breathe and ventilate.

7. Social workers operate with the police as part of a coordinated or helpful model. Except if the association between social specialists and the police is clear, social workers are frequently constrained to attempt to do 'delicate' policing. As past models have appeared, it will get perilous for the social worker if the social help clients accept that they are by and large secretly observed.

8. If social workers need to go about as 'delicate' police, at that point there is no 'government assistance' and social service becomes solely a monitoring and social control activity. This leads to a lot of stress on the already isolated victims of terrorist trauma.

9. It had been perceived that there is a solid need and want for instruction and progress in the affected zones in terms of the following:
   a. Intense discussions with various stakeholders;
   b. Operating with centres of resistance, influence and power. This has a few ramifications for the social worker–social help–client relationship:
   c. Understanding societies as 'sets of implications,' impacts and varieties;
   d. Risk examination aptitudes and managing hazard;
   e. Political and experiential state of affairs in war zones.

SUMMARY

This chapter provides a theoretical introduction to the practice of social work in terrorism. It presents the reader with two goals: one of which is theoretical—to define the concepts and terms related to the field of social work in terrorism, in addition to a brief presentation on the history of terrorism; and the second goal is to delineate its forms, classifications, causes, motives and effects on the individual and the society and their characteristics, which in turn give the reader a clear and complete idea of the phenomenon of terrorism, in order to enable the students, specialists and other interested persons to go into combating terrorism. The chapter attempts to present the methods of providing social services in the context of terrorism and combating the damage caused by it, explaining the role of the social workers in dealing with terrorism as a phenomenon, and their interaction with young people, the family and society, while clarifying the opinions of scholars and thinkers. In addition, it explains the assistance the various institutions in society offer at all levels—individual, family, group and community—to prevent the pernicious ideas behind terrorism from spreading in society and causing further trouble.

REFERENCES

Abdullatif, Sawsan Osman, & Afifi, Abdulkhaliq. (1999). *Community organization and professional practice.* Ain Shams Library.

Al-Massaad, Abdulla. (2006). Technical inspection procedures for the terrorist event. Unpublished master thesis, Graduate school, Police Science Department, Naif University for Security.

Al-Buraq, Salem. (1987). *Terrorism prevention and treatment.* Higher Institute of Security Sciences in Riyadh, Arab Center for Security Studies.

Al-Hadidi, Hisham. (2000). *Terrorism: Its seeds, the revolution of its time, its place and its characters,* I. The Egyptian-Lebanese House, pp. 15–16.

Al-Qahtani, Mohammed Fahad. (2006). *Criminal liability for the crime of concealment,* Tasalih Study on Terrorist Crimes in Saudi Arabia, unpublished, Naif University for Security Sciences.

Al-Shalawi, Hamdan bin Gharib Bin Abdulla. (2004). *Terrorism and the role of Saudi Arabia in combating it.* Naif University for Security Sciences.

Al-Shamrani, Hamdan Bin Ali. (2002). *The impact of shifts in the international system on the phenomenon of terrorism.* Unpublished study, Naif Arab University for Security Sciences.

Al-Yousef, Abdullah bin Abdulaziz. (2006). *Social welfare and its role in combating terrorism.* Naif University for Security Sciences.

Al-Zahrani, Moussa Ben Yahia. (2008). *Terrorism effects—Prevention.* Tabuk.

Al-Zahrani, Nasser bin Meafer. (2004). *Terrorism harvest.* Obeikan Bookshop.

Aqeel bin Abdulrahman bin Mohammed. (2004). *Terrorism, the scourge of the times.* Riyadh, King's National Library.

Attalla, Imam Hassanein. (2004). *Terrorism and the legal structure of the crime*. University Publishing House.

Badawi, Ahmed Zaki. (1974). *Dictionary of social float terminology*. National Center for Social and Criminal research.

Combs, C. C. (2000). *Terrorism in the twenty-first century* (2nd ed.). Pearson.

Fraidlin, N., & Rabin, B. (2006). *Social workers confront terrorist victims: The interventions and the difficulties* (pp. 115–132). International Social Health Care Policy, Programs and Studies, Haworth Press.

Houari, Anwar Mashhour. (2002). *Terrorism: Concept, causes and remedies*. System Publishing House.

Ismail, Ezzat. (2010). *Psychology of terrorism and violent crimes*. Kuwaiti Series Publications.

Itzhaky, H., & York, A. S. (2005). The role of social worker in the face of terrorism: Israeli community based experience. *Social Work, 50*(2), 141–149.

Khalifa, Mahrous Abdulaziz. (1987). *Social work and methods of care*. University of Knowledge.

Khawaldeh. (2005). *Theories of the interpretation of terrorism*. Dar al-Shorouk.

Kushner, W. H. (2003). *Encyclopedia of terrorism*. SAGE Publications.

Marei, Ibrahim. (1996). *Professional practice and supervision in the context of working with groups*. Arab Bureau for Publishing and Distribution.

Matroudi, Abdul Rahman. (2008). *A view of the concept of terrorism and its position in Islam* (p. 35). Saudi Arabia Publications.

Meyer, C. (1987). *Direct practice in social work. Encyclopedia of social work* (Vol. 2). NASW Press.

Robert, B. (1998). *The social work dictionary* (3rd ed., p. 289). NASW Press.

Sadiq, Nabil Mohammed. (2001). *Community organization: 'Theories–skills–practices'*. Cairo.

Shoaib, Mokhtar. (2004). *Terrorism: International industry*. Dar Nahdet Misr.

Taleb, Hassan. (2004). Arab newspapers address the phenomenon of terrorism. Unpublished study, Naif Arab University for Security Sciences.

Zayton, Ahmed Wafa. (2000). *Studies in poverty and development*. Al-Safwa Library.

Chapter 9

Disaster Management in India
Perspectives from Social Work Practice

Subhasis Bhadra

INTRODUCTION

Disaster in human life has various grave impacts that cause threats to the development and normal life of any society. India as a country is called the 'Theatre of Disaster' because of multiple hazards and vulnerabilities that cause different types of disaster in diverse geographical and social situations. Disaster as a term is not new, but understanding disaster in a scientific manner and analysing the consequences of the same for the purpose of prevention and management is comparatively new in the professional field of social work practice in the 21st century. It is pertinent to mention that the aftermaths of the disaster are more crucial to manage than focusing only on the event of disaster. Survivors with multiple negative life events and experiences require a series of constructive engagements for rehabilitation and resiliency building. Equally, pre-disaster phases are critical for designing prevention and mitigations strategies among the individuals and communities. 'Prevention is better than cure'—a commonly used phrase—is equally important in case of management of disaster, where adequate prevention can considerably reduce the damage/losses and the rebuilding efforts also become easier. Disaster unfolds with its grave impact on society and human life. Thus, a disaster, while being a matter of concern in itself, additionally causes great crisis in human life and living. Flooding in barren fields, landslides on terrains, earthquakes in deserts—these events happen where no human habitat is present, and thereby the events do not cause any negative impact on human life. Such events are therefore not called disasters. Thus, the impact of disasters on human society and human lives is an essential concern for social work practice in disaster management. In this chapter, I would like to explore the concept of disaster, the role of social workers in disaster management, the vulnerability profile of India, and the policies and programmes of disaster management in India.

The definitions of social work profession clearly indicate the definite role of the social workers in helping the survivors of disaster. The definition given by IFSW (2014) explained social work as a profession that underpins the practical orientation of the academic discourse that highlights the developmental changes, liberating and empowering people to establish the value of human rights and social justice. Ultimately, social work essentially tries to enhance human well-being, by encouraging people and structure to target the challenges and make effective changes through collective responsibilities.

Disasters cause significant impact on human life in the form of destruction, death, displacement, degradation of the living conditions and of nature. This has multidimensional immediate, short- and long-term impacts. There are needs for material goods such as food, water, clothing, shelter, medical care and livelihood provisions along with a number of non-materialistic requirements such as care, protection, safety, security, feeling of belonging and re-establishing hope to support the well-being of the survivors. Disaster imposes threats and challenges, not only for the surviving communities but also for the civic authorities, institutions, organizations and professionals to deal effectively with, respond to and manage the situation. A complex problem arises out of every disaster, based on severity and impact. Thus, disaster interventions and management are practically problem-solving efforts to promote the desired social change and development. The interventions are to empower people to re-establish the relationships, social support and restore the sense of well-being with enhanced resiliency. While doing so, it is obvious to work in a trans-disciplinary manner with other human service professionals to ensure holistic care and rehabilitation. Thereby, promoting human rights, ensuring social justice, engaging the communities and the diverse groups, and inclusion of the marginalized sections become crucial for successful disaster response programming. Understanding indigenous practices and developing a culturally sensitive, contextualized programme is also essential. The core skills of social work practice become the key to work in tandem with physicians, nurses, psychologists, psychiatrists, engineers, civic administrators, journalists, lawyers and others in different phases of disasters, that is, rescue, relief, rehabilitation, rebuilding, mitigation and preparedness (Des Marais et al., 2012). Social work as a profession made considerable contributions in the field of disaster management and also contributed to a large extent in developing the models of disaster interventions through different phases of disasters by using the basic methods of social work practice. All the three primary methods of social work, that is, case work, group work and community organization are used simultaneously in various interventions in disasters. Psychological First Aid (PFA), a single session therapy for emergencies, has been routed through casework theories, while group and community organization are the most common to facilitate recovery as well as to build preparedness among community people by mobilizing and engaging the communities through various group interventions and community initiatives. The secondary methods such as social welfare administration are also essential to mobilize the funds and for adequate management of a project in such humanitarian crisis. Social action plays a critical role in advocating the rights of survivors; and social work research is the key method to develop the relevant data and scientific information about the damage, and the success of rehabilitation efforts. For social work practice, a disaster is understood by its diversity, intensity and complexity of impact on human life immediately after the event and in the long term. The impact on the humans, other living creatures and the environment are at the focus of disaster management (GOI-UNDP, 2012). In the phases of disaster intervention, that is, rescue, relief, rehabilitation and long-term recovery, the survivor community becomes the largest stakeholders in the process with other agencies, institutions and governments at different levels. Therefore, the community has all the time a key role to play in the disaster response programme through the participatory model of disaster management (Bhadra, 2013).

DEFINITION OF DISASTER

Disaster is defined from different angles considering the damage, extent, consequence, cause of a disaster, status as a social event and so on. A disaster is a grave occurrence having ruinous results. Quarantelli's (1999) perspective in 'What Is a Disaster' focused on a combination of seven elements, out of which the initial three elements are physical in dimension and the next four are psychosocial. These seven elements are mentioned here.

1. Physical aspects (earthquakes, floods, cyclones or any physical force causing such disasters)
2. Physical impact or damage (the destruction or loss due to the disaster)
3. Assessment of damage (the damage must exceed certain thresholds for the event to be called a disaster)
4. Disruption of social system (due to physical damage, destruction and loss)
5. Reality check and developing social interpretation (taking cognizance about the seriousness of the impact)
6. Political considerations (official declaration of a situation as disaster)
7. Demands for specific directed action (in case the normal response capabilities are not sufficient and so additional strategies need to be adopted).

Quarantelli (1999) emphasized that a disaster must be considered as a social construct. WHO explained disaster as an event that causes damage and severely disrupts the ecological balance. Therefore, living becomes quite challenging for the survivors. The damage also imposes huge psychosocial difficulties and thereby the severity of the event is beyond the coping capacity of the surviving community (WHO, 2009). Disaster and its impact is not only limited within the time of the disaster events, but rather the stress, trauma and the problems emerge and linger on for long due to the challenges which the survivors face in their post-disaster life. For the purpose of social work practice, Bhadra (2010) defined disaster as 'a physically, psychosocially, ecologically devastating event of such a nature which exceeds the coping capacity of the individuals and the community. It demands external help to rejuvenate the life by facilitating the psychosocial resources of the survivors to reduce the stress of various life events immediately as well as in the long term at individual, family and community level'. The degree of development of a community is a determinant fact about the nature and intensity of the disaster. So, for the purpose of working with the situation of the population that has been affected in the disaster, the resulting difficulties can be considered based on five criteria that have been mentioned as follows:

1. The local community and the available resources are not enough to provide required support to the affected population.
2. Physically the observable destruction of the usual support system (housing, water supply, electricity, medical care, education, etc.) causes a wide range of problems, which are typical in the disaster situation.
3. Disasters are unfortunate events that leave a long trail of devastation, mortality and morbidity. Every disaster invariably causes disabilities and so adds to the factors of vulnerability and threat to life and environment.
4. Any disaster takes the society into depression and impedes its development for years together. This takes a considerable time to bounce back to normalcy.
5. Political consideration is important and also essential (in some cases) to consider a calamity as disaster.

The Disaster Management Act 2005 (GOI, 2005) described disaster as:

A catastrophe, mishap, calamity or grave occurrence in any area, arising from natural or manmade causes, or by accident or negligence which results in substantial loss of life or human suffering or damage to, and destruction of property, or damage to, or degradation of environment, and is of such a nature or magnitude as to be beyond the coping capacity of the community or the affected area.

TYPES OF DISASTER

The causes of disaster can be broadly divided as natural disaster, that is, due to natural forces, and human-made disaster, that is, due to human actions or inactions. This broad division is followed though it is theoretically established that there is no disaster without human hands (Steinberg, 2000). Some examples of natural disaster are floods, tsunamis, earthquakes and cyclones, while examples of human-made disaster are riots, wars, terrorist attacks and industrial accidents. For better understanding of social work practice, human-made disasters are further divided into two types, namely disaster caused due to human error and disaster due to human intentions (Sekar et al., 2005, p. 10). In terms of intention and gravity of the disaster, these two types vary widely and also need different response strategies to work with their survivors. The different categories of disasters, as described by the High Power Committee on Disaster Management (1999) and further elaborated by UNDP (GOI-UNDP, 2012), are given in Box 9.1.

This typology of disasters is essential for understanding the uniqueness of each of the disaster situations and its impact on human lives. For the purpose of disaster preparedness, management and timely interventions, understanding the unique characteristics of the disaster is crucial, as disaster management is a multidisciplinary task for different professionals. Likewise, the engineers' role to prevent floods and earthquakes is largely to deal with structural safety, while a doctor has to deal with the health emergencies in disasters. Social workers have roles in each of these disasters in terms of analysis of the factors connected with the lives and behaviour of people as individuals, family/group members, communities and human society as a whole.

CYCLE OF DISASTER

The term 'cycle of disaster or disaster management cycle' (Baas et al., 2008) denotes the different phases of disasters that are important from the perspective of managing the eventualities due to disasters and preparing the community for dealing with future eventualities. In the disaster management cycle, the first phase is prevention. Prevention denotes adopting strategies to avoid negative impacts of hazards, and

Box 9.1 *Categories of Disasters*

A. *Disasters due to climatic condition and water-related issues:* Tsunamis, floods, overflowing river and drainage system, thunder, lightning, cyclones, hurricanes and tornadoes, heat and cold waves, cloud blasts, avalanches, hailstorms, coastal zone erosion, droughts.

B. *Disasters related to geological condition:* Earthquakes, landslides, minor fires, dam blasts.

C. *Disaster caused by accidents:* Incidents of fire in urban/village area, collapse of building/bridge/other infrastructure, forest fires, oil spills, serial bomb blasts, disasters in festivals, electrical disasters, air/road/rail accidents, boat capsizes.

D. *Industrial disasters:* Industrial accidents impacting a large number of individuals.

E. *Chemical disasters:* Chemical poisoning, leakage of chemicals and similar conditions.

F. *Disaster related to biological incidences:* Food poisoning, cattle epidemics, pest attacks, epidemics, use of biological weapons.

G. *Radiological and nuclear disasters:* Leakage of disposed of radioactive substances into the environment, nuclear accidents/disasters.

The categories E, F and G together are called CBRN (chemical, biological, radiological and nuclear) disasters.

Source: Author

further, taking every possible action in advance to negate the impact of the disasters. Examples are the construction of earthquake–resistant structures in earthquake-prone zones, building levees and creating flood channels to prevent flood in low-lying flood-prone areas. The second step is mitigation, which explains the efforts for reducing or limiting the adverse impact of the hazards and dealing with different facets of existing vulnerabilities for enhancing the capacity of the environment, structures and communities. For example, imposing traffic rules will reduce accidents, and likewise, planting mangroves will help in reducing the impact of severe waves and tsunamis. The next step is preparedness, which explains the gain of knowledge and capacity by all the stakeholders for responding to the disaster situation. As part of preparedness, the government, civil society organizations, communities, institutes and professionals have important roles in taking various steps to effectively design and implement actions to anticipate a disaster, further develop response strategies and ultimately facilitate recovery subsequent to the disaster. Hence, a substantial number of activities of preparedness are supposed to be taken up well in advance, considering the hazards and vulnerability profile of the particular region. Thus, effective and timely response is possible. Examples of such activities include conducting evaluation drills, capacity building of the staff, enlisting community volunteers with rescue skills, installing warning systems for tsunamis and cyclones, evacuating people well in advance, marking evacuation routes, construction of cyclone shelters and storage of life-saving materials are some important actions as part of preparedness. For example, school safety planning, community safety planning, regular fire drills and earthquake evacuation drills are part of disaster preparedness. Response is the step immediately after the disaster or during the events of the disaster. Effective preparedness is crucial for efficient and timely response. This specifically deals with the provision of emergency services and assistance for rescue and survival. At this time, providing medical care, supply of basic necessities, ensuring safety and reducing further damage are important. This also includes relief to facilitate the basic life-saving support in the temporary shelters, relief camps to ensure well-being and preventing health and psychosocial damage. Rehabilitation starts after the rescue and relief. The purpose is restoring the way of life of the survivors to bring back normalcy, by taking various actions such as facilitating livelihoods and rebuilding dwelling units, communication systems, educational and health facilities and so on. Thus, rehabilitation involves specifically restoring key services, support systems and lifelines of the battered community. Reconstruction is a process to reorganize and rebuild permanent structure and support services that are sufficiently resilient. This may include restoring electricity, sewerage system, water connection and roads, and construction of permanent housing, schools, community halls, hospitals and other facilities that are designed to withstand threats and hazards of similar disasters. As a result, living conditions of the survivors improve, vulnerabilities are tackled and disaster risk factors are reduced. Further, the recovery phase begins where survivors regain confidence and start progressing (ISDR, 2010). Finally, the motto of disaster management is build back better (BBB), which implies enhancing resiliency of the nation and communities by mainstreaming the disaster management as part of development work, with a significant focus of risk reduction by adopting appropriate measures for restoration of infrastructure and social systems throughout the phases of recovery, rehabilitation and reconstruction (UNISDR, 2017a). It is also crucial to note that the world is working for holistic, integrated development through international commitments transcended from Millennium Development Goals to Sustainable Development Goals. All these goals have close linkage with the effective management of disasters, and working on disaster management by keeping the SDG goals in the forefront is important for developing resilience of the local communities (UNISDR, 2017). Bhadra (2017) explains that reduction of vulnerability factors, and rehabilitation of women in disaster and conflict situations, depends on effective implementation of the programme for achievement of SDGs. Therefore, the disaster management cycle should be covered with the agenda of development, sustainability, building resiliency and ultimately building back better. Here, it is named the 'extended cycle of disaster management' (see Figure 9.1).

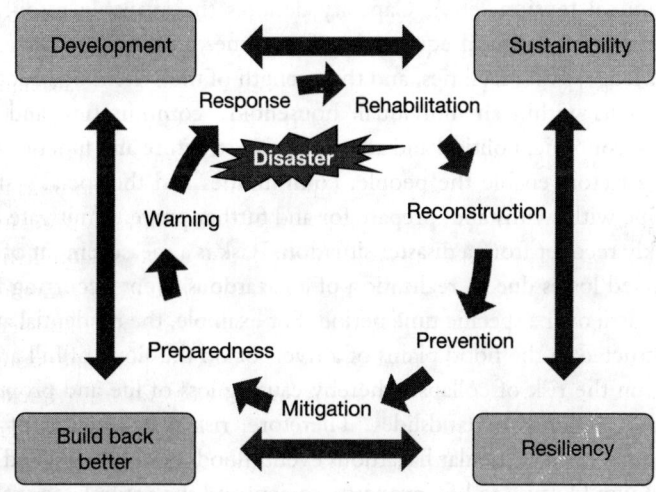

Figure 9.1 *Extended Cycle of Disaster Management*
Source: Author

CONCEPTS OF DISASTER MANAGEMENT

To understand disaster management, social workers need to be clear about the basic concepts of hazard, vulnerability, capacity and risk (HVCR). The UNISDR in its publication of terminology has given the standard concepts which are widely used (UNISDR, 2009). A disaster is caused by hazards and vulnerability in the environment and for dealing with the disaster, the capacity to respond to the situation and reducing the risk are crucial. A hazard is a dangerous condition or event that threatens or has the potential for causing injury to life or damage to property or the environment. It causes damage to lives, livelihoods as well as physical and social structures. In every situation, there are hazards. Vulnerability can be explained as the condition that makes the structure, situation or people weak and exposed in front of the hazard. It shows to what extent a community, physical structure, facilities, services or geographic area is likely to be damaged or destroyed due to the impact of a particular hazard. Vulnerabilities can be from the physical condition (e.g., poor building construction, settlement located near sea or flood zone, etc.) or socio-economic condition (poverty, lack of education and knowledge, lack of cyclone shelter, poor governance, lack or warning or other information, higher than usual communal tension, etc.). Capacity denotes the available resources, possession of technical equipment (for rescue, providing relief, etc.), knowledge, skills, facilities, and the strength of the system or structure that exists within an individual, households, communities, and the socio-economic, political and administrative structure and functioning. These factors enable the people, communities and the social system to cope with, withstand, prepare for and further prevent, mitigate and quickly recover from a disaster situation. Risk is a measurement of the expected losses due to realization of a hazardous event occurring in a given area over a specific time period. For example, the residential areas constructed in the flood plains of a river, or on the slope of hill areas, will run the risk of collapse, thereby causing loss of life and property in case of floods or landslides. Therefore, risk is a function of the probability of a particular hazardous event (floods or landslides) and the loss it would cause to life, property, society and the natural ecosystem. Thus, risk depends on the nature of hazards, the specific hazardous events and the vulnerability of the elements which are affected. All these components are closely linked with developing sustainable solutions in the long term. This can be represented as follows:

Risk (R) = (Hazard [H] × Vulnerability [V])/Capacity (C).

This formula denotes that risk can be reduced by either increasing the capacity, reducing the potential for hazards or reducing the vulnerability of a given population in a particular area in a specific time frame.

For example, if an area is highly earthquake prone, this denotes the hazard (H) component for the area. The poor construction of buildings, overcrowded living conditions and the lack of skill and knowledge about earthquake safety represent the vulnerability (V) of the people living in that area. Therefore, this area can be considered as having higher risk (R) of damage in an event of earthquake (i.e., disaster). Through interventions such as training on earthquake safety, construction of earthquake-tolerant buildings and keeping open spaces (escape routes) between the buildings, the authorities can increase the capacity (C) of the population to withstand a hazardous event (such as an earthquake) and thereby reduce risk (R). While this community will be actually affected by an earthquake (hazardous event) anyway, the loss of life and property will be minimum. Thus, the hazardous event will not cause a disaster and the risks will be largely nullified.

Thus,

Disaster = Hazardous event + Vulnerability

or disaster is realization of risk.

Disaster management is well defined in the Disaster Management Policy (GOI, 2009, p. 7). Disaster management is a multi-stakeholder-oriented integrated process that includes systemic goal-directed efforts of planning, budgeting, coordinating, deployment of disaster intervention personnel and implementation of different measures for the following purposes:

1. Developing the vulnerability profile of each area considering the geological, sociopolitical and human factors;

2. Planning and adopting preventive measures based on risk, hazard and vulnerability factors;
3. Initiating and institutionalizing the disaster mitigation and risk-reduction activities;
4. Adopting and practicing strategies for limiting the negative consequences of the disaster;
5. Capacity building of the multiple stakeholders at different levels, starting from government officials, first responders, medical professionals, teachers, community volunteers and others;
6. Allotting utmost priority to preparedness planning and implementation, and further, practice of disaster drills at frequent intervals;
7. Keeping the response mechanism in place to ensure prompt response to any eventualities or disaster-like situations;
8. Quickly assessing the situation after the disaster to understand the severity and magnitude of the event;
9. Initiating with priority life-saving actions such as evacuation, rescue from disaster-affected areas and ensuring relief and basic supplies for survival.
10. Finally, hastening the rehabilitation and reconstruction of the surviving community.

Scientifically, an ideal disaster management continuum includes two phases—pre-disaster and post-disaster. While the pre-disaster phase comprises prevention, mitigation and preparedness, the post-disaster phase comprises immediate response, rescue, relief, rehabilitation, reconstruction and recovery.

Disaster risk reduction (DRR) is an essential component of disaster management for social workers to understand and practise as disaster intervention professionals. DRR means designing policies and programmes and adopting strategies for practice before disasters to protect lives, save valuables and important documents, and limiting the damage due to disasters. In doing so, strengthening the capacity of the stakeholders and facilitating quick recovery of the survivors are also crucial. DRR is aimed at strengthening the resiliency and attaining sustainable development by preventing new disasters, reducing the risk of disasters, and continuously focusing on higher achievements (UNISDR,

2017). It is essentially important to understand the need of DRR in three major dimensions.

Ethical dimension: It is morally preferable to prevent human suffering than to save lives in the aftermath of a disaster. Being protected from disasters is an essential human rights consideration too.

Financial dimension: 'Risk reduction pays', that is, the cost of reducing disaster risk is on average lower than the overall cost of responding to and recovering from a disaster.

Political dimension: A government has political interest and responsibility involved in protecting its citizens and enforcing DRR legislation. Failure to do so may cause political instability and unrest for a long period.

DRR is a continuum with four major components that lead to humanitarian action and development. These components are preparedness, early warning, mitigation of disaster and safe-sustainable development. Preparedness deals with various activities to ensure timely and effective 'first line of response' as and when a disaster happens. For this, disaster drills, first-aid training, search and rescue training of community volunteers, contingency planning at community/school level, stockpiling relief goods, community emergency funds, etc., are important steps. Early warning is about the forthcoming hazardous event, a crucial factor for DRR. The provision of timely information enables people to take action to avoid or reduce risk and prepare for effective responses. Early warning requires involvement, ownership and participation of communities, local organizations, government administration, the meteorological department and other administrative authorities. Some hazards are predictable (e.g., cyclone and flood) and some others cannot be predicted well in advance (e.g., earthquake and landslide). Disaster mitigation deals with structural (physical) and non-structural measures undertaken to limit the adverse impact of natural hazards. This includes planting mangroves, development of flood channels, construction of flood/cyclone shelters and hazard-resistant construction of houses. Safe and sustainable development is a concept that encourages development of new structures with some standards represented by safety codes, such as safe land use, safe construction standards and construction of settlements at a safe distance from potentially hazardous locations. The development plan must ensure a sustainable solution. Specifically, important public structures, such as school buildings, hospitals, offices, multi-storeyed buildings and bridges, should be constructed with maximum caution in order to make these safe and sustainable.

EVOLUTION AND INSTITUTIONAL FRAMEWORK OF DISASTER MANAGEMENT IN INDIA

Disaster Management in India started in British era during the 20th century. In British period, relief departments were set up during the disaster to respond to the emergencies. At that time, most of the disaster management strategies were reactive in nature, which meant actions used to be initiated only after the event of a disaster. Gradually, the proactive disaster management concept was adopted and evolved by engaging multiple stakeholders such as governments at different levels, various civic authorities, army personnel and the community representatives. Thus, holistic recovery became the main focus considering the approaches that are part of the disaster management cycle.

In the post-independence period, the Central Relief Commissioner was appointed to coordinate with the relief commissioners stationed in each state. The office of relief commissioner was the main authority for responding to the disasters and also to develop adequate storage of basic supplies such as food items and medicines to deal with disasters. Further, the 'Irrigation, Command Area Development and Flood Control' programme was developed as part of the Five-Year Plans to reduce the intensity of the frequently occurring devastating incidents of flooding across the nation.

The UN General Assembly declared the decade of the 1990s as the 'International Decade for Natural Disaster Reduction' (IDNDR). Further, in compliance with the UN declaration, the government of India took active steps for institutionalizing the disaster management strategies by setting up the disaster management cell under the Ministry of Agriculture. Until 2001, disaster management was a portfolio under Ministry of Agriculture. Further, under the chairmanship of Mr J. C. Pant, the government of India appointed a high-powered committee for developing an appropriate system of disaster management. The

Box 9.2 *Different Nodal Ministries for Disaster Management*

1. Ministry of Agriculture and Cooperation is responsible for dealing with drought situations.
2. Ministry of Environment and Forest is responsible for the management of all environment-related concerns, climate change, air and water pollution and also the industrial and chemical disasters.
3. Ministry of Science and Technology has two departments: Department of Science and Technology and Department of Ocean Development. This ministry plays an important role in scientific and technological research towards the prevention and mitigation of disasters in the country.
4. Ministry of Health and Family Welfare is primarily concerned with all health-related disasters (biological disasters) including epidemics, pandemics and so on. Emergency health management in the country is looked after by this ministry.
5. Department of Space has an important role in facilitating early warning of disasters through remote sensing, space research and other technological inputs.
6. Department of Atomic Energy is responsible for dealing with any nuclear-related emergencies and radiations.
7. Ministry of Civil Aviation is responsible for managing air accidents, and Ministry of Railways is responsible for dealing with railway accidents.

Source: Author

committee recommended establishing a separate ministry and further, in February 2001, National Disaster Management Authority (NDMA) was established under the Ministry of Home Affairs (MHA), and the Prime Minister of India was nominated as the Chairman. Subsequently, disaster management was handed over to MHA. Some further major milestones in disaster management in India are the formation and implementation of the Disaster Management Act (2005). Further, in line with NDMA, State Disaster Management Authority (SDMA) at the state level and district authorities at the district level were formalized. In addition, a National Crisis Management Committee (NCMC) was constituted at the centre and different ministries were identified as nodal ministries to deal with different types of disaster, as shown in Box 9.2. This structure encouraged the stakeholders to interact adequately in a timely manner at different levels within the disaster management framework.[1]

In accordance with IDNDR, a National Centre for Disaster Management was established in 1995 at New Delhi. Further, on 16 October 2003 the Centre was elevated as National Institute of Disaster Management (NIDM). The key responsibilities of NIDM are capacity development, training, research and documentation for disaster management. As per provision of the Disaster Management Act 2005, National Disaster Response Force (NDRF) is constituted by upgradation/conversion of eight standard battalions of Central Para Military Forces to respond to disaster or disaster-like situations including chemical, biological, radiological and nuclear (CBRN) emergencies. The states/union territories are advised to incorporate disaster management training for the police forces, through police training colleges, in-services courses and also for the gazetted and non-gazetted officers[2] in the similar pattern. The Civil Defence Act (1968) has been amended in 2010 to utilize the services of civil defence volunteers for the disaster management throughout the country.

DISASTER MANAGEMENT POLICIES AND GUIDELINES

India has developed various policies for dealing with different disasters. The first comprehensive policy is 'The National Policy on Disaster Management (NPDM)' approved by the central government on 22 October 2009 (GOI-UNDP, 2012, p. 71). This guideline made a holistic approach to incorporate the concerns of all sections and different institutional mechanisms of India. The guideline has specifically focused on the transparency, accountability and responsibility fixed at different levels.

The NDMA has a major emphasis to develop various guidelines for streamlining the disaster response in different nature of disasters.

---

[1] http://nidm.gov.in/idmc/partner.htm
[2] National Policy on Disaster Management, Government of India, Ministry of Home affairs, 2009, New Delhi, p. 14.

At present, there are 26 different guidelines available in India[3]. These guidelines are developed through a broad-based consultative process by engaging disaster management practitioners, government, non-governmental organization (NGO), stakeholder representatives, academic, research institutions and other significant role players. Some of the important guidelines are on management of earthquakes, tsunamis, cyclones, floods, urban flooding, droughts, landslides and snow avalanches, nuclear and radiological emergencies, chemical disasters (industrial), chemical (terrorism) disasters, biological disasters and heat waves. There are few guidelines dealing with the creation of a safety culture such as guidelines for safety in schools and hospitals. A few guidelines are developed to standardize the services provisions, such as psychosocial support and mental health, incident response system, disaster management information communication system, training of fire service and so on.

National Action Plan on Climate Change (NAPCC)[4] (Pandve, 2009) was unveiled on 30 June 2008, considering the increasing threat of climate change and disasters. Within NAPCC, there are eight core 'national missions' initiated in 2008 looking into the consequences of global warming and climate change. These are National Solar Mission, National Mission for Enhanced Energy Efficiency, Sustainable Habitat, Sustaining the Himalayan Ecosystem, Water Mission, Mission for Green India, Sustainable Agriculture, and Strategic Knowledge on Climate Change.[5] All these missions have special focus on dealing with the climatic conditions, as the intensity and frequency of grave natural disasters are going to increase if the environmental dilapidation cannot be controlled at the right time.

Over the years, it is being focused that developing a culture of prevention and of creating an enabling environment are most crucial for integrating disaster management as part of development planning and strategy. There is a need of participatory process, collective decision-making and multi-stakeholder engagement. Therefore, National Platform for Disaster Risk Reduction (NPDRR) was established on

---

[3] https://ndma.gov.in/en/ndma-guidelines.html

[4] http://pmindia.gov.in/climate_change_english.pdf

26 February 2013[5] to engage the different stakeholders and make an effective contribution towards policymaking, decisions and disaster management.

COMMUNITY AS KEY STAKEHOLDER IN RECOVERY

Community should always be engaged as the key stakeholder in the recovery process in the aftermath of a disaster. While community is at the receiver's end, the survivors become the passive recipients and fail to recognize their own capacity. Social work practice recognizes the importance of community participatory approach and importance of engaging the community through community organization practices, but lack of trained social workers in the field of disaster intervention at the community level sometimes causes higher dependency of the survivors on the external agents for recovery. The presence and support of external agency is most crucial for disaster recovery, but how the support to be utilized and maintained for strengthening the community capacity has to be firmly planned and implemented using the basic methods of social work practice. While working with the individual survivors, use of casework method is important. Specifically, for the survivors with traumatic experiences of loss such as death of close relatives, loss of house, business, self-injuries causing permanent disabilities, and in such other cases, individual interventions become vital for recovery and gaining normalcy. Group work is essential to building the community groups for strengthening the recovery initiatives. While livelihood groups are crucial for reviving the livelihood ventures, the youth groups become volunteers for relief distribution, conducting survey, and in many such other essential works towards community recovery. Developing self-help initiatives through group engagement is also an important strategy for recovery. Considering the community after a disaster as an essential stakeholder means a greater responsibility of the external supporting agencies and professionals to engage the survivors meaningfully in the process of recovery by building their capacity, recognizing their efficiency and identifying the cultural strength and indigenous practices of the

---

[5] http://nidm.gov.in/npdrr/

community. The community as key stakeholder is a continuum of engagement that starts with higher engagement of the external agencies at the initial stage with gradual decrease towards the end of intervention with the gradual increase of community engagements with higher degree towards the end of the intervention. With the pace of time, the engagement of external agencies decreases and the community's ownership engagement increases (Bhadra, 2014).

Every community has certain indigenous practices and skills for dealing with disasters and crises. Communities traditionally have certain common pools of resources that they usually use for all. Likewise, the communities often have common places, common kitchen utensils, water resources, grazing land, jungle and so on. While disasters threaten the existence of the community, people try to pull these resources and support each other to win the struggle of survival. Until today, it is seen that even before the government support reaches, people pool their resources for initiating various rescue efforts and relief work. There are many examples where the neighbouring communities support, provide shelter and food to other community people in a situation of disaster. Therefore, recognizing the strength of indigenous resources, knowledge and skills is important for effective disaster intervention.

ROLE OF SOCIAL WORKER IN DISASTER MANAGEMENT

Disaster management in India has started getting included within the formal social work curriculum. A large number of professional social workers have been working in the area of disaster management over the past few decades. The social workers have been involved in the activities pertaining to livelihood restoration, microfinance, right-based issues, community participation, rehabilitation of the vulnerable groups and psychosocial care. In all these areas, the social workers play a prominent role in creating community resources by training the community-level workers (government and NGO workers, such as anganwadi workers, health workers, self-help group leaders and teachers of formal schools) and volunteers to facilitate the process of rescue, relief, rehabilitation and reconciliation in the aftermath of disaster. They also help create the culture of safety through preparedness activities in pre-disaster phases. The generic roles which the social workers need to carry out in any event of disaster are as follows.

1. *Provision of basic needs:* Immediately after the disaster, serving the basic survival needs is the priority. Organizing the basic services by utilizing different contributions and also organizing government provisions and international support are essential.
2. *Assessment of the situation:* Immediately after any disaster, to ensure adequate services and provision of various materials, it is essential to conduct an effective assessment. A professional assessment is a combination of different dimensions of the impact, including the services required immediately as well as in the later months and subsequent periods. Repeated assessment is crucial to track the impact of services and to understand the changing needs of the survivors.
3. *Facilitating timely report:* In any disaster situation, while the government and national or international organizations try to provide support, it is essential to create the disaster report on time. Even these days, there is a dearth of adequate reporting to facilitate support to the survivors. Therefore, generating timely reports keeping in mind the objectives of different organizations is very crucial to organize the support and to communicate the situation and changes at different phases after the disaster.
4. *Mobilizing community to join in the effort of recovery:* The community-based approach is most crucial for the recovery. Involving the affected community as equal partners in the effort has to be practised from the very first day onwards. Therefore, involving the community by engaging them in needs assessment, as care provider (being a community-level worker), for implementation (preparing list for distribution, organizing meeting for housing support, livelihood, etc.) as well as in the information sharing and monitoring process is vital to bring about effective changes after a disaster.
5. *Capacity building for disaster intervention workers at different levels:* The basic object of capacity building in the context of disaster management is to provide the essential skills, sensitization and

awareness about the needs and ensure required support to the survivors in a culturally appropriate manner according to the context. The content and length of capacity building may differ according to the needs and the level of the participants. Extensive training is needed for the people who are going to train others or going to work intensively with the people or have bigger responsibilities. In the rehabilitation phase, DRR programme capacity building of the community-level workers and volunteers is most important. The cascading model of capacity building is crucial to transfer the knowledge to the grassroots level. 'The cascade model involves the delivery of training through layers of trainers until it reaches the final target group' (Elder, 1996, p. 13).

6. *Coordination with various serving government departments and non-government organizations:* It is very important in disaster response programme to develop an effective coordination mechanism at the local, state or district and other higher levels. Facilitating participation of all the supporting organizations, developing working groups, collecting and disseminating information, and organizing sub-committees based on sectors of needs (livelihood, housing, water and sanitation, health services, psychosocial services, etc.), are some of the vital issues in coordination.

7. *Networking with the existing systems (administration, health system, education, social welfare) at the local/district and state:* Networking is essential to organize the effective delivery of the materials and services at the ground level. In any disaster, the existing system of the government has to be revoked, used, or in severe cases a system needs to be initiated. Usually, working with the district and state administration is very important. Networking with the government systems of health services, education, social welfare and supporting the survivors through the existing structure and personnel needs to be emphasized as part of an immediate and long-term response plan.

8. *Information sharing at different levels:* Dissemination of information is essential to ensure service and resources for the affected communities. The information should be made relevant according to the target audience and also based on the need of the forum. Therefore, organizing workshops and conferences, publishing local

newsletters and sending messages to other relevant authorities on various issues are beneficial for the development of the area.

9. *Budgeting and financial implication:* Disaster response is a huge investment for any organizations. Usually the budget depends on the extent of loss and destruction, as the exact implications need to be factored in. Though it requires a specific professional qualification to deal with budgets, for a social worker it is important to participate in the budget making and forecast the cost, ensuring adequate allocation based on the needs at different levels (local, state, organizational, national or international as needed) and requirements.

10. *Fund raising:* Many a time, social workers have worked and working with different organizations to mobilize funds for different programmes. Disaster intervention is one of the areas where a large amount is often available because of its urgency and the overwhelming nature of the problems. Therefore, mobilizing funds and convincing donors with adequate logistics and documents are among the most technical as well as crucial parts of the job. For a social worker, focusing on the needs with justification and reference from the past experiences, facilitating alternative resources in the communities, convincing donors about the sustainability and uniqueness of the proposed intervention and having well-defined goals and objectives with specific, measurable, achievable, relevant and time-bound indicators becomes priority.

11. *Support and supervision:* Social workers working as coordinator, manager, team leader and director (as per the position and organizational designation) assume the responsibility of support and supervision of a team, which may be scattered in the field at different locations. In a disaster intervention, support and supervision is very crucial as the situation is largely abnormal, demanding and stressful. Ensuring personal safety of the team members, imparting adequate skills to respond effectively, maintaining adequate communication, developing support among the members and encouraging self-care practices are vital.

12. *Monitoring and evaluation:* Monitoring is the process to take the programme towards the desired direction through identification of the problems, responding to the same, ensuring adequate

resource allocation and making effective use. Evaluation is to understand the impact of various humanitarian actions and suggest the possible ways of improving the situation by changing practices, designing new policies and fixing accountability of stakeholders. Therefore, involving the stakeholders in the process and ensuring effective implementation of the programme is a crucial step, where professional social workers have a greater role to play.

13. *Advocacy and ensuring adequate policies:* There is a continuous need of improving the existing knowledge based on the experiences and translating the same in the policies. Therefore, advocacy and ensuring adequate policies are very crucial on different issues of rehabilitation. These may be used to deal with livelihoods, compensation packages, rehabilitation, allocation of houses, benefits for the vulnerable groups and so on

14. *Ensuring rights of the survivors:* The principles of human rights and social justice are core to the profession of social work. Supporting the needs of the survivors is not a work of charity; it is the right of the survivors to get help with adequate dignity and respect. Human rights violations in disasters are common phenomena until date. Various forms of violation of human rights, such as discrimination in relief, resource allocation, providing support, caste domination, unorganized services leading to chaos among the survivors, not giving basic information and corruption among the officials/NGOs, are common. Professional social workers have a greater role to ensure the best practices by considering the rights of the survivors and various marginalized groups.

15. *Research and documentation:* For enhancing the professional knowledge as well as to track the changes in a scientific and systematic manner, research and documentation are most crucial. Social work research could focus on the present situation, changes over time, social dimensions, impact of interventions on specific groups, impact of specific interventions (e.g., livelihood, housing, self-help group initiatives), and any other topics which have relevance to the present situation or for future interventions. In the field of disaster, research work should ideally be conducted with service components to the community. Similarly, periodic documentations are essential for identifying the changes and looking for best alternatives.

16. *Handling media:* This is one of the most important administrative and social responsibilities. At times, the news gets reported in a distorted form if adequate relevant information is not provided to the media. Therefore, dealing with media is a very sensitive issue, which social workers have to be very careful and aware of. Misrepresentations of the facts cause various kinds of damage to the programme, and at times some local media may even have a tendency to provide distorted news for serving vested interests. Therefore, providing relevant information in the form of report and organizing press conferences on behalf of the coordination committee are safer options. At times, the community-level workers also need to be provided with adequate relevant information to enable them to become effective spokespersons for a community.

All the different roles of social workers in the context of disasters are shown in Figure 9.2.

CONCLUSION

Human rights are one of the main considerations for disaster intervention. The stakeholdership of the community members is very crucial to ensure human rights fulfilment by enhancing people's participation in the programme from the first day onwards. There is always high chance that some survivors based on caste, gender, physical status or due to any other reason may get marginalized and continue to suffer for long (Bhadra, 2014). It is seen that while disaster is not managed efficiently, it cause further trauma and disorganization—that is termed 'the second wave of disaster' or 'humanitarian aid-induced social problems' (Inter-Agency Standing Committee [IASC], 2007, p. 2). This is in addition to emergency-induced problems and pre-existing social problems, which complicates the situation further. While working in disaster interventions, hostility or non-cooperativeness of the survivors can occur due to inappropriate and inadequate services or lack of coordination with the survivors, community leaders and other volunteers. Hence, it is always important to involve the community members in the discussions and make them equal partners in the process

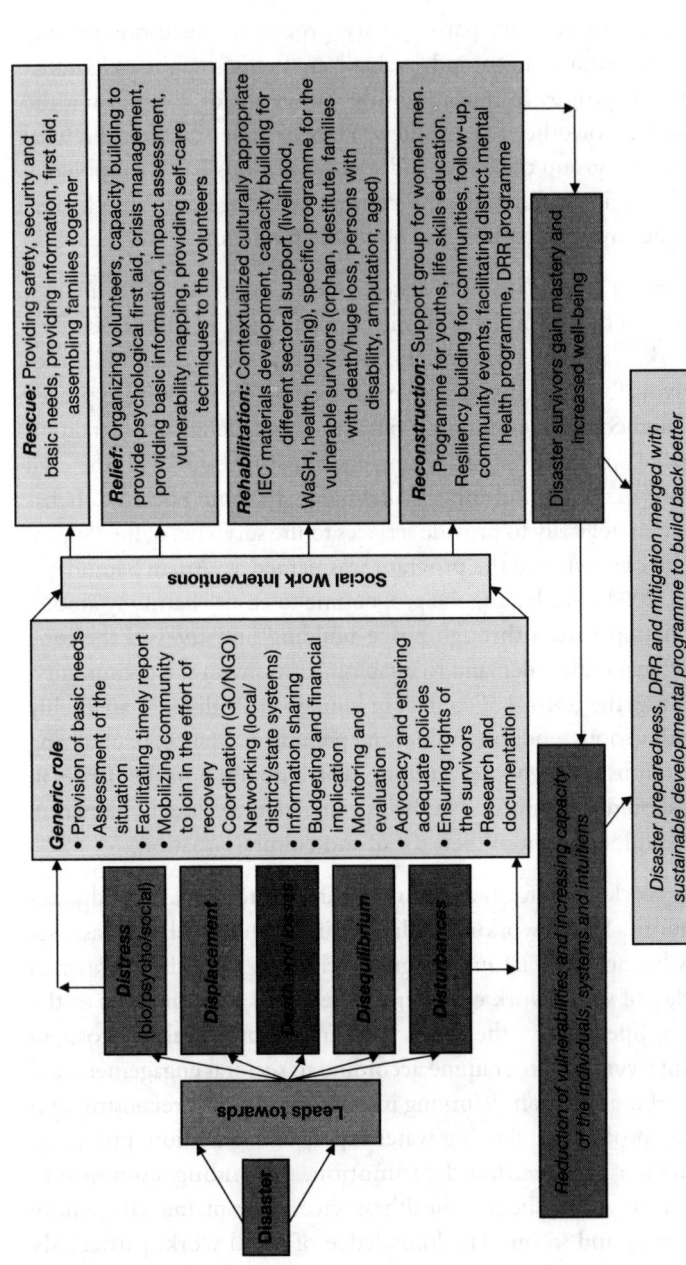

Figure 9.2 *Role of Social Workers in Disaster Management*

Source: Author

of recovery through the participatory process of decision-making, planning, implementation and evaluation. Being caught in conflict between the groups in a community causes major trouble for the social workers or other practitioners. Hence, understanding the local and prevailing group dynamics and social equations based on political opinions, religious affiliations and cultural beliefs are crucial to handle conflict and provide the best and equitable services.

Further, in human-made disasters, such as riots, terrorist attacks, bomb blasts, border conflicts, ethnic conflicts and in CBRN disasters, social workers need to have specific knowledge about the problems of the survivors for delivering effective services. While working in peace-building and conflict resolution programmes, maintaining neutrality is most crucial and developing a strong coordinating body with the civil society organizations and other stakeholders become effective. It has been done strategically to provide services to the survivors of the Gujarat communal conflict, and the program was named as 'Aman Samudaya' (Chachra, 2004). Facilitating the programme to ensure harmony among the conflicting parties through peace-building initiatives in the long term is often a critical demand to establish harmony in the community. Many a time, the reasons of conflict in human-made disasters are highly toned with various emotions, values and prejudices. Hence, neutralizing those emotions through interventions, which do not hurt the parties in conflict, should be planned. This helps cultivate the values of pluralism, tolerance and inclusion in their social and cultural situation.

Social workers perform all such roles in different phases of disaster interventions. While working in disaster intervention, all the basic six methods become crucial in strength, as derived from the theoretical knowledge of social work considering the ethics and principles of the profession. Specifically, the social workers perform multiple roles in disaster intervention programme according to sectoral engagement and demands of the situation. Working in any sector such as reconstruction of housing projects, facilitating water supply and sanitation, providing microfinance for livelihood promotion, rebuilding community infrastructure, strengthening health services, organizing safe school programming and so on. The knowledge of social work, particularly for community mobilization, group engagement, rebuilding individual resources (i.e., hope, self-respect, self-esteem) and community resources (trust, faith, mutual support, neighbourhood networks, social support) are crucial for ensuring a successful disaster intervention programme.

REFERENCES

Baas, S., Ramasamy, S., DePryck, J. D., & Battista, F. (2008). *Disaster risk management system analysis.* Food and Agriculture Organization of the United Nations, Rome.

Bhadra, S. (2010). Social work and disaster interventions. In B. Gunjal & G. Molankal (Eds.), *Fields of social work practice* (pp. 355–386). Baraha Publishing House.

Bhadra, S. (2013). Community based psychosocial support programme for resiliency building in Tsunami rehabilitation of Kanyakumari District. *Journal of Social Work, Special issue on Building Resilient Communities: Communitarian Social Work, 3*(8), 66–86.

Bhadra, S. (2014). Community as the key for disaster recovery: A case of long-term intervention in Kanyakumari district. In Sanjay Bhatt & Neera Agnimitra (Eds.), *Social work response to environment and disaster* (pp. 133–147). Shipra Publication.

Bhadra, S. (2017). Women in disasters and conflicts in India: Interventions in view of the Millennium Development Goals. *International Journal of Disaster Risk Science, 8*(2), 196–207. https://doi.org/10.1007/s13753-017-0124-y

Chachra, S. (2004). Disasters and Mental Health in India: An Institutional Response: Action Aid India. In Diaz, P., S. Murthy and Lakshminarayana (Eds.) *Disaster Mental Health in India.* Indian Red Cross Society Publications, pp.151–160.

Des Marais, E., Bhadra, S., & Dyer, A. R. (2012). In the wake of Japan's triple disaster: Building capacity through international collaboration. *Advances in Social Work, 13*(2), 340–357.

Elder, H. (1996). The cascade model of training: Its place in the Pacific. *Pacific Curriculum Network, 5*(1), 13–15.

GOI. (2005, December 23). *Disaster Management Act.* Government of India. https://www.ndmindia.nic.in/images/The%20Disaster%20Management%20Act,%202005.pdf

GOI. (2009). *National policy on disaster management.* National Disaster Management Authority.

GOI-UNDP. (2012). *Disaster management in India.* Ministry of Home Affairs.

Inter-Agency Standing Committee (IASC). (2007). *IASC guidelines on mental health and psychosocial support in emergency settings* (data set). American Psychological Association. https://doi.org/10.1037/e518422011-002.

IFSW. (2014, November 29). *Global definition of social work*. International Federation of Social Workers. https://www.ifsw.org/what-is-social-work/global-definition-of-social-work/

ISDR. (2010, 21 May). un-spider.org/glossary/term/6016.

NIDM. (1999). *High Power Committee on Disaster Management*. https://nidm.gov.in/PDF/pubs/HPC_Report.pdf

Pandve, H. T. (2009). India's national action plan on climate change. *Indian Journal of Occupational and Environmental Medicine, 13*(1), 17. https://doi.org/10.4103/0019-5278.50718

Sekar, K., Bhadra, S., Jayakumar, C., Aravindraj, E., Henry, G., & Kumar, K. K. (2005). *Facilitation manual for trainers of trainees in natural disaster*. NIMHANS and Care India.

Steinberg, T. (2000). *The acts of God: The unnatural history of disasters in America*. Oxford University Press.

Quarantelli, E. L. (1999). *The disaster recovery process: What we know and do not know from research*. Disaster Research Center.

UNISDR. (2009). *UNISDR terminology on disaster risk reduction*. https://www.unisdr.org/files/7817_UNISDRTerminologyEnglish.pdf

UNISDR. (2017a). *Build back better in recovery, rehabilitation and reconstruction*. https://www.unisdr.org/files/53213_bbb.pdf

UNISDR. (2017b). *Disaster risk reduction and resilience in the 2030—Agenda for sustainable development* (p. 21).

UNISDR. (2017c, February 2). *Terminology*. Retrieved December 26, 2018, from https://www.unisdr.org/we/inform/terminology.

WHO. (2009). *Disaster management guidelines: Emergency surgical care in disaster situations*. Retrieved May 9, 2017, from http://www.who.int/surgery/publications/EmergencySurgicalCareinDisasterSituations.pdf

Chapter 10

Integrated Social Work Intervention with Drug Dependents
Cure to Care

Kirti Arya and Ravi Ranjan Kumar

INTRODUCTION

Drug dependency is a universal problem, which has affected almost all the nations—both developed and developing—across the globe. According to the World Drug Report (2019), in 2017, an estimated 271 million people lying in the age group of 15–64 had used drugs at least once in the last year, corresponding to 5.5 per cent of the global population, representing 1 in every 18 persons worldwide.

Since the prehistoric era, drugs were the mediums for reducing pain and altering states of consciousness, which were certainly limited to the individuals who had reached maturity or were in a particular situation (World Drug Report, 2015). The same report also denotes that the root cause of drug consumption may be traced to physiological factors (tiredness, heightening sexual experience or overcoming sexual problems), psychological factors (relieving tension, depression, inhibition or boredom, or experiencing pleasure or ecstasy) or socio-economic factors (custom, company, social gathering, boosting prestige and social status).

Drug abuse prevention programmes have evolved considerably during the last two decades, including progressively improved pharmacological and psychological treatments. The consequences of the problem of drug dependence include sexual problems, psychological distress (paranoia, depression, anxiety, aggression, hallucinations and other similar problems), or socio-economic factors (joblessness, poverty, family breakdown, crime and delinquency).

To understand the roots of the drug problem on a large spectrum, one cannot ignore the international politics and India's geographical proximity to the countries such as Pakistan, Afghanistan, Iran, Myanmar, Thailand, Laos People's Democratic Republic (PDR), which are important locations for illicit production and supply of opiates in the world, making it the transit country for drug trafficking. Some of the border states, such as Jammu and Kashmir, Punjab, Rajasthan, Gujarat, Uttar Pradesh, Manipur, Nagaland, Mizoram and Arunachal Pradesh, are worst affected, which indicates a geopolitical angle to the issue.

DRUG DEPENDENCE: MEANING AND IMPLICATIONS

Drug or substance dependence is defined by the World Health Organization (2000) as dependence on a psychoactive drug or substance in any chemical form, which on consumption alters the functioning of the human mind and leads to intoxication. This usage is intentionally broad. It includes not only medications intended primarily for the treatment of patients, but also pharmacologically active substances. Examples of such substances are alcoholic beverages, opioids, cannabis and tobacco products (cigarettes, chewable tobacco, etc.).

The existence of drugs can be traced back to the Greek and Roman civilizations, which deified wine with the statues of Dionysus and Bacchus. Historically, magical-religious celebrations, rituals and social events were linked to drugs and alcohol. Gradually, their use became widespread in other contexts. Primarily, tobacco or cannabis was used, as they were natural in origin. With time, the list of substances used

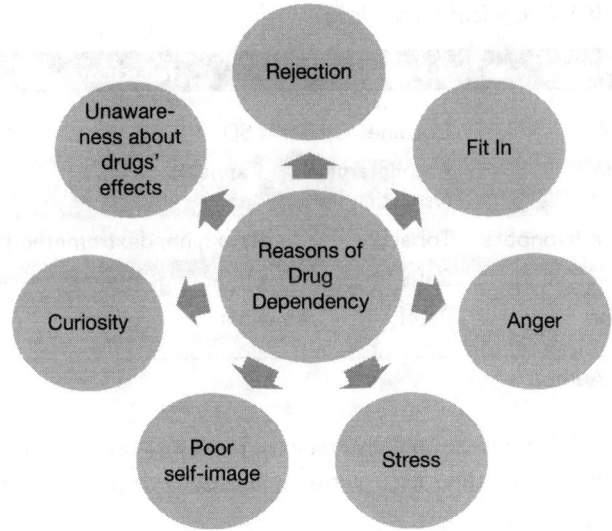

Figure 10.1 *Key Reasons for Drug Dependence*
Source: Author

expanded to other chemical substances obtained after fermentation and distillation of grains/fruit juices. Later on, synthetic and drugs used for psychiatric purposes were produced artificially.

A person may take drugs due to various reasons, and so it is not feasible to provide an exhaustive list. However, a few key reasons emerging out of studies are depicted in Figure 10.1.

There are other reasons too, abbreviated as 3 Fs, that is, Fun, Forgetting and Functionality woes which instigate people to start using drugs, later causing dependency. Psychoactive substances alter the users' cognition and behaviour, for example, when a person consumes alcohol, he may feel happy (change in mood), have difficulty in concentrating (cognition) and may have an unsteady gait or slurred speech (behaviour).

TYPES OF DRUGS

Classification of drugs (as depicted in Table 10.1) helps in understanding and estimating their effects, possible harm potentials and potential

Table 10.1 Classification of Drugs

Depressants	Stimulants	Hallucinogens
Alcohol	Cocaine	LSD
Opioids	Amphetamine-type stimulants	Cannabis
Sedative-hypnotics	Tobacco	Ketamine, dextromethorphan
Volatile solvents	Caffeine	Other (e.g., nutmeg/mace)
Cannabis	Betel	Khat

Source: Author

withdrawal features. Several criteria exist to classify drugs. Drugs may be classified as per their legal status, application- or properties-based action depicted as follows:

- *Legal status:* Based on compliance with the laws, drugs are classified *licit or legal* substances allowed for consumption and trade, for example, alcohol and nicotine (tobacco), while the substances strictly prohibited are termed as illicit or illegal substance, for example, cannabis and opioids.
- *Medical applications:* Opioids are used for pain alleviation (e.g. morphine and diamorphine).
- *Classification based on properties-based action*

Drug Dependence: Micro and Macro Implications

International Statistical Classification of Diseases and Related Health Problems 10th Revision (ICD-10)–WHO defines drug dependence as a cluster of physiological, behavioural and cognitive phenomena which develops after the repeated use of substance typically with the strong urge to consume it, failing in controlling it, persisting despite harmful consequences, ignoring other activities and obligation, increased tolerance and at times physical withdrawal symptoms.

As per ICD-10, 'dependence' is characterized by three or more symptoms as detailed below.

- *Tolerance:* Need to enhance the quantity of intake to get the same effect over a period.
- *Physiological withdrawal state:* Physical and psychological discomfort on missing the dose.
- *Loss of control:* When the substance is consumed in a large amount for a prolonged time, reducing or controlling substance use becomes unsuccessful.
- *Continuity:* Continued use in spite of clear evidence of harmful consequences.
- *Craving:* Strong desire to use the substance.

Drug (Ab)use in India: Extent and Intensity

It was in the 1980s when drug dealers looked at India as a possible destination for the drug trade. In 1982, when the silver prices crashed, Indian smugglers, previously taking silver out and bringing in gold, switched to heroin as a profitable substitute (Allana, 2018). Writing in 1986 for *India Today,* Raj Chengappa observed:

> Three years ago hardly anyone [had] heard of smack addicts. But today it has become the number one problem concerning officials and psychiatrists combating drug addiction in the country … In four major government hospitals in Delhi which treated only 50 patients in 1982, almost 3000 addicts came for treatment last year and 1000 of them had to be refused admission because of lack of beds.

Historically, India has a long history of socially accepted drug use without apparent crisis. Consumption of raw opium, *ganja, bhang* and alcohol was prevalent in the Indian communities. Norms and cultures showcased long history and tradition regarding the usage of drugs. Drugs were even cultivated traditionally in many regions without little or no inhibition to the usage of drugs. Age-long usage and customs of indulgence in cannabis and opium were also observed in social gatherings like "Madak" and "Chandu" in northeast tribal communities, as offered in socio-religious ceremonies.

Geographically, India is sandwiched between the two largest opium-producing areas—Golden Crescent (Afghanistan, Pakistan and Iran) and Golden Triangle (Myanmar, Laos PDR and Thailand). Unfortunately, proximity to the Golden Triangle, growing demand for drugs among the local population, political instability, insurgency and the poorly guarded (porous) borders have resulted in drugs proliferating the North-Eastern states majorly, turning India into a narcotics haven.

United Nations Drug Control Programme (UNDCP, 2003) conducted an in-depth study on the drug scenario in North-Eastern India and stated the situation as "fast going beyond one's control". It has also exposed the deep-rooted nexus of drug mafia and politicians, suspected patronage of politicians and security personnel to traffickers.

According to the National Crime Records Bureau (NCRB, 2014), more than 25,000 people, young and adults, committed suicide due to drug abuse in the last 10 years. There were more than 4,000 cases of drug-related suicides in 2012 and 4,500 cases a year later in 2013, while United Nations estimates suggest that more than 2 lakh people are killed in the world due to drugs every year.

In a 2015 report, the Narcotics Control Bureau (NCB) stated that there were about four million drug dependents in India. Tobacco and alcohol, the most commonly abused substances, serve as a gateway drug to hard-core substance use. Children as young as 9 years old start smoking *beedi* and *marijuana* and graduate to opium and heroin from the age of 12 onwards.

The United Nations Office on Drugs and Crime (UNODC) in 2012 framed a hypothetical timeline (as depicted in Figure 10.2) to understand the drug use pattern among the people who inject drugs in India in a study conducted on 'Association of drug use pattern with vulnerability and service uptake among injecting drug users'. This timeline depicts the multiple windows of opportunity to design and implement interventions in people with drug dependency.

For primary prevention, the young age of onset of legal drugs has obvious implications. To prevent transition from the use of illegal non-injecting drugs to the use of injecting drugs, which has a window of 6 years and long enough to institute evidence-based effective drug

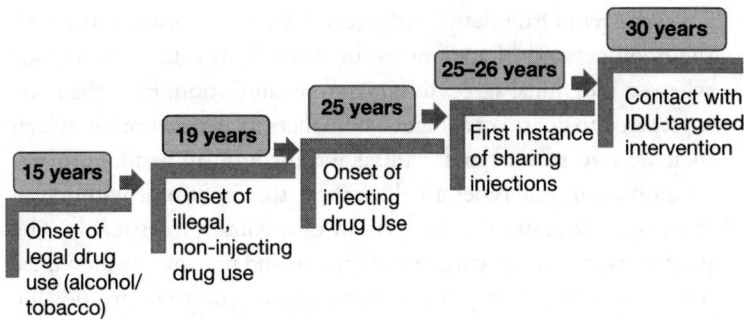

Figure 10.2 *A Hypothetical Time Scale of Drug Use Career of a Typical IDU*

Source: Author

treatment and opioid substitution therapy (OST). Once drug users begin injecting, a period of five years is lost to engage them in targeted interventions.

DRUG REHABILITATION: A COMPREHENSIVE PROCESS

Drug rehabilitation is a comprehensive process, which requires 10 per cent treatment and 90 per cent psychotherapy for the care and treatment of people who use drugs. It is a blend of effective, efficient and ethical treatment services specifically planned for an individual on the basis of level of severity. It includes screening and brief intervention, outreach services, evidence-based and comprehensive psycho-social assessment, in-patient/out-patient treatment services, long-term residential treatment, recovery support services and rehabilitation.

The aim of the rehabilitation process is to recover from and rectify maladaptive behaviours, avoid relapse in the long run and rehabilitate patients to a balanced life. In the rehabilitation process, patients learn strong coping mechanisms, impulse control, controlled emotional regulation skills and drug-refusal strategies.

The process involves three stages before the patient's plans for undertaking the rehabilitation patient.

1. *Detoxification:* Drug detox and alcohol detox is a process in which the body gets rid of addictive substances. This is the initial phase when an individual agrees to undergo rehabilitation. First, the body is prepared to get rid of addictive substances by detoxification, which includes two major types: natural and medical. In natural process, an individual undergoes a cold turkey, that is, abrupt withdrawal from opioids under the supervision of medical professionals. The purpose is to manage withdrawal systems and prepare the individual for the rehabilitation process. Withdrawal symptoms are not life threatening but are discomforting leading to relapse.

2. *Psychotherapy:* Rehabilitation process comprises pharmacological and psychotherapeutic treatment. In this phase, psychological aspects of drug dependency are addressed, which further decides the course of rehabilitation. Regular sessions are conducted either with one-on-one meetings (individual counselling), or with groups (group counselling) and at times with the immediate family members (family counselling).

3. *Aftercare:* Aftercare is planned once the patient completes the residential rehabilitation. This includes follow-up and provides long-term support and services to help them make successful transition back into society.

So, the rehabilitation process faces an immense struggle in rehabilitating individuals in society. Along with this, individuals through the span of life face identity crisis and declining social value in the society they live in.

DRUG DE-ADDICTION CENTRES: NEED FOR A PATIENT-FRIENDLY ENVIRONMENT

The last decades have seen the problem of drug dependence at an alarming rate. De-addiction centres are mostly privately owned and their focus is on de-addiction of the person. They do not focus adequately on rehabilitating the person, which is a much more comprehensive procedure of reinstating the person back into the society. When this procedure is not followed and the focus remains only with detoxifying the person's body, then the person will again take the drug whenever available to him/her. Therefore, the rehabilitation procedure is necessary.

Looking in its subtleties, it becomes clear that the centres are not very patient-friendly and there are times when the person is seen bound in the room. They are treated as inmates like that of a prison. Their condition is not less than any inmate of a jail. They are not treated properly. In contrast, in the government-owned facilities, the faculty members working in the rehabilitation centres are more educated and well trained. They are at least mandated to treat the person with compassion and give them proper treatment.

Treatment includes medicine as well as recreational activities through which the withdrawal symptoms can be controlled. The person can have a better life and a proper rehabilitation. However, the boundaries of the facility can scare a person. Despite these facilities, the dropout rate from the government facilities is higher than the private facilities. The treatment and the procedure of rehabilitation may be studied through the visits to the rehabilitation centre, de-addiction centres and discussions with the drug dependents.

ADVERSE EFFECTS OF SUBSTANCE ABUSE AND RELATED CONSEQUENCES TO VULNERABLE POPULATIONS

People who use drugs and their family members both succumb to the adverse effects of drugs in various ways, which include physical, social and psychological consequences. However, the impacts are long lasting and adverse when it comes to vulnerable populations such as women, economically disadvantaged/children from low-income families, the elderly population, and the people living with HIV and other chronic health conditions, including severe mental disorders, differently abled, homeless and the rural population who have inaccessibility to healthcare services.

When it comes to children, the drug dependency becomes lethal. They have to suffer significant emotional and behaviour problems in substance-using families, as stated by the key informants. Also, the elderly and the disabled in such families require additional attention

Table 10.2 *Adverse Effects of Drugs on Vulnerable Populations*

	Adverse Effects	
Social	Psychological	Physical/Health
1. Poor performance	1. Mental health	1. Economic hardships
2. Stigma and discrimination	2. Depression	2. Prone to health issues and infectious diseases such as HIV/AIDS, HCV, TB, STDs
3. Marital discord	3. Suicidal thoughts	
4. Fear of identification	4. Anxiety	
5. Homelessness	5. Aggression	3. Lethargy
6. Child abuse	6. Sleeplessness	4. Pain
7. Domestic violence		5. Physical weakness
8. Lack of support		
9. Unemployment		

Source: Ministry of Social Justice and Empowerment (2014)

and care. Lack of vision and a complete absence of *empathetic* attitude towards patients on the behalf of service providers as well as policymakers for the same appears to be the fundamental cause of this neglect and below par arrangement.

The adverse effects on vulnerable populations can be divided into three categories: physical, psychological and social factors, as depicted in Table 10.2.

SOCIAL WORK IMPLICATIONS: CLIENT-CENTRIC APPROACH

Social Work being a practice-based profession and an academic discipline (Global Definition, IFSW & IASSW, 2014), demands a practice-based model to implement any programme in the field. With this perspective, an attempt can be made where cure should be supplementary to care and not vice versa. Treatment should be a matter of collective care by a team of multi-disciplinary service providers. Experts should be held duly accountable for their negligence, and similarly health care should be a collective responsibility of society and not just of patients and/or their immediate family.

Studies on the issue of drug dependence and rehabilitation (Arya, 2018) suggest that the therapeutic model for treatment is being predominantly used across de-addiction centres in India instead of the social model of health. The basic tenet of the social model that *cure* should be secondary to *care* was blatantly neglected in basic modus operandi across Drug De-addiction and Rehabilitation Centres (DRCs). The onus of client-centric approach across DRCs was found lying only with the counsellors, as they were the ones who were responsible to provide individual attention. When the individual needs and expectations were not addressed separately, it gradually developed into poor coping mechanisms, leading to dropouts. There is a need for a paradigm shift towards the social model and incorporating rights-based approach in the treatment process with the involvement of social workers and soft skills training for medical practitioners.

Inclusion of behavioural therapy followed by relapse prevention will help in better treatment of the patients. Types of behavioural therapies are stated below:

1. *Cognitive-behavioural therapy:* Helps patients to recognize, avoid and cope with situations in which they are likely to relapse.
2. *Multidimensional family therapy:* Designed to support recovery of the patients by improving family functioning, that is, family-based support in the recovery process.
3. *Motivational interviewing*[1]*:* Focus on expectations, attributions and behaviour of clients. It builds on developing a comprehensive understanding among service users regarding the causes and their effects associated with drug dependence.
4. *Motivational incentives:* Uses positive reinforcement to encourage abstinence, for example, acknowledgement of small milestones in the overall process of recovery and rehabilitation.

It can easily be inferred that not addressing the impact of drug dependence in terms of adequate emphasis on psychotherapy and

---

[1] Propounded by Miller (1983). Motivational Interviewing is particularly useful for individuals in the contemplation stage. Although, it can be beneficial for individuals in all stages of treatment.

counselling at rehabilitation centres was a prominent reason for high relapse or dropout cases. One core aspect to this issue also relates to the shallowness of rehabilitation mechanisms at centres neglecting the vital aspect of 'client in and as a system', which asks strongly for a holistic intervention as proposed in Integrated Social Work Practice. The Pincus and Minahan Model of Integrated Social Work Practice with its emphasis on client system, action system, target and change agent systems suggests the critical need for such a holistic intervention in complex social issues, among which drug dependence takes centre stage.

Drug dependency today claims its victims from all sections of society despite class, gender, status, age, religion, caste, community or social group. No section of society is immune—be it a rag picker, peon, lorry driver, manager, student, executive or professional. It is estimated through numerous studies such as the World Drug Report, United Nations Drugs Control Society and Narcotics Bureau of India—Annual Reports that at present there are 8 to 10 lakh drug dependents in India.

As per the report "Magnitude of Substance Use in India" published in 2019 by the Ministry of Social Justice and Empowerment, Government of India established that a substantial number of people in India used psychotropic substances in the last one year. Alcohol was consumed widely by 14.6 per cent of the population (between 10 and 75 years of age) of the country. Cannabis and opioids are the next commonly used psychotropic substances in India. About 2.8 per cent and 2.1 per cent of the population consumed cannabis and opioids, respectively, within the year.

With the extensive number of people who use drugs, it is becoming an alarming situation in various states of India. Based on these figures, the dreadful picture which is likely to emerge after a couple of decades or so defies imagination. With this scenario, rehabilitating the drug users is emerging as a major challenge for India just like in the United States where half of the beds in general hospitals are reportedly occupied by the drug dependents (inclusive of alcohol-dependent patients).

The severity of the problem heightens with increasing political and business interference. Youth, which is the central figure of any society in terms of its future prospects, happens to be the most adversely affected. There are generations being affected and the problem of drug dependency and the rehabilitation centres have virtually failed in either responding to or curbing the menace; the need of the hour hence is a patient-centric social model of rehabilitation instead of a cure-based therapeutic model as prevalent across DRCs and other institutional services.

CLIENT-CENTRED APPROACH IN SOCIAL WORK PRACTICE: RESTORING CLIENT SELF-DETERMINATION

When it comes to the social work profession, self-determination is defined as an ethical responsibility towards the client, which is considered among the highest values. Social work professionals are trained to foster maximum self-determination among their clients in order to ensure comprehensive treatment.

In our country, when it comes to the treatment for substance use disorders, there is a huge 'treatment gap', that is, people who need treatment do not receive treatment. Rehabilitation in India is basically focused on inpatient treatment/hospitalization, which again has its own consequences. The traditional focus on medicines rather than psychotherapy for the rehabilitation of drug dependents acts as the biggest hurdle in the treatment of the patients. There is a dire need of implementing scientific evidence-based treatments for the people with substance use disorders to reduce the overall social and public health burden.

The situational analysis of the present scenario of rehabilitation services in the hospital settings presents an unnerving condition, which creates a space for addressing the urgent need for a paradigm shift in focus to a 'Social Model of Health' ensuring patient-centric healthcare services. The administration has to be conveyed strictly that modern medicine has its own limitations and the solution to the complex human problems cannot be found within the traditional treatment method, that is, medicine. The people who use drugs encounter issues related to short- and long-term effects on their health, stress, anxiety, emotional breakdown, stigma and discrimination, financial instability, poverty, distortion of interpersonal family relationships, and violence, etc. The common concerns on the behalf of family included denial, blaming, suppressed anger, depression, bargaining, preoccupation, change of personality and co-dependency. This happened due to lack of motivational activities and monotonous counselling sessions. At present, there is a dire need to understand the health perspective from the purview of 'people' instead of 'medicine'.

The medical social work practitioners in the rehabilitation centres are among the frontliners in providing psychological support and help to the patients and their families. They need to practise various patient-centric therapies within the purview of the humanistic approach, emphasizing empathetic relationships for the treatment of the patients.

SUMMARY

The chapter outlines the present understanding and scope of integrated social work intervention for the social work practitioners working in the field of substance use disorders and the rehabilitation of drug dependents. The emphasis, however, is laid on building a better understanding about drug dependency.

Further, it focuses on the current scenario of drug dependency in India and its implications on the people who use drugs and their family members both succumbing to the adverse effects of drugs in various ways, which includes the physical, social and psychological consequences. However, the impacts are long lasting and adverse when it comes to vulnerable populations such as women, economically disadvantaged, children from low-income background, the elderly population, and the people living with HIV and other chronic health conditions including severe mental disorders, differently abled, homeless and the rural population who have inaccessibility to healthcare services.

The chapter also highlights the urgent need for a paradigm shift with focus on the 'Social Model of Health', ensuring patient-centric healthcare services.

REFERENCES

Allana, A. (2018, June 12). In the black hole. Fountain Ink. https://fountainink.in/reportage/in-the-black-hole

Arya, K. (2018). *Rehabilitation of drug users: A study of district rehabilitation centres in the state of Punjab* [Doctoral thesis]. University of Delhi.

Balhara, Y. P. S., Prakash, S., & Gupta, R. (2016). Pathways to care of alcohol-dependent patients: An exploratory study from a tertiary care substance use disorder treatment centre. *International Journal of High Risk Behaviors & Addiction*, 5(3), e30342.

IFSW & IASSW. (n.d.). Global Definition of Social Work. https://www.ifsw.org/what-is-social-work/global-definition-of-social-work/

Miller, W. R. (1983). Motivational interviewing with problem drinkers. Behavioural Psychotherapy, 11(2), 147–172. https://doi.org/10.1017/S0141347300006583

NCRB. (n.d.). Executive Summary. In Crime in India. https://ncrb.gov.in/sites/default/files/crime_in_india_table_additional_table_chapter_reports/Chapter%201_2014.pdf

Robinson, S. M., & Adinoff, B. (2016). The classification of substance use disorders: historical, contextual, and conceptual considerations. *Behavioral Sciences*, 6(3), 18.

UNDCP. (n.d.). *Problem of Drug addiction in north east region.* In Drug abuse and juvenile delinquency in north east region. https://shodhganga.inflibnet.ac.in/bitstream/10603/67730/14/14_chapter%207.pdf

UNODC. (2015, May). World drug report. United Nations publication. https://www.unodc.org/documents/wdr2015/World_Drug_Report_2015.pdf

UNODC. (2019, June). World drug report. United Nations. https://wdr.unodc.org/wdr2019/prelaunch/WDR19_Booklet_1_EXECUTIVE_SUMMARY.pdf

World Health Organization. (n.d.). Drugs (psychoactive). https://www.who.int/health-topics/drugs-psychoactive#tab=tab_1

Chapter 11

Social Casework with Juvenile Delinquents
A Psychosocial Model

Mohd. Shakil and Asif Khan

INTRODUCTION

The social work profession is considered an enabling and practice-based profession that helps out people with problems of living and human relationships and with the dysfunctional complexities of a range of social institutions. Indigenous social work practice in India has various cross-cultural and diverse characteristics due to different socio-religious beliefs, customs, norms and values of different sections of the community. Today, the social work profession in India is practised in a variety of settings and agencies within the discourse of social policies, human rights and social justice with contemporary perspective. Some of the noteworthy ones are psychiatric, medical, marriage and family counselling, school, juvenile delinquency, corrections, rehabilitation, public welfare, drug abuse, women and child welfare and social policies. Social work profession makes certain that social workers widen scientific knowledge and qualified skills to address human problems, recognize their needs and access available resources to provide solutions at the individual, group and community levels. Social work profession can be classified into two broad methods, that is, primary method and secondary method. Primary method is practised with its three sub-methods, namely social casework, social group work and social work with community organization. In contrast, secondary method is practised with another three sub-methods, namely social action, social welfare administration and social work research (Shakil, 2015). The definition approved by the IFSW General Meeting and the IASSW General Assembly in July 2014 reflects that social work is not only an academic discipline but also a practice-based profession. The aim of this profession is to promote social change, development, social cohesion, empowerment as well as liberation of people (IFSW, 2014).

SOCIAL CASEWORK

Social casework is practised for the adjustment and development of the individuals to facilitate their life in terms of more satisfying human relations. Individuals need better family life, better housing, improved school facilities and infrastructure, availability of more hospitals and medical care facilities, safety, security and protection from adverse economic conditions and harmonious relations between various religious groups. All these factors come together in helping the individuals achieve their all-round growth and development. But, their adjustment and development depend on the resources available to them. Sometimes, they fail to avail all the existing opportunities and facilities just because of certain intrinsic and extrinsic factors. In this situation, the social caseworker facilitates them at all the levels of awareness, education, sensitization and recommendations to come across the solution of the conditions. Thus, the objectives of the social casework profession may be enumerated:

- To observe and analyse the internal problems of the individuals.
- To reinforce their ego power.
- To remediate the problems and challenges in their social functioning.
- To assist them in prevention of problems in their social functioning.
- To facilitate in the development of resources for improving social problems (Misra, 1994).

As part of the primary practice method of the social work profession, the social caseworker tries to assist individuals in a systematic and organized way, based on scientific knowledge of human behaviour and several tested approaches. Each and every individual including child, adolescent, adult and the aged have various needs such as psychological, physical and social to fulfil in order to grow, develop and find satisfaction. The concept of 'social functioning' in social casework practice has a significant place. This concept defines the meaning of the adjective 'social' very explicitly and clearly employs it together with the words 'casework', and this helps in differentiating it from psychologically based work such as psychotherapy. The resources can be understood in terms of the personality potential of the individual as well as the social or material provisions available in the community or agency of the individual (Upadhyay, 2012).

SOCIAL CASEWORK SETTING AND ITS COMPONENTS

The social casework setting functions with the following components: a person, a problem, a place and a given process. A social caseworker assists an individual using these four components:

1. *Person:* The 'person' refers to a client or an individual such as a child, adolescent, adult or an old aged individual, irrespective of sex or gender, in need of help in terms of social-emotional living—irrespective of whether the need is some tangible provision or counselling.
2. *Problem:* The 'problem' refers to the association of the individual with a problematic state, which arises from some want, need, obstacle, hindrance, concentrated state of anxiety or other frustration and maladjustment. This specifically weakens the social functioning of the individual and affects his or her competency and efficacy.
3. *Place:* When a person with some problem is supposed to visit a social service agency or social service department under a human welfare context, such an agency is referred to here as the 'place'. The place is set up to deal with socio-psychological problems at large and with human beings who experience such types of problems and challenges.

4. *Process:* The 'process' in social casework is very important in the sense that the social caseworker comes across the client and starts the intervention. Rapport building is also an important factor to take the whole process of the practice forward step by step. The steps are intake, study, diagnosis, analysis and adjournment. It regards a series of problem-solving operations carried on within a consequential relationship. The end of this process is enclosed in its means to persuade the individual that he or she has attained effectiveness in coping with the problem (Perlman, 2011).

SOCIAL CASEWORK AND ITS PRINCIPLES

Felix Biestek has discussed seven principles of social casework relationship, which are:

1. *Individualization:* Social casework is based on the principle of individualization, as each and every individual has a unique combination of personality traits. These are the resources that the individual needs to rely on to obtain relief from his or her problems and challenges and work out the solution. Social caseworker recognizes and understands each individual or client's unique qualities and employs particular methods, approaches, skills and techniques to assist the person in resolving his or her issues and problems.

2. *Purposeful expression of feelings:* Through this principle, the social caseworker recognizes and understands well about the specific needs of the client to be expressed by his or her feelings freely, particularly negative feelings.

3. *Controlled emotional involvement:* This principle guides the social caseworker to extend sensitivity towards the client's feelings, to understand the meaning of the emotions to be involved, and work out the appropriate and purposeful response to the feelings of the client.

4. *Acceptance:* Social caseworker applies this principle with recognition of the unique personality of the individual, without any presumed perception of the strength or weakness, congenial or uncongenial qualities, positive or negative feelings, constructive or destructive

behaviours and attitudes at the time of diagnosing and assessing the problems and needs of the client.

5. *Non-judgemental attitude:* Social caseworker adopts a non-judgemental attitude as a quality of the casework relationship. This principle is based on the conviction that the casework function excludes discussing the guilt or innocence or the degree of client responsibility for the causative position of the issues, problems or needs.

6. *Self-determination:* This principle of social casework profession practically recognizes the rights and needs of the clients to freedom in making their own choice, responsibility and final decisions in the process of social casework.

7. *Confidentiality:* This is a very important principle which reflects the preservation of confidential and secret information regarding the client. This is considered to be a matter of great importance in professional relationship. The principle of confidentiality is considered an ethical obligation of the social caseworker and is very pertinent as well as necessary for effective and efficient casework service delivery (Misra, 1994).

PROCESS OF SOCIAL CASEWORK

The social casework process can be better understood in terms of the following main four steps.

Study: In the phase of study, the client is engaged with the social caseworker to discuss the problem and its causative factors in depth. Study is regarded as one of the main strands of the process that is continued in an interwoven manner throughout. This way the initial participation, involvement and interaction of the client with the social caseworker is strengthened.

Social diagnosis: Social diagnosis is also termed 'social assessment' and is intended to provide a differential approach for the treatment that is based on the client's individual differences and needs. It undoubtedly distinguishes the uniqueness of every state of affairs, the importance of treatment planning related to a particular awkward situation, an instance of family dysfunction or trouble within a life situation.

Social treatment: Social treatment is also termed 'intervention' and starts with the very first contact of worker and client. Social treatment begins when the social caseworker assists the client to clarify the issues and problems, and makes changes in the life situation of the client, resulting from mutual understanding. Treatment goals are determined by social caseworker and client together. Intervention is determined by the client's needs, and when the agency does not provide the service indicated, the worker has the responsibility to help the client tap other resources.

Termination: It is part of a decision to accept a 'case', to intervene professionally, to provide aid to an applicant (an individual or to a family) needing help, with the inbuilt assumption that at some point in the process, the intervention will end. Termination is the last phase of the process of social casework (Skidmore et al., 1991).

DELINQUENCY AND RISK FACTORS

The research literature reflects that there can be no single factor responsible for the delinquency and emphasizes that multiple factors rather than a specific factor are to be studied as being responsible for augmenting the chances of offending by the youths. Various factors responsible for youth's chances of offending multiply the consequences and several studies have come to the conclusion that these different factors are to be analysed differently. To describe the kind of relationship between outcomes and variables, different theoretical models can be employed (Farrington, 2000). Researchers have categorized the risk factors in different ways. Those factors can be broadly classified under the subdivision of individual, social and community levels. Furthermore, the subdivided risk factors can be again sub-classified into other sub-categories, for example, family- or peer group–related risk factors can also be grouped as social group risk factors. The foremost risk factors which can be associated with juvenile delinquency are recapitulated:

1. *Perinatal and prenatal factors:* Several studies have concluded that for criminal or later delinquent behaviour, perinatal and prenatal factors of complexity are most probably responsible. Frequently,

these factors can lead to a variety of health issues that can negatively affect the all-round development of the individual.

2. *Psychological, behavioural and mental characteristics:* Social work principle specifies that every individual has a unique combination of components for the particular personality. The child who has been continuously reflecting association with low level of confidence in personality, growth and development, along with low level of attendance in classes, less interest in study and enjoyment of superfluous entertainments can be at elevated risk factor for being a child delinquent in comparison to other children.

3. *Structure of family:* Family is the first and foremost primary group and social institution, in which an individual experiences his or her growth and development in terms of proper health, safety, security and protection, educational process and other roles, and status and responsibilities in the family. Juvenile delinquency is indicated by such prominent factors as large family size, home discord, low level of parental education and skills, child abuse and maltreatment.

4. *Influences of peer groups:* Several studies reflect that there is dependable relationship between delinquent behaviour and delinquent peer group. Between 12 and 14 years of age, a vital predictor variable for child delinquency is a kind of antisocial peer company which serves to make the child deviant by promoting delinquent behaviours. It has been analysed that certain prominent factors such as allegiance or attachment to such peer groups, spending time with such peer groups, participating in the delinquent behaviours of peer groups and peer pressure result in adolescent or child antisocial behaviour.

5. *Policies of school:* The available studies also conclude that the kind of decisions taken by the school administration also affects the behavioural status. The decision of suspension or expulsion of the student from school also goes against any effort to curb the undesirable behaviour of the individual and increases the scope of the delinquency.

6. *Neighbourhood:* According to sociological theories of deviance which hypothesize that disorganized neighbourhoods have pathetic social control networks, weak social control, consequential from isolation among residents and elevated residential turnover, lets criminal activity go unmonitored. Even if researchers debate the interactions

between environmental and personal factors, most have the opinion that living in a neighbourhood where there are elevated levels of poverty and crime augments the risk of participation in serious crime for all children growing up there (Shader, 2001).

Thus, the issue of juvenile delinquency is not related to any specific community or society, but it pervades all areas of social stratification. It can be observed everywhere irrespective of any religion, language, race, ethnic group, tradition, culture, class or caste. Its association is completely related to the kind of nature of the social order, parameters of social health, ways of treating juvenile adolescents, how far the scope is for tolerance and how the juveniles are responded to with certain patterns towards their holistic growth and all-round development. Other factors increase the frequency of the predictor variables such as societal values and inter-generational gaps that they have while violating social norms (Encyclopaedia of Social Work in India, 1997). Apart from behavioural influences, other studies conclude that an individual may suffer from mental and psychological tensions, disorders for which only circumstances are to be held responsible. But the adolescent falls into conflict with law and he or she becomes more delinquent. There are several debates that give voice to the innocence of the delinquent on account of his fundamental and human rights and urge to protect the individual from all these maladies. These delinquents are to be treated with best possible efforts of the professionals and the kind of diagnostic system which will lead to better treatment needs to be upheld (Encyclopaedia of Social Work in India, 2020).

To be worried by the question of who takes delivery of social welfare is to fail to spot an essential point about a social institution. The needs a social institution is designed to address and the people who show signs of having those needs may be neither good nor bad in themselves. The needs and the institutions created to serve those needs are a result of the connectedness of all parts and all people within a specified society. To censure those who are in need and to put a stigma on them is to make them answerable for aspects for which they alone cannot be held responsible. The part social work plays in serving the needs of people within the institution of social welfare is a natural and practical one inside society. Such meanings and values connected with social welfare should be cautiously examined. Social workers must definitely contract with people who are undervalued by society and compact with a society which undervalues social workers (DuBois & Miley, 1999). Social work practitioners and agencies take part in a vital role in working with juvenile delinquents through their research, service delivery and advocacy for this vulnerable group. In the majority of cases, they are an element of a multidisciplinary team that works for the welfare of juvenile delinquents. Many agencies propose specialized interventions through personalized support and counselling to make sure that they have access to necessary services. They also try to reduce the negative effects of withdrawal by making accessible specialized services such as complaint and reporting mechanisms, support for drug abuse, psychosocial counselling, trauma therapies, empowerment through sports and support services that can help them to reconnect positively with family and local community services. The tailor-made and modified interventions by social workers can go a long way in ensuring access to such indispensable services and in making sure their best interests are served. The social caseworkers have the skills and training to put together a relationship of trust with juvenile delinquents with a non-judgemental attitude. They are also efficient counsellors who strive to stimulate them toward positive behaviour and place realistic goals for social reintegration. Their skills for networking are of immense aid in linking them with different agencies and persons who can support the juvenile delinquents in their journey towards advancement as self-reliant and responsible adults (Dabir, 2014).

Case Example: Psychosocial Model

The psychosocial model applies to individuals as a perspective on the combined influence that psychological factors and the surrounding social environment have on the physical and mental wellness of individuals and their ability to function. The indigenous sociocultural factors bind the individual personality towards wellness or deviation. This depends on the surrounding or extrinsic environment as well as the intrinsic traits of the individual.

Study: Such factors as the following, revealed in the interview, are noted and taken into consideration for assessment and intervention:

Soham (changed name of a client), a 14-year-old boy, belonged to an economically feeble and less educated family in a slum area of Delhi. Hence, poverty became a noteworthy variable in relation to his delinquent activities and behaviour. So, the culture of the slum supported him to engage in theft and he involved himself in such a delinquent offence. When he found it very easy to commit such a crime, he became accustomed to continue the criminal activity, sometimes for supporting his family and sometimes for his own pleasure. Being child from a migrant family and living in a clustering population of slums with bleak and deprived life, he attributed all his delinquent behaviour towards his lifestyle. His justification was based on denied equal opportunity to avail all the sociocultural and socio-economic facilities, which made him susceptible to abuse and forced him to join a culture of deviance.

Assessment: The kind of social order found in the rural setting was replaced with the migration of the family from rural to slum setting. The social controlling factors were also changed a lot, and this enabled him to adopt a new kind of lifestyle. He started not only to accommodate but also to assimilate the sociocultural and socio-economic atmosphere of the slums. In fact, the social control related to the principles of a rural neighbourhood was also diminished and he found freedom from all rural morals to be responsible for his behaviour. Thus, the client (Soham) did not only find himself out of the way of proper socialization, but also created the grounds for joining the new gang and commit the illegal activity to earn the money for family and for his daily expenditure. This also helped him to join a delinquent group of thieves and antisocial individuals and then fall into a fertile ground of delinquent behaviour towards society such as indiscipline and moral squalor.

Intervention: The goal was to support the client in his efforts to become more self-reliant and to help him earn a proper livelihood. He was encouraged to make decisions affecting his life. He was helped to question himself about the source of his earnings. He attended quite a few short counselling sessions, helping him stay away from situations that may propel him towards deviance. The client was facilitated to restart his life with a self-reliant member of the community. He was assisted to earn money from his fair skills, moulding his behaviour by role-playing, sessions on positive reinforcement and consciousness-raising such as involvement of community members, rewards and other techniques to bring about changes in his life prospects and lifestyles.

Termination: When the client obtained for himself a viable source of income, started contributing to the livelihood of his family members and reintegrated into a dignified lifestyle, he became ready to move on and also realize his capacity to carry on his future endeavours.

CONCLUSION

The aim of social casework is to lend a helping hand to the juvenile client to resolve his delinquency problem, in such a way that he makes himself competent in dealing with such problems at present and in the future. Before studying the delinquency problem of the client, the caseworker needs to do rapport building, which is an inevitable part of the social casework process. While involving themselves in the social casework process, the caseworkers abide by the professional social casework principles, goals, values and norms for application along with its knowledge and skills.

REFERENCES

Dabir, N. (2014). *Children and adolescents, clinical and direct practice, international and global issues, populations and practice settings, poverty.* Oxford University Press.

DuBois, B., & Miley, K. K. (1999). *Social work: An empowering profession.* Allyn & Bacon.

Encyclopaedia of Social Work in India. (1997). Volume 2. Publications Division, Ministry of Information and Broadcasting, Government of India.

Encyclopaedia of Social Work in India. (2002). Volume 1. Publications Division, Ministry of Information and Broadcasting, Government of India.

Farrington, D. P. (2000). *Explaining and preventing crime: The globalization of knowledge.* The American Society of Criminology.

Hoge, R. D. (2001). *The juvenile offender.* Springer Science & Business Media.

IFSW. (2014). *Global definition of social work.* https://www.ifsw.org/global-definition-of-social-work/

Misra, P. D. (1994). *Social work: Philosophy and methods.* Inter-India Publications.

Parris, M. (2012). *An introduction to social work practice: A practical handbook.* Open University Press.

Perlman, H. H. (2011). *Social casework: A problem-solving process*. Rawat Publications.

Shader, M. (2001). *Risk factors for delinquency: An overview*. Office of Justice Programs.

Shakil, M. (2015). Social work with individuals: Social diagnosis and social treatment of psycho-social problems. *International Journal of Research, 2*(3), 332–342.

Skidmore, Thackeray, M. G., & Farley, O. W. (1991). *Introduction to social work*. Prentice-Hall.

Thompson, K. C., & Morris, R. J. (2016). *Juvenile delinquency and disability: Advancing responsible adolescent development*. Springer International Publishing.

Upadhyay, R. K. (2012). *Social casework: A therapeutic approach*. Rawat Publications.

Conclusion

This book, *Social Work Education: Indigenous Perspectives*, discusses select topics on contemporary issues and practices in social work education from indigenous perspectives. It covers diverse and emerging issues and practices that were hitherto neglected in the social work discipline. Each chapter in this book focuses on a specific issue which is of contemporary relevance and identifies relevant social work skills, techniques and methods that may be useful in tackling that issue. The theoretical background, empirical insights and case examples presented in each of these chapters not only expand the knowledge base of the concerned issue, but also enable the readers to think and reflect on the issue. In this book, the various chapters deliberate upon the following broad themes:

- Medical and psychiatric social work practice
- Importance of fieldwork in medical and psychiatric social work
- Trends in clinical social work and problem-solving models
- Social work with families and children
- Scope and challenges in working with families and children
- Emergence and development of professional social work in correctional settings
- Major work areas of correctional settings
- Roles and professional obligations of social workers in correctional settings
- Palliative care as an emerging field of social work practice
- Approaches, models and agents of palliative care in India

- Emerging practice areas of counselling in social work
- Psychosocial approaches and application of various social work therapies in counselling
- Emergence of social enterprises as self-sustainable models in social work
- Importance of goal attainment model in the field of social enterprises
- Social work response to environmental problems
- Environmental justice and social justice mandate of social work
- Holistic green agenda for social work •
- Importance of social work theories and models to understand terrorism
- Social work response to terrorism and its remedies
- Theoretical and institutional framework of disaster management
- Role of social workers in disaster management
- Social work interventions with drug dependents
- Importance of client-centric approach in drug rehabilitation
- Social casework with juvenile delinquents
- Importance of psychosocial model in the treatment of juvenile delinquents.

While dealing with all these themes in various chapters, the authors mostly follow the indigenous perspectives. They firmly believe that 'the West to the rest' approach did not fit in the context of developing countries of Asia, Africa and South America due to its inherent limitations. They have, thus, tried to approach the identified issues from the locally relevant indigenous perspectives. At the same time, they have retained the universal character of social work theories and methods in their application to these identified issues with necessary adaptation. Adequate care has also been taken in each chapter to highlight the gaps between theories and practices of social work, and various ways have been suggested to bridge those gaps. Each chapter of this book is written keeping in view the following points:

1. The relevance of the issue/topic in social work discipline;
2. Historical background of the concerned issue/topic;
3. The need of solving the concerned issue;

4. The identification and application of suitable social work skills, techniques, methods, therapies and models to solve the concerned issue; and

5. The identification of a set of roles of professional social workers in dealing with the concerned issue.

In the selection of the issues/topics covered under this book, due care has been taken to suit the needs and interests of all the actors involved in the process of social work education.

This book consists of 11 chapters, each dealing with a specific topic relevant to social work. The overviews and conclusions of each of these 11 chapters are presented here for providing a quick recap to the readers.

The first chapter of this book traces the origin and history of medical and psychiatric social work practice both in the USA and in India and reflects upon the emergence and development of clinical social work. It discusses medical and psychiatric social work as two main branches of clinical social work. It then provides a glimpse of the stages involved in the treatment of the client in clinical social work such as the identification of the client, assessment/diagnosis of his or her problem, treatment of his or her problem and rehabilitation of the client with the society at large. It also highlights the application of various social work models in the treatment of the client's problem. These include problem–solving model, behaviour modification model, crisis intervention model and public health model. It then delves upon the importance of fieldwork in medical and psychiatric social work and identifies a set of relevant roles of the social worker to be played in the field of medical and psychiatric social work. In the end, it describes the current state of clinical social work in international as well as in Indian contexts.

The second chapter traces the historical evolution of social work with families and children globally as well as in Indian contexts. It then examines the relevance of social work interventions with families and children. In the context of families, it discusses the family casework, family counselling, couple counselling, crisis intervention, legal aid, family therapy and so on. In the context of children, it discusses two types of services—statutory and non-statutory. Statutory services, which are governed by a number of legislations, mainly include care, protection and rehabilitation of children kept in various correctional centres such as children's homes, observation homes, aftercare organizations and so on. Non-statutory services, which are mostly provided by the non-government organizations (NGOs) and other civil society organizations, cover a wide variety of services in the areas of health, education, skill development, vocational training and such other areas. Lastly, it underscores the bottlenecks and challenges that social workers are likely to encounter during the fieldwork practice in the area of social work with families and children.

The third chapter deals with the emergence and development of professional social work in correctional settings, primarily in the Indian context. It begins with theorizing the correctional settings as a specialized branch or domain of criminal justice system, and discusses five major work areas of correctional setting, namely, (a) public interest litigation, (b) bail system, (c) prison system, (d) legal aid and services and (e) compensation to the victims of crime. It then discusses a number of correctional institutions such as prisons, observation homes, special homes, children's homes, aftercare organizations, protective homes for women, short-stay homes, beggar homes, courts, probation and parole boards and borstal schools. In this context, it identified different role set performed by social workers in various types of correctional institutions noted above. Among others, it includes the roles of probation officer, parole officer, counsellor, therapist, broker, rehabilitator, activist, facilitator, planner, implementer, researcher and change agent. Further, it discusses a variety of skills social workers are required to possess while working in different correctional institutions. This included rapport building skill, documentation skill, presentation skill, leadership skill, network building skill, negotiation skill, coordination skill, motivational skill, rehabilitative skill and termination skill. It then discusses various kinds of professional obligations social workers are supposed to maintain while working in the field of correctional setting. This includes maintaining the privacy of sensitive information of clients, respecting the dignity and individuality of clients, respecting client's right to self-determination, treating clients of different backgrounds alike, protecting the integrity of law-enforcing officers, devaluing crimes but not criminals, and balancing between the needs of clients and public safety of the country. The chapter ends citing three case studies—social casework with an economic offender, social group work with alcoholics and social work with communities—to provide the readers with real life illustrations of social work practice in correctional setting.

The fourth chapter discusses palliative care as an emerging field of social work practice and traces its origin in the efforts of Dame Cicely Saunders in England and M. R. Rajagopal in India. It then goes on to discuss the two broad approaches to palliative care—traditional approach and modern approach. The traditional approach consists of two components—curative treatment and palliative care—whereas the modern approach comprises supportive services and palliative care, which even extends beyond death as bereavement care is necessary for the family and caregivers. Further, it elaborates the existing models of palliative care in India, which include pain and palliative medicine centres, home care units, day care centres, hospice care and community-based model. In this respect, it describes hospitals, NGOs and community as the main agents of palliative care. The chapter ends with the deliberation on the current state of palliative care in India and with a set of useful suggestions to develop and scale it across the country.

The fifth chapter discusses the contemporary and emerging practice areas of counselling in the social work profession and underscores the huge potential scope of counselling practice in India. It then provides an overview of the four main therapeutic schools of counselling, namely the psychodynamic school, the humanistic-existential school, the cognitive behaviour school and the postmodern school. Corresponding to these four therapeutic schools of counselling, it provides a list of various remedial therapies used in the social work. This includes classical psychoanalysis, analytical therapy, person-centred therapy, Gestalt therapy, transactional analysis, reality therapy, existential therapy, logotherapy, behaviour therapy, rational emotive behaviour therapy, cognitive therapy, multi-model therapy, solution-focussed therapy and narrative therapy. It then emphasizes the importance of professional competency and the use of self in counselling. The chapter ends with describing the social work values and skills required in the practice of counselling.

The sixth chapter discusses the emergence of social enterprises as a self-sustainable model in social work and identifies various social work values which are applied in the field of social enterprises. These values include service, social justice, dignity and worth of the person, importance of human relationships, integrity and competence. It then presents a case study of Goonj—an internationally recognized Indian NGO—to illustrate the self-sustainable elements of social enterprises in carrying out the social work mandates. Apart from describing the vision, mission, goals, organizational structure, projects and campaigns of the organization, it discusses the charity model, barter model and economic model followed by the organization for the attainment of its various goals. The chapter finishes off with emphasizing how social enterprises as a self-sustaining model can lead social work to a highly professionalized sector in a short span of time.

The seventh chapter presents the social work response to various environmental problems of contemporary times. In this regard, it discusses the person-in-environment approach, ecosystems approach and eco-critical approach of social work to deal with environmental problems of present times. From the feminist viewpoint, it underscores how ecofeminism has contributed to the conservation and protection of the nature/environment. It reinvigorates the environmental justice and social justice mandate of social work and advocates for breaking down the artificial barriers created between environmental issues and social justice issues. Further, it talks of the introduction of environmental social work, green social work and conservation social work in the social work education and underlines the importance of developing environmental consciousness in the students of social work. The chapter ends with laying down the holistic green agenda for social work.

The eighth chapter presents a comprehensive theoretical under-pinning of terrorism and social work response to combat it. It describes terrorism as one of the most serious problems of the present century facing humanity. Tracing the concept of terrorism from historical to present times, it has identified a number of typologies of terrorism on various parameters. This includes sensory and moral terrorism, internal and external terrorism, individual and organized terrorism, political and non-political terrorism, voluntary and sanctioned terrorism, dynastic and mass terrorism, religious and non-religious terrorism, military and intellectual terrorism. It then discusses the psychological, social, economic and educational causes of terrorism. In addition to these, it discusses social construction theory and differential mixing theory to develop theoretical insights into the causes and process of terrorism. It then offers several strategies and tactics to combat terrorism. The strategies include communication strategy, change directions strategy, capacity-building strategy, solidarity strategy and education strategy. The tactics include collective discussion tactic, open communication tactic, exchange of views tactic and teaching tactic. The chapter sums up by identifying the various roles of social workers in dealing with terrorism.

The ninth chapter details out the evolution and institutional framework of disaster management in India from the colonial period to the present time. In its analysis, it projects India as a 'theatre of disaster' and suggests that prevention of disaster is better than its cure. It describes various types of disaster by clubbing them into two broad, universally accepted categories: natural and human made. Natural disasters, which occur due to natural forces, include earthquake, cyclone, flood, tsunami and so on, and human-made disasters, which occur due to human actions or inactions, include riots, war, terrorist attacks, industrial accident and so on. Further, it argues that there is no disaster without human hands, and expands the list of disasters to include climatic disasters, geological disasters, chemical disasters, biological disasters, radiological disasters and nuclear disasters. It then describes the disaster management cycle which includes prevention, mitigation, preparedness, response, rehabilitation and reconstruction in a cyclic form. It then examines the gaps between the motto of disaster management, that is, 'build back better' and the ground realities. Next, it describes certain basic concepts closely associated with the concept of disaster or disaster management. This includes the concepts of hazard, vulnerability, capacity and risk. Thereafter, it discusses the concept of disaster risk reduction and its four major components namely, preparedness for response, early warning, disaster mitigation and safe-sustainable development. The chapter ends by describing the roles of social workers in disaster management.

The 10th chapter underscores the need and importance of integrated social work interventions in the treatment and rehabilitation of drug dependents. It describes various types of drugs such as licit and illicit or legal and illegal, based on their compliance with the laws, morphine and diamorphine based on the medical applications, and some other types of drugs. It then elaborates various characteristic symptoms of drug dependents such as preoccupation with substance, intolerance, physiological withdrawal state, loss of control and so on. Thereafter, it assesses the current state of drug use or abuse in India and statistically compares the drug dependence and suicide rates across the Indian states. In this regard, it points out to various key reasons for drug dependence such as anger, stress, rejection, curiosity, lack of awareness about drug effects and so on. Next, it describes the process of drug rehabilitation, which includes screening and brief intervention, outreach services, evidence-based and comprehensive psychosocial assessment, inpatient/outpatient treatment services, long-term residential treatment, recovery support services and rehabilitation. In addition to these, it discusses three preliminary stages/processes, namely detoxification, therapy/counselling and aftercare, which precedes the actual drug rehabilitation process. Next, it discusses the adverse effects of drugs on its consumers which are broadly grouped into three categories: physical/health, psychological and social. As part of drug dependency prevention measures, it presents a case of Punjab Model of De-addiction as worth emulating in other places for the treatment and rehabilitation of drug dependents. The chapter ends by calling for the adoption of a patient-centric approach and utilization of Social Model of Health in the treatment and rehabilitation of drug dependents or drug users.

The 11th or last chapter of this book highlights the importance and utility of social casework method of social work in rehabilitation of juvenile delinquents. It begins by detailing out the objectives, components and principles of social casework, and how they are useful while working with juvenile delinquents. Among others, it enumerates the following objectives of social casework: (a) observing and analysing the internal problems of the individuals, (b) reinforcing their ego power, (c) remediating the problems and challenges in their social functioning, (d) assisting them in prevention of problems in their social functioning and (e) facilitating in the development of resources for improving social problems of society at large. It discusses person, problem, place and process as the main components of social casework. It then proceeds to discuss the seven fundamental principles of social casework, which includes principle of individualization, purposeful expression of feelings, controlled emotional involvement, principle of acceptance, principle of non-judgemental attitude, principle of client's self-determination and principle of confidentiality. Thereafter, it elaborates the process of social casework, which broadly includes study, social diagnosis, social treatment and termination. Next, it discusses various risk factors leading to juvenile delinquency. This includes perinatal and prenatal factors, psychological, behavioural and mental factors, size/structure of family, influences of peer groups, disorganized neighbourhoods and school policies. The chapter ends by presenting a case example using the psychosocial model of social casework to provide practical exposure to the readers.

In the end, I must express my thanks to all the readers of this book and hope that they enjoy reading the book.

About the Editor and Contributors

EDITOR

Sanjoy Roy, MSW, MPhil, PhD, LLB, believer and promoting Indigenous Social Work in India, is Associate Professor at the Department of Social Work, University of Delhi. Previously, he taught in various other universities in India, such as Visva-Bharati University, IGNOU, Assam University (Central) and CSJM University. He has written more than 50 articles/research papers published in different referred journals and books and 12 books in national and international publications in the area of social work education. He is also associated in various capacities internationally with many professional bodies, such as International Advisory Board Member in *Encyclopaedia of Social Work*, Editorial Board member of the *Journal of Historical Archaeology and Anthropological Sciences*, Associate Editor of the *International Journal of Religion and Spirituality in Society*, Editorial Board Member of the *International Journal of African and Asian Local Government Studies*, Editorial Board Member of the *International Journal of CPQ Medicine (CPQME)*, Editorial Board Member of the *Sociology International Journal*, Review Board Member of the *International Journal of Social Work Values and Ethics*, Editorial Board Member for the *Journal of Ecology and Natural Resources (JENR)*, Associate Editorial Board Member for the *Women's Health Science Journal* and so on.

Dr Roy's research interest areas include development studies, social exclusion, justice, law and human rights and empowerment for disadvantaged groups, social work practice and critical social work. He has many honours and awards to his credit, including the Bharat Ratna; Dr Radhakrishnan Gold Medal Award 2019 by Global Economic Progress and Research Association (GEPRA), Tiruvannamalai, Tamil Nadu, India; Shelter Award 2019 along with Certificate of Excellence by Shelter Promotion Council (India), Kolkata, for contributions in various areas; Best Academician of the Year Award (Male), 2018, by Global Education and Corporate Leadership Awards 2018 by LWT and MIET, India; Rising Personality of the Year 2018 by Rifacimento International, Group of Editors for dedication and achievement in the profession; Neelkanth Samman Award 2018 and Scroll of Appreciation for Defender of Democracy by the Kabir Ke Log and Centre for Dalit Study, Delhi, on the occasion of 69th Constitution Day of India, 2018.

CONTRIBUTORS

Neera Agnimitra is Professor and Head of the Department of Social Work, University of Delhi. She has teaching experience of more than three decades and teaches courses on community practice, environmental social work, disaster management and research. Besides having many publications to her credit, she figures on many core university committees, boards of research studies and is also an expert member on several government and non-governmental panels/committees. She has written many articles in reputed journals and also guides MPhil and PhD students in the department.

Kirti Arya is a Medical Social Service Officer in AIIMS, New Delhi, in the Medical Social Welfare Unit. She has also completed her PhD from the Department of Social Work, University of Delhi, on the 'Rehabilitation of Drug Users in the State of Punjab'. She has worked in the project of John Hopkins University, Maryland, on the Behavioural Survey of the Injection Drug User. She has written nine publications in the national and international journals, including chapters in edited volumes and more than a dozen research paper presentations.

Subhasis Bhadra is Associate Professor at the Department of Social Work, Central University of Rajasthan. He started his professional career in 2001 from intervention in Gujarat earthquake rehabilitation programme and subsequently worked in various disaster interventions in India and abroad. His research interest includes peacebuilding, conflict-resolution, life-skills education, disaster mental health, community and school mental health, psychosocial support and livelihood interventions.

Tushti Bhardwaj is Assistant Professor at the Department of Social Work, Dr Bhim Rao Ambedkar College, University of Delhi. She holds BA, MA, MPhil and PhD degree in Social Work from the University of Delhi. She received specialized palliative care education (MSc Palliative Care) from King's College, London. She conducted her academic research on psychosocial aspects of cancer care focusing mainly on quality of life and care-giving burden on families. With teaching experience of almost 16 years with the University of Delhi, she authored many research papers in reputed national and international journals and a book titled *Living with Breast Cancer: Dynamics and Challenges*. She has developed a care-giving burden assessment scale for family caregivers of cancer patients in Indian setting. She is currently supervising PhD scholars in the area of health care.

Basem Youssief Mohamed Elmoazen, MSW, PhD, is Assistant Professor at the Department of Community Organization, Faculty of Social Work, University of Helwan, Egypt. He has 10 years' experience in teaching at university level. He has also gained numerous administrative experiences as Director, Field of Training, Department of Social Work, University of Helwan, as manager of volunteering development centre, as manager of various projects related to community research and community development and so on. He has written more than 20 articles/research papers published in different refereed journals and 5 books in national and international publication. He is a member of many of the community organizations especially in Egypt.

Preeti Jha is a Doctoral Research Fellow at Department of Social Work, University of Delhi. Her areas of interest include social entrepreneurs and social enterprises, women empowerment, social development, corporate social responsibility and human resource management. She has worked in the development sector as well as taught at the Department of Social Work, University of Delhi.

Archana Kaushik is Associate Professor at the Department of Social Work, University of Delhi. She has wide experience in the field of social work with families and children and gerontological social work.

She has many books and research articles on these issues in journals of national and international repute to her credit. She is guiding MPhil and PhD scholars in the department.

Asif Khan is Guest Lecturer at the Department of Social Work, University of Delhi. He did his PhD in Social Work from Aligarh Muslim University. Earlier, he served as an Academic Associate in Communication Area at Indian Institute of Management Kashipur, Uttarakhand. He has more than a year experience working as a research assistant in an Indian Council of Social Science Research–funded research project on disaster mitigation at the same place. He has published research papers in double-blind peer-reviewed journals.

Ravi Ranjan Kumar is Assistant Professor in Rajiv Gandhi (Central) University, Arunachal Pradesh. Young Social Science Awardee of the Year 2016 by Indian Social Science Association, Gold Medal for Masters in Social Work and Gian Pandit Award by Delhi School of Social Work are his major recognitions. He has completed PhD from the Department of Social Work, University of Delhi, in the field of Women's Participation in the Panchayati Raj Institutions in Bihar. He has teaching experience of nearly four years. He has 15 publications in journals of national and international repute, including chapters in edited volumes and more than a dozen research paper presentations. He has contributed in the capacity building, faculty development programmes and delivered lectures across institutes over a decade-long association with social work.

Shashi Rani is Assistant Professor (Senior Scale) at the Department of Social Work, University of Delhi. She has written articles and chapters in many reputed journals and books. She has also written a book. She is also involved in many administrative responsibilities in the university. Her interest areas are social justice and empowerment, public health, social work and counselling.

K. Sathyamurthi, MA(SW), PhD, EDI-Fellow, is Professor and Controller of Examinations at the Madras School of Social Work, Chennai, Tamil Nadu. He has completed 22 years of professional service in teaching and research and training in social work field. Earlier, he worked as HOD, IQAC Coordinator (Addl) in the Department of Social Work (Aided); Coordinator (Trg i/c), TORC; Head of the Department of Social Work, SCPJ College; Welfare Officer for Child Adoption, VCA-TN; Research Officer, Research and Development Wing, RICA, CLEP; Programme Coordinator, CD Wing, TNSCB; and Social Scientist, TNIP-NIN, Hyderabad. He teaches Medical and Psychiatric Social Work at postgraduate level and has been guiding MPhil and PhD scholars for more than two decades. His fields of expertise are Youth and Adolescents at Risk, and Children and Slum Entrepreneurship. He has produced 6 PhD and 12 MPhil scholars.

Mohd. Shakil is Assistant Professor at the Department of Social Work, NIMS University Rajasthan. He has worked as a Guest Faculty (Consolidated) in the Department of Social Work, Gautam Buddha University, Greater Noida. He did his PhD in Social Work from Aligarh Muslim University. He has qualified both JRF and NET under the scheme of UGC, India.

Index

All India Conference of Women
and Indian Council of Child
Welfare, 32
Aman Samudaya program, 186
American Counselling Association
(ACA), 85
American social work, 31
anticipatory bail, 57

Beavers Systems Model, 32
British Association of Social Workers,
134

Calgary Family Assessment Model,
32
Calgary Family Intervention Model,
32
Central Social Welfare Board, 33
child rights, violation of, 41
Circumplex Model of Marital and
Family Systems, 32
Civil Defence Act (1968), 176
clinical social work (CSW)
defined, 19
focus of, 19
opportunities and challenges in,
24–26
professionals, 19
Collaborating Center of the World
Health Organization (WHO)
for Mental Health Research and
Training, 23
community organization, 3, 85
Companies Act (1956), (2013),
105

correctional settings in India, 65
bail system, 57
case studies, 65
compensation to victims of crime,
59
institution, types of, 59
legal aid and services, 58
prison system, 58
professional obligations of social
workers, 62–63
professional social work in,
emergence and development of,
54–56
public interest litigation, 57
skill required by social workers,
60–62
social workers role in, 59–60
work areas in, 56
correctional social work education,
objectives of, 54
counselling
and application of psychosocial
approaches, 89–92
and professional competence,
93–95
and professional relationship,
92–93
and social work, 85–87
contemporary and emerging
practice areas of,
87–89
couple, 218
defined, 86
family, 218
importance of, 98–99

supervision and application of
skills, 95–98
use of self in, 93–95
counsellors, 75, 86, 93, 106
criminal justice social work, 54
criminal justice system, 65
components of, 52
corrective function of, 53
criticism of, 54
defined, 53
feature of, 53
importance of, 53

Darlington Family Assessment Model,
32
Department of Social Work, 102
Disaster Management (DM)
defined, 170–172
extended cycle of, 169
Disaster Management Act (2005),
175
disaster management in India, 223
community role as stakeholder in
recovery, 178–179
in post-Independence, 174
nodal ministries for, 176
origin of, 174
policies and guidelines, 176–178
social workers role in, 179–184,
167
disaster risk reduction (DRR)
components of, 174
defined, 172
ethical, 173
financial, 173
political, 173
disaster
categories of, 166
cycle of, 166–170
defined, 165
human-made, 166
mitigation, 173
natural, 166
District Legal Services Authority, 59

drug abuse in India
history of, 193–194
rate of suicides, 194
drug abuse prevention programmes,
190
Drug De-addiction and Rehabilitation
Centres (DRCs), 196–197,
199
drug or substance dependence
behavioural therapy inclusion for,
200
consequences of problem, 190
defined, 191
hypothetical time scale of drug
use, 194
micro and macro implications, 193
reasons for, 191
restoration of client self-
determination, 201–202
social work implications, 198–201
World Drug Report (2019)
estimation, 189
drug rehabilitation
aim of, 195
defined, 195
process involved in, 196

ecofeminism, 122
ecoliteracy, 135
Encyclopaedia of Social Work in India,
32
environment in social work, 130–133
environmental
activism, 126
apartheid, 121
consciousness, 133–135
decimation, 122, 136
engagement of social workers,
123–130
environmental
justice mandate of social work,
120–123

Family Capacity Model, 32

Family Cycle of Health and Illness Model, 32
family system
  defined, 29
  functional perspective, 29
  interventions, 39–40
  universal presence, 28
Family Systems Stressor-Strength Inventory, 32
Family Systems Theory/Model, 32
family-centred care
  defined, 29
Foreign Contribution Regulation Act (2010), 105
Friedman Family Assessment Model, 32

gender disparity in India, 35
Global North, 121
Global South, 121
Goonj (NGO), 117
  employees at the organization, 114
  goal of, 110
  mission of, 110
  models followed by, 113
  networking with other, 113
  organizational structure of, 110–113
  profile of, 107–109
  projects and campaigns at, 114–116
  vision of, 110
Goyal, C.P., 18
green agenda for social work, 135–139
green social work, defined, 129–130
group work, 85

habitat destruction syndrome, 126
hazard, vulnerability, capacity and risk (HVCR), 170

Income Tax Act (1961), 105
Indian Conference of Social Work (1947), 31

Indian Journal of Psychiatric Social Work, 18
Indian Trusts Act (1882), 105
Institute of Almoners, 17
Integrated Child Development Services (ICDS), 33
Integrated Child Protection Scheme, 42
interim bail, 57
International Association of Schools of Social Work (IASSW), 2
International Decade for Natural Disaster Reduction (IDNDR), 174
International Federation of Social Work, 34, 102
International Federation of Social Workers (IFSW), 2, 127, 134

judicial activism, 137
juvenile delinquency, risk factors in, 209–212
Juvenile Justice (JJ) Act, 33, 42

Kerala Sastra Sahitya Parishad (KSSP), 137–139
Kumarappa, J. M., 18

Mandela, Nelson, 29
McMaster Model, 32
medical and psychiatric social work, field-based practice, 23
medical social work (MSW), 17
Ministry of Agriculture, 174
Ministry of Home Affairs (MHA), 175
Mission Flexipool under National Health Mission (NHM), 71
Mission for Green India, 177

Narcotics Control Bureau (NCB), 194
National Action Plan on Climate Change (NAPCC) (2008), 177

National Association of Social
Workers (NASW) Journal of
Social Work, 126
National Association of Social
Workers (NASW), USA, 15
National Cancer Control
Programmes, 71
National Centre for Disaster
Management, 176
National Crisis Management
Committee (NCMC), 175
National Disaster Management
Authority (NDMA), 175
National Disaster Response Force
(NDRF), 176
National Institute of Disaster
Management (NIDM), 176
National Institution of Public
Cooperation and Child
Development, 32
National Mission for Enhanced
Energy Efficiency, 177
National Palliative Care Programme,
71
National Platform for Disaster Risk
Reduction (NPDRR) 2013,
178
National Policy on Disaster
Management (NPDM),
176
National Solar Mission, 177
Neighbourhood Network in Palliative
Care (NNPC), 77–78
NIMHANS, 18

opioid substitution therapy (OST),
195

palliative care in India, models and
agents
community based model, 77–78
day care centres, 76
home care units, 75
hospice care, 77

pain and palliative medicine
centres, 72–74
palliative care in India
national strategies, development of,
79–82
present scenario, 78–79
palliative care
aim of, 70
defined, 69–70
modern approach, 72
origin of, 71
traditional approach, 72
people as place, notion of, 127
person-in-environment approach, 120
person-in-environment framework,
124
prakriti-manav (environment-human)
relationship, 120
prison in India, types of, 58
prison system, 54
Prisons Act, (1894), 57
professional counselling, defined, 89
professional practice of social work,
concept of, 145
professional social workers, 86
psychiatric social work (PSW), 16, 17
psychiatric social worker, appointment
of first worker, 17
psychological first aid, 20
psychosocial model, 212–214

Rajagopal, M.R., 71
regular bail, 57

services for children, categories of, 42
Sir Dorabji Tata Graduate School of
Social Work, (now called Tata
Institute of Social Sciences,
TISS), 31, 55
Sir Dorabji Tata Trust (SDTT), 55
social action, 3, 99, 163
social case work
methods of, 85
social casework

defined, 205
objectives of, 205
principles of, 207–208
process involved in, 209
setting functions and components,
    206–207
social enterprises (SEs)
defined, 103
emergence of, 103–105
necessity of, 112
registration of, 105
self-sustainable model, 116–117
sustainable model to social work
    profession, 102–103
to follow social work profession
    values, 105–107
social entrepreneur, 106
social entrepreneurial framework, 107
social group work, 3, 220
social interventions, 102
social welfare administration, 3
social work, 27, 84, 218
Social Work Forum, 32
social work profession, 205
methods of, 3
social work professional, rise in
    demand for, 101
social work with families and children
areas of intervention, 38–39
bottlenecks and challenges in
    fieldwork practice, 46–49
fieldwork engagements, 44–46
historical evolution of, 30–33
interventions, relevance of, 33–36
learning requirements in fieldwork,
    43–44
scope of, 36–38, 40–43
social work
aim of, 15
as a profession in India, 102–103
clinical, 17
defined, 2, 15, 85–86
education, 54, 133–135

educational institutions, 32
gaps between theory and practice
    in, 3–4
generic vs specialized, 7–8
indigenous perspectives in, 4–7
medical, 17
paradigms, 16
research, 3
techniques used in, 20–21
social workers, 16
behavioural modification model,
    22
crisis intervention model, 22
problem solving model, 21
public health model, 22
role of, 24
State Disaster Management Authority
    (SDMA), 175
Strategic Knowledge on Climate
    Change, 177
strength perspective, 60
supportive counselling skills, 87
Sustainable Agriculture, 177
Sustainable Habitat, 177
Sustaining the Himalayan Ecosystem,
    177

Tata Institute of Social Sciences
    (TISS), 16, 55–56, 102
terrorism, 222
terrorism, causes of
economic, 151
educational, 151
psychological, 149–150
social, 151
terrorism, theories and models
differential mixing theory, 147–148
social construction theory, 147
terrorism
classification of, 146, 152–153
defined, 145–146
manifestations of, 146
problem of, 144

professional strategies against,
153–155
professional techniques against,
155
social work commitments in fight
against, 156–158
social workers role to deal with,
156
The State of Social Enterprise in
India, 2016, 106
theatre of disaster, India as,
161

United Nations Convention on the
Rights of the Child (UNCRC),
33, 40
United Nations Development Fund
for Women (UNIFEM), 56
United Nations Development
Programme (UNDP), 56
United Nations Office on Drugs and
Crime (UNODC), 194

Water Mission, 177
west to the rest approach, 217